# The Political Economy of Independence in Europe

This book examines secessionism, separatism, and calls for independence in the European Union in recent history and within an economic context. It contributes to the deeper understanding of factors influencing the individual decision-making processes around secession, using economic analysis to answer a set of simple questions about who the secessionists are, what they really want, what their incentives are, and why it is easier to declare their secessionist tendencies than to vote for secession.

This a highly topical theme, given the secessionist referenda in Catalonia, Scotland, Ukraine, Kosovo, and the United Kingdom, and this book offers a unique contribution to the debate. It is based on an exclusive survey carried out among members of the pro-independence parties and movements across 17 European countries and 56 European regions. It uses the instruments of the Political Economy of Conflict to reveal the importance of romantic and economic factors influencing the drive towards secession. Secessions have been regarded as a purely romantic phenomenon that cannot be rationalised, whereas this book connects the sensibility of romantic factors such as language, religion or ethnicity with the sense of economic factors through its rational, economic approach. Furthermore, it applies the standard methodology of microeconomic analysis to discover the impact of individual pro-secessionist factors. An integral part of the text presents a brief historic overview, uncovering the lesser-known path dependency.

The book will find an audience among researchers, scholars, and students of economics and political science, as well as policy-makers and professionals engaged with a secessionist agenda.

**Hana Lipovská** is a lecturer at the Faculty of Economics and Administration, Masaryk University, Czech Republic.

## Routledge Studies in the European Economy

**Centrally Planned Economies**
Theory and Practice in Socialist Czechoslovakia
*Edited by Libor Žídek*

**SME Finance and the Economic Crisis**
The Case of Greece
*Alina Hyz*

**Russian Trade Policy**
Achievements, Challenges and Prospects
*Edited by Sergei Sutyrin, Olga Y. Trofimenko and Alexandra Koval*

**Digital Transformation and Public Services**
Societal Impacts in Sweden and Beyond
*Edited by Anthony Larsson and Robin Teigland*

**Economic Policy, Crisis and Innovation**
Beyond Austerity in Europe
*Edited by Maria Cristina Marcuzzo, Antonella Palumbo and Paola Villa*

**The Economics of Monetary Unions**
Past Experiences and the Eurozone
*Edited by Juan E. Castañeda, Alessandro Roselli and Geoffrey E. Wood*

**Economic History of a Divided Europe**
Four Diverse Regions in an Integrating Continent
*Ivan T. Berend*

**The Political Economy of Independence in Europe**
*Hana Lipovská*

For more information about this series, please visit www.routledge.com/series/SE0431

# The Political Economy of Independence in Europe

**Hana Lipovská**

Routledge
Taylor & Francis Group
LONDON AND NEW YORK

First published 2020
by Routledge
2 Park Square, Milton Park, Abingdon, Oxon OX14 4RN

and by Routledge
52 Vanderbilt Avenue, New York, NY 10017

*Routledge is an imprint of the Taylor & Francis Group, an informa business*



*British Library Cataloguing-in-Publication Data*
A catalogue record for this book is available from the British Library

*Library of Congress Cataloging-in-Publication Data*
Names: Lipovská, Hana, author.
Title: The political economy of independence in Europe / Hana Lipovská.
Description: Abingdon, Oxon ; New York, NY : Routledge, 2020. |
Series: Routledge studies in the European economy | Includes
bibliographical references and index.
Identifiers: LCCN 2019058994 (print) | LCCN 2019058995 (ebook)
Subjects: LCSH: Europe—Economic conditions. | Europe—
Economic policy. | Nationalism—Europe. | Secession—Europe.
Classification: LCC HC240 .L54 2020 (print) | LCC HC240 (ebook) |
DDC 330.94—dc23
LC record available at https://lccn.loc.gov/2019058994
LC ebook record available at https://lccn.loc.gov/2019058995

ISBN: 978-0-367-89647-8 (hbk)
ISBN: 978-1-003-02029-5 (ebk)

Typeset in Times New Roman
by Apex CoVantage, LLC

# Contents

# Figures

# Tables

# Appendices

# Acknowledgements

I am incredibly grateful for the research help, advice, critiques, and support to Professor Germá Bel, Eva Bidania Ibargutxi, Jana Bobošíková, Jakub Fischer, Petr Hampl, Ondřej Hýsek, Dalibor Moravanský, Professor Václav Klaus, Jiří Ovčáček, Jindřiška Šedová, Professor Robert A. Young and Libor Žídek.

This book is dedicated to my dear friends Professor Hans-Werner Sinn, Dr. h.c. mult. and Gerlinde Sinn.

# Abbreviations

| | |
|---|---|
| ANOVA | analysis of variance |
| AT | Austria |
| BE | Belgium |
| CIA | Central Intelligence Agency |
| HR | Croatia |
| CZ | Czech Republic |
| DGI | Degree of international economic integration |
| DK | Denmark |
| DG | Directorate-General |
| EC | European Commission |
| EFA | European Free Alliance |
| EU | European Union |
| EV | expected value |
| FI | Finland |
| FR | France |
| DE | Germany |
| GR | Greece |
| GDP | Gross Domestic Product |
| HHI | Herfindahl-Hirschmann Index |
| HU | Hungary |
| ISCO | International Standard Classification of Occupation |
| IT | Italy |
| LU | Luxembourg |
| NL | Netherlands |
| NUTS | Nomenclature of Territorial Units for Statistics |
| NAFTA | North American Free Trade Agreement |
| OLS | Ordinary Least Squares |
| OECD | Organisation for Economic Cooperation and Development |
| OPEC | Organisation of the Petroleum Exporting Countries |
| PL | Poland |
| PEC | political economy of conflict |
| PPP | Purchasing Power Parity |
| SAPIM | survey on autonomist and pro-independence movements |

| | |
|---|---|
| SNP | Scottish National Party |
| ES | Spain |
| SITC | Standard International Trade Classification |
| SE | Sweden |
| UEFA | Union of European Football Associations |
| UK | United Kingdom |
| UN | United Nations |
| UNCTAD | United Nations Conference on Trade and Development |

# Introduction

Imagine a hypothetical situation in which every single economic subject has homogeneous preferences that would be connected to the homogeneity of the individual utility functions. The single omniscient and benevolent social planner (as defined, for instance, by Boettke 2000:3) could therefore, be a simple maximiser of the aggregate social utility function, which would also maximise each individual utility function. Such a situation would be a simple exercise in pure economic science. On the contrary, political economy as a science deals with decision-making based on the existence of heterogeneity of interests and preferences. Finally, heterogeneity leads to conflicts among economic actors (Drazen 2000:6), and such conflicts are being solved using the political economy of conflict as a specific economic subdiscipline.

The aim of this thesis is to examine secession as the conflict resulting from the heterogeneity of preferences. Two main objectives are identified to reach the aim:

1 identifying causes of the secessionist processes;
2 determining their importance for the citizens of the European secessionist regions and estimating the contribution of the romantic and economic factors to their secessionist utility function.

Various conflicts emerge in the daily life of economic actors, most of which could be studied by the political economy of conflict. Nevertheless, the most obvious are violent conflicts such as wars, uprisings, or terrorist attacks. If the history of humankind is a history of war as, for example, Flynn claims (Flynn 2007:2), then the history of war is not only a history of annexations, occupations, terrorist attacks, and territorial or power disputes but also of numerous secessionist and separatist tensions, movements, and successful as well as unsuccessful attempts to gain independence and establish a new state. Some of the key wars that changed Western society – the American Civil War (1861–1865) as well as the First World War (1914–1918) – were secessionist wars, whether they reached or missed their aim.[1] A vast majority of all recent European states drew (or many times redrew) their borders after the secessionist wars (compare Vaubel 2013): The Swedish-Norwegian War (1914) and the Estonian, Latvian, and Lithuanian Wars of Independence (1918–1920) serve as examples. All wars in the post-Cold War Europe were and still are secessionist (Baev 1999). The Yugoslav Wars (1991–2001), the Kosovo War (1996–1999), or the Russo-Georgian War (2008) are all based on the effort of one group to receive either autonomy or full independence of the central government. Moreover, the recent European Union (EU) is subject to numerous secessionist "cold wars" of political forces and national movements seeking to reach greater autonomy within the existing state or gain full independence. There were independence referenda in Scotland, Catalonia, and Venetia, as well as secessionist and separatist movements in Flanders, the Basque Country, Navarra, Corsica, Sardinia, and Aosta Valley or South Tyrol. Moreover, the secession *sui generis* includes Brexit and all other exit attempts by current member states of the EU, though they are not the subject of our study.

The increase in the secessionist tensions in modern Europe is connected to the end of the Cold War. As Baev (1999) mentions, most of the conflicts emerged on the (political, not geographical) periphery of the European integration as there was a "gravity field centred on Brussels [that] gradually subsidis[ed] towards . . . Central Asia".[2] European integration accelerated disintegration tensions, which are being solved either by negotiation between secessionists and the central government or by the armed conflicts.

The interactions of these factors motivate secessionist movements. These are common topics in the political sciences (Cabada 2009), international law (Walter et al. 2014), ethics and philosophy (Buchanan 1991b; Boykin 1998; Rosůlek 2014), history (Doyle 2010), game theory (Young 2004), and economics (Bookman 1993; Speir 1994; Alesina and Spolaore 1997). All the conventional approaches assume that the declared secession is the ultimate goal of the secessionist movements (or the players in terms of game theory). Secessions have been largely discussed from the ethical, legal, philosophical, ethnographic, geographic, linguistic, and fiscal points of view. However, the nature of secession is as well economic, not solely in the sense of pecuniary conflicts and fiscal decentralisation but also and foremost in terms of the allocation of scarce resources, negotiation over property rights, and searching and finding the effective long-run equilibrium. The macroeconomic dimension of secession is based on economic variables, which can be studied under public finance and public economy, for example, as a problem of fiscal decentralisation. Nevertheless, it has also and above all its microeconomic dimension based on optimising the utility function. This dimension is the subject of the political economy of conflict.

As we mentioned, research on secession was, for a long time, based merely on anecdotal evidence which first sprang from the case study of the American Civil War (Yates in Gordon 2002:35). The 20th-century case model is represented by the Quebec sovereignty movement (Young 1998; Young 1999; Buchanan 1999; Millard 2008; Delledonne and Martinico 2018). Rigorous study of secession using economic tools has for a long time been questioned because of the lack of adequate data (Speir 1994). Notwithstanding, when it was studied by economists, only anecdotal evidence was used, with the considerable exception of Bookman (1993).

This study therefore deals with the *secession* as the economic phenomenon. Movements in Catalonia, Scotland, or even South Tyrol ostensibly depend more on the historic development, differences in the religion, language, or ethnicity, as well as psychological and social circumstances than on the rationality of the financial accounting and careful calculation of the costs and benefits. That might be the reason why secession has not been, until the recent century, the point of interest of economic *Ars et Scientia*. The second reason why the economists largely ignored problems of secession was chronic lack of data. Secessions provided us just with the anecdotal evidence, which does not allow us to use the statistical and econometric method.

Nevertheless, the same was true even for most other aspects of our lives, which are now, thanks to the approach introduced primarily by Gary Becker and his followers, the object of the economic science. Our study is based on conviction that if there is the subject who makes some decision, who chooses between alternatives, who tries to maximise his individual utility function in accordance with his set of preferences an at the given set of restrictions, there is always space for the application of the unique economic way of thinking. From such point of view, the secession is the standard economic problem. There are the economic subjects – citizens of the region within other country – who make decisions when answering the simple question: "To leave or to remain?" Every decision is connected to some individual as well as aggregate costs and inconveniences and to some benefits and pleasures. Each subject, when being homo economicus, wants to maximise his own particular utility function. The role of the decision-makers – and the space for the economists – is to choose such set of constraints that leads to the optimal situation maximising the total utility of the country as a whole.

To reach the aim of examining secession as the conflict resulting from the heterogeneity of preferences, the survey among the members of the secessionist movements in the European countries was conducted. Furthermore, the conventional statistics and econometric approach was used. For a description of the results and for testing the hypotheses, we used

- descriptive statistics (such as the arithmetic and geometric mean, standard deviation, variance, frequency, and Pearson coefficient of correlation);
- standard tests (non-parametric Chi-squared test, t-test); and
- econometrics methods (Analysis of Variance, linear regression estimated by the OLS model).

To estimate the Cobb-Douglas function, two vectors, reflecting weights of both the romantic and economic factors, had to be distinguished. Based on the survey data, the Factor Analysis was run. Using the factor loadings based on the orthogonal rotation and Principal components extraction method, romantic and economic factors were estimated and normalised. The Cobb-Douglas function was then computed in the logarithmic form using the Ordinary Least Squares method and finally re-transformed to the convenient parametric form. Heterogeneity of preferences was approximated by the Herfindahl-Hirschman index.

The structure of this study is as follows. The first chapter is devoted to specifying the political economy of conflict within the political economy and its application on the subset of conflicts concerning secessionism. Firstly, the *Political economy of conflict* is introduced. Then, the secession as subject of the political economy of conflict is defined. Finally, the secession is viewed as the conflict over the territory, people and resources. The subchapter 1.3 covers the practice of the secessions: it summarises the historic secessionist waves in the Europe since the 19th century, which lead to the born of the new states and which formed the recent face of the Europe, introduce the list of the secessionist parties and movements as well as with their attitudes towards the European Union, and the role of their leaders. The first objective (identification of the causes of the secessionist processes) is fulfilled in the subchapter 1.4, which summarises the theoretical background for two large sets of the reasons for secession: so-called romantic and economic factors. The final part describes the theoretical approach to the potential economic solutions of the secession: the law and economics as well as the fiscal decentralism as the possible cure for the secessionist pressures.

To meet the second objective (determining their importance for the citizens of the secessionist regions) and thus, to shift the economic analysis of secession from the anecdotal evidence approaches to the data approach, we conducted an original *Survey on autonomist and pro-independence movements* (SAPIM) among the members of the European secessionist parties and movements associated in the political group European Free Alliance (EFA). Survey data enabled us to analyse their preferences, incentives for supporting the secession, and political and economic opinions. Thus, this study identifies both the economic and romantic causes of secessionist tensions to evaluate the impact of purely economic factors. Secessions are, for the sake of this study, considered to be an economic problem, which can be described and understood by economic analysis.

SAPIM, as well as other data sources and methodology, are introduced in the second chapter. Subchapters 2.1 and 2.2 introduce the focus group of respondents and explain the questions used in the questionnaire in detail. Additional data sources necessary for understanding of the longitudinal development (e.g. data from Eurostat, Organisation for Economic Cooperation and Development, numerous national as well as academic institutions, or European Election Database) are described in the subchapter 2.3. The inconvenient and novel source of data is available due to the web-based tool Google Trends and Google Correlate. This service provides researchers with data on the development of searching for the key words among time as well as among the regions all over the world. If we are correct, these data are being used for the research of secessionist conflicts for the first time. Finally, the statistical and econometric methods used for our analysis are briefly described in subchapter 2.4.

The core of this study forms the third chapter, which introduces detailed results of the survey. Survey descriptions including the basic description of dataset as well as the simple statistical description of the respondents are explained in subchapter 3.1. Part 3.2 deals with the romantic factors in terms of the informal institutions (for example, heterogeneity in language, religion, and ethnicity; culture; and education) as well as formal institutions (political parties and political preferences as revealed in the election). Subchapter 3.3 is devoted to the macroeconomic as well as microeconomic factors. Finally, subchapter 3.4 leads to fulfilling the third objective as it summarises the estimation of the Cobb-Douglas function including the weights of the romantic and economic factors.

The last part introduces a short case study of two specific secessionist regions. Flanders in Belgium (subchapter 4.1) represents typical secessionist regions which have been widely studied in the recent secessionist literature. On the contrary, the region of South Tyrol in Italy (subchapter 4.2) is less recognised even because it does not call for the full independence, but it considers kind of irredentism – reunification with Austria based on historical development.

This study does not suggest a solution to existing or potential secessionist conflicts nor can its economic science prevent the existence of heterogeneity in the interests of different nations living within the same state. Nevertheless, economic understanding of secession enables policy-makers to avoid deepening tensions, mitigate conflicts, and ultimately maximise the aggregate social utility function.

## Notes

1 Although it is not mentioned in the secessionist literature, we could claim, with a great deal of precaution, that even the "first total war" (Bell 2007), the Napoleonic Wars (1803–1815), were an unfortunate legacy of secessionist movements. In 1769, Corsica was conquered by France. In the very same year, Napoleon Bonaparte was born in the capital, Ajaccio. At the beginning of his career, young Napoleon carried strong sentiments towards Corsican independence. In his *Letters on Corsica*, he wrote: "Corsica's history is nothing but a perpetual struggle between a small nation who wants to live in freedom and its neighbours who want to dominate it" (Krajewska 2005).

2 However, Belgium case is ambiguous as the country is in the core of the integration but at the same time it deals with the secessionist tensions.

# 1 Secession in political economy of conflict

The origins of the economic *ars et scientia* might be recognised in the political economy as formed by the classical school of political economy (Drazen 2000). This chapter is devoted to specifying the political economy of conflict within the political economy and its application on the subset of conflicts concerning secessionism. In the first subchapter, the relatively novel branch of the *Political economy of conflict* is briefly introduced. The second subchapter deals with the theory of secession in terms of the political economy. Various definitions of secession are discussed. At the end of this subchapter, the secession is viewed as the conflict over the territory, people, and resources. The third subchapter covers the practice of the secession: it summarises the secessionist waves in the Europe since the 19th century. The next three parts deal with the recent secessionist parties and movements as well as with their attitudes towards the European Union and the role of their leaders. The fourth subchapter summarises the theoretical background for two large sets of the reasons for secession: so called romantic and economic factors. Finally, the fifth subchapter describes theoretical approach to the potential economic solutions of the secession. First of all, instruments of the Law and Economics are implemented to solve the secession as the case of the property rights definition. Secondly, the fiscal decentralism is discussed as the possible cure for the secessionist pressures. The whole chapter provides us with the sufficient theoretical background for the rest of this book. It enables us to study the recent secessionist pressures as the economic problems of the recent European Union (EU).

## 1.1 Political economy of conflict

Imagine an economy whose subjects are perfectly homogeneous in their preferences and differ only in the initial endowment. In such an economy, the Pareto-effective state could be reached by a simple textbook-like optimisation calculated by the benevolent social planner or, even better, artificial intelligence. Nevertheless, real-life economic players are usually heterogeneous in their preferences, which leads to the heterogeneity of interests and, ultimately, conflict of interest (Drazen 2000:10).

The political economy itself supposes existence of the conflict of interests, which is the result of the heterogeneity of preferences. The political economy of conflict (PEC) as a distinct discipline that emerged at the turn of the 20th and 21st centuries is therefore the subset of political economy with the *conflict* as its subject. The word *conflict* itself has roots in the Latin *cōnflīgere* (to strike together), which is composed of the prefixes *com-* and *fligere* (strike). *Conflictus* also means *competition*. In the narrowest sense, the subject of PEC can be understood as **armed conflict** (Vaďura 2010). Armed conflicts are also variously defined. For instance, the *Armed Conflict Report* defines it as "a political conflict in which armed combat involves the armed forces of at least one state (or one or more armed factions seeking to gain control of all or part of the state), and in which at least 1,000 people have been killed by the fighting during the course of the conflict" (Malley-Morrison et al. 2012). However, the *Uppsala Conflict Data Program* defines armed conflict[1] as a "contested incompatibility where the use of armed force between two parties results in at least 25 battle-related deaths in one calendar year" (Melander et al. 2016).

Other authors consider *armed conflicts* as just one part of the PEC's point of interest. For instance, Anderton (2001) spreads the PEC's field to cover all criminal activity, legal disputes, strikes, rent-seeking, as well as the redistribution policy. PEC is, therefore, more varied and richer in subjects than just *peace economics*[2] or *defence economics*.[3] It can, certainly, study the causes and consequences of war; however, it also deals with any other conflicts including terrorist attacks, space races, corruption (Braddon and Hartley 2011), the behaviour of hooligans (Leeson et al. 2012), and natural resource shortages (Soubeyran and Tomini 2012).

Political economy as a science has its roots in the economic discussion of wars. Wars, as the most obvious example of conflicts, had always had their consequences not only for the national economy but also for the economic theory. It is not surprising that the building blocks of the PEC as a serious economic theory were always laid during or after armed conflicts. English Political Economist William Petty, in his study *Treaties of Taxes* (1662), explains that defence is a public charge of the state because it is (in current terminology) a public good which should be financed from the collected taxes.[4]

A considerable contribution to the war and peace economy was presented by John Maynard Keynes' retrospection of the First World War and, following the Paris Peace Conference, *The Economic Consequences of the Peace* (1920):

> [French] future position remained precarious in the eyes of one who took the view that European civil war is to be regarded as a normal, or at least a recurrent state of affairs for the future, and that the sort of conflicts between organized great powers which have occupied the past hundred years will also engage the next.

However, the First World War chiefly gave birth to the first significant theoretical study on the field of PEC. English neoclassical economist Arthur Cecil Pigou published *The political economy of war* to explain the "anatomy and physiology" of the "economy of the world-shattering war". In this opus, he deals with the costs of expecting potential armed conflict; thus, the necessity of keeping and feeding the army. He mentioned that the *Brussels Financial Conference* stated in 1920 "that, on average . . . some 20 per cent of the national expenditure is still being devoted to the maintenance of armaments and . . . preparations for war" (Pigou 1921:6). The second theme of his study lies in the economic causes of war, which he finds in the *desire for domination* and *desire for gain* (Pigou 1921:16).

The Second World War brought a further breakthrough in the PEC, as it had claims on the economic science and economists. Shortly after its start, Keynes wrote a study on *How to Pay for the War* (1940), which according to Coyle (2014:17) led to the first modern estimates of national accounting in the United Kingdom. The Cold War in the second half of the 20th century led to the development of the Game theory. One of its founding fathers, John von Neumann, co-operated on cold war strategies for RAND Corporation.[5] The first Nobel Prize in economic science for "having enhanced our understanding of conflict and cooperation through game-theory analysis" was awarded in 2005 to Thomas C. Schelling and Robert J. Aumann (The Royal Swedish Academy of Sciences 2005).

We have seen that each war conflict has its political-economic dimension either in financing the war or in dealing with particular interests of economic subjects. Nevertheless, it was not until the end of the Cold War that conflicts were shifted to the focus of the political economy as a science (Andreas 2012). Simply, until the 1990s, the political economy was just one aspect of conflicts. Nowadays, conflict is one of the study subjects of the political economy.

In this study, the PEC is defined as the *economic subdiscipline dealing with the armed and unarmed, interregional, intraregional, as well as spatially unbounded conflicts* (compare Vaďura 2010; Anderton 2001; Braddon and Hartley 2011).[6] It studies the reasons and conditions of the conflict as well as the economisation of the conflict motives (Weiss 2008) using standard methods of the political economy. The name of the subdiscipline does not suggest its uniqueness in terms of method (the PEC uses the full palette of standard methods of the Political Economy) but rather its special field. In the following sections, "conflict" will be further narrowed as a subset of secessions. *Cum grano salis*, we could also speak about the "political economy of secession" without prejudice to accuracy – as, for instance, Collier and Hoeffler (2002) did.

## 1.2 Theory of secession

The term "secession" has its roots in Latin *secedere* (go apart). According to Doyle (2010), it was first used in the 16th century to describe the temporary withdrawal of the commoners who were leaving Rome between 494–287 BC. The main aim of *Secession Plebis* was for the noble class (*patricians*) to accept their requirements through a kind of strike: *plebeians* were the working class serving the *patricians*, who took them under their patronage (Fiordelisi and Molyneux 2006:24). Later in the 18th century, the term *secession* was used to describe leaving the union, especially in terms of the emerging Scottish secession church split (Clark et al. 2018). In central Europe, *secession* is closely connected to the art movement,

*Wiener Secession* (Art Noveau), which was founded by a group of young artists who seceded from the *Association of Austrian Artists* (Charles and Carl 2014).

The current political meaning in terms of leaving the common state appeared in the 19th century, which described the southern secession and the following war of secession (American Civil War) in 1861–1865 (Gordon 2002). This is why the word "secession" bears a negative connotation in American literature, reflecting "slavery, war, and anarchy" – as mentioned by Clark et al. (2018).

Secessionist tensions, which are the subject of this study, can exist exclusively within the state as "a human community that (successfully) claims the monopoly of the legitimate use of physical force within a given territory" (Weber 1946:78).[7]

This study is, however, not aimed at comparing the details of numerous definitions of the state.[8] Unless otherwise indicated, the state is considered to be the entity defined in line with the *Montevideo Convention* (1933). The *State* is considered to be the *person of international law*, which meets four definition features:

1 permanent population;
2 a defined territory;
3 government; and
4 capacity to enter into relations with other States.

(Dugard 2013:27)

There is no one unique, official, all-encompassing definition of secession. The literature dealing with decentralisation, independence movements, and disintegration distinguishes several terms used occasionally and erroneously as synonyms: secession, separatism, irredentism, and dissolution. In the Anglophone world, *separatism* is used more often to mean radicalism. It describes movements whose fight for independence is violent, often connected to the terroristic attacks such as the *pro-Russian separatists* in the Donetsk or Bosnia and the Herzegovina or *Basque separatists* in Spain. Wood (1981), however, noticed that *separatism* is a less precious term than *secession*, as *separatism* describes, even, the effort on gaining greater regional autonomy or federalisation tendencies. However, *secession* expresses the peaceful effort to withdraw the existing state legitimately (Doyle 2010).[9] In this section, several definitions of secession are introduced to select the most proper definition which will be used within this study.

Griffiths (2016) conceives of secessionism as the "formal demand for independence by a nation from its existing sovereign state" (p. 5). Radan defines secession as "the creation of a new state upon [an] existing territory previously forming part of, or being a colonial entity of, an existing state" (Griffiths 2016:6). Such secession pressures have been seen as justifiable because they are seen to be based on natural law (Andreotti 2017). For instance, Althusius claimed yet in 1609 that "citizens have a right to forswear allegiance to the king in the case of an abuse of power", as he considered secession as "ultima ratio" just after the failure of other attempts of maintaining the state unity through, for example, subsidiarity (Andreotti 2017).[10]

The leading authority in moral theory of secessionism, Alan Buchanan, highlights that secession "is an effort to remove oneself from the scope of the state's authority . . . by redrawing the boundaries so that one is not included within them" (Buchanan 1991b:11). Rosůlek worked out a more complex and detailed definition of secession as a "complex and successful withdrawal", which occurs when a "political movement . . . supported by the majority of inhabitants in the potentially secessionist region articulates the intention to establish its own state within its borders . . . proclaims independence, establishes authorities of the new state, exercises control over the regional territory, and gains full recognition from the existing states, international organisations, as well as from the state, from which this group together with its territory hived off" (Rosůlek 2014:53). On the contrary, Doering and Backhaus offer a simpler definition. This is useful, especially, for modern Europe, which is under pressure not only from the secessionist region but also from the states or political groups seeking to leave the EU. According to them, secession is a "separation of a territory from a nation state or a fully consolidated federal state", while an exit is a "separation from a loose confederation" (Backhaus and Doering 2004:14).

Modern secession in democratic states of the 21st century differs from the secessionism of the 19th century because they emphasise the relationship with supranational and international organisations (the EU and the United Nations), instead of the state frontiers, army, or external sovereignty (Calvet ND:19).[11]

Several secessionist waves occurred as the aftermath of a hostile occupation of the territory. As Pigou (1921:17) mentioned, the central governments are

> humiliated, outraged, [and] dishonoured if a subject population passes out from their yoke. . . . For continuing to hold these places against their will, ruling powers have offered many reasons – their duty to civilisation, the white man's burden, the need for a strategic frontier, and so forth. These reasons are often put forward sincerely; sometimes they are sound; but, in addition to and behind everything else, there is the will of dominant Powers to continue dominant. Against that clashes the will of the dominated to be free. There is the seed of wars of liberty, of irredentist wars, of wars of nationality!

Besides these secessionist waves, there exist permanent autonomy forces, which form together with secessionist movements: the *disintegration tendencies*. While *secession* should be understood as a radical approach to disintegration, *autonomism* is considered a modest approach (Massetti and Schakel 2013). Rosůlek (2014) distinguishes the following forms of disintegration:

- decolonisation (such as that in Latin America after 1810);
- break-up, fragmentation, dissolution, status quo ante, restoration, or even partition (especially, in post-communist countries after the fall of the Iron Curtain);
- irredentism (such as Sudeten Germans in the Czechoslovak Republic, 1938);
- exclusion (the relationship between the United States and Puerto Rico in the case where Puerto Rico wanted to become part of the US without US agreement);

- expulsion (such as in Singapore from Malaysia);
- separation; and
- pure secession.

Beside the pure secession, especially the *irredentism* and *restoration* are – for the aim of our research – in quest.

Secession denies the sovereign authority of the existing state in similarly as revolutions, riots, or emigration. Buchanan (1991a) suggests that the main aim of secessionists (unlike the autonomists) is not overthrowing the government or changing the constitutional order. Secessionists do not question the state's authority. On the contrary, they want to exclude part of the territory from the authority. This differentiates secession from mass emigration: while secession restricts the state's authority over the territory, emigration restricts its authority over the citizens (Table 1.1). In terms of Buchanan and Faith (1987), the Jewish Exodus from Arab countries can be described as an external exit while the Palestinian Independence Declaration from 1988 as an example of a secessionist tension is an internal exit.

Hereafter, if it would not be suitable to precisely define it, we use *secession* as the common term for all kinds of separatism, dissolution, and irredentism to mean the permanent and intentional separation of existing state territories and its citizens to found an independent sovereign state.

### *1.2.1 Secession as a conflict in the political economy*

In this section, we introduce secession as a conflict. Probably the first and most pronounced secession which had been studied by the political economy of conflict was the American Civil War (1861–1865).[12] This so-called "war of secession" was driven by two economic drivers: on the one hand, there was a deep and unsolved debt problem of the Union, and on the other hand, there was a rivalry for cheap labour (Sinn 2018).

Lincoln's legendary speech[13] proves that, from the very beginning of secessionist tensions, secession is considered to be **political divorce** (compare Doyle 2010 of Buchanan 1991b). Secession should be, from its very nature, studied under the

*Table 1.1* Requirements on the governmental power distribution according to secessionists, autonomists, and migrants

| | *Governmental power over the* | | *Change of the government* |
|---|---|---|---|
| | *Territory* | *people* | |
| State | Yes | Yes | No |
| Secession | No | No | No |
| Autonomy | Yes | Yes | Yes |
| Emigration | Yes | No | No |

Source: Author.

PEC as it is "hardly ever achieved without some degree of conflict" (Rodríguez-Pose and Stermšek 2014; compare Young 2013).

As the American Civil War and the Ukraine crisis show, the ultimate result of such conflict can be articulated as regular wars decreasing the standard of living of both fighting countries – or worst, of both warring parties of the same country. Violent secessions are quite common (Young 1994a). However, most of them do not become total wars (Wood 1981). The most violent event connected to secessionism broke out in Corsica during the 1970s when the siege of Aleria ended in bloodshed (Lefevre 2003). This violence resulted in the establishment of the separatist militant group, National Liberation Front, in 1976.

Nevertheless, even non-violent secessions have conflict features. They are always accompanied by political battles, which divide elites and the people (Young 1994a). The resulting economic and cultural divergence is usually so deep that the reintegration of the following states seems impossible. Due to this divergence (or, in other words, heterogeneity in preferences), secessionist conflicts might be fully solved as the standard economic problem based on the optimisation of the utility function.

In case of secession, the utility function $u$ is determinated by the vector $\vec{x}$ and weight vector $\vec{\omega}$. For each two utility functions $u_i$, $u_j$, $i \neq j$ the vector $\vec{x}$ is the same, but the parametres in the weight vectors might differ. Thus $\overrightarrow{\omega_1} \neq \overrightarrow{\omega_2}$. Suppose utility function

$$u = x_1^{w_1} \cdot x_2^{w_2} \cdot \ldots \cdot x_n^{w_n}; \sum_{i=1}^{n} w_i = 1 \tag{1.1}$$

Then the utility function of the citizen living in the secessionist region might be of the form

$$u_s = x_1^{w_{1,s}} \cdot x_2^{w_{2,s}} \cdot \ldots \cdot x_n^{w_{n,s}}$$
$$\sum_{i=1}^{n} w_{i,s} = 1, w_{i,s} = \begin{pmatrix} 0 & 0.2 & \ldots & 0.08 & 0.5 \end{pmatrix} \tag{1.2}$$

while the utility function of the citizen living in the rest of the country has the form

$$u_R = x_1^{w_{1,R}} \cdot x_2^{w_{2,R}} \cdot \ldots \cdot x_n^{w_{n,R}}$$
$$\sum_{i=1}^{n} w_{i,R} = 1, w_{i,R} = \begin{pmatrix} 0.1 & 0.25 & \ldots & 0 & 0 \end{pmatrix} \tag{1.3}$$

If the vector $\vec{x}$ chosen by the central government (with the given and uniform budget line) maximises utility function $u_s$, it does not maximise utility function $u_R$ and vice versa. The observed utility $u_i$ is then lower than the optimal utility $u_i^*$ which leads to the dissatisfaction of the people and the origination of potential conflict.

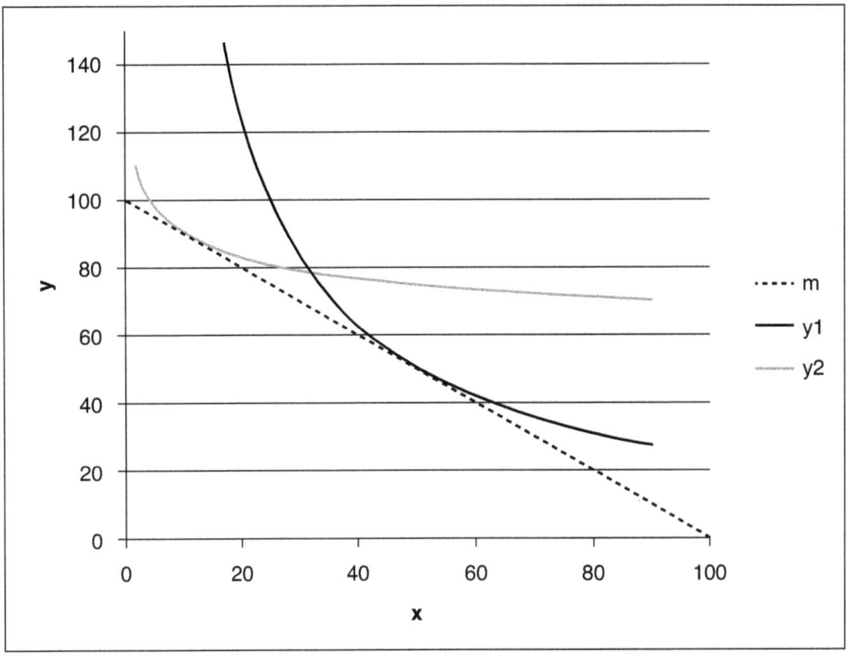


*Figure 1.1* Heterogeneity of preferences render using the indifference curves

Source: Author.

### *1.2.2 Secession as a conflict over territory*[14]

Conflict, in simple terms, is usually *over* something. As Table 1.1 shows, secessionist conflict can be considered as conflict either over the territory, the people, or the governmental power. This section deals with conflict over the territory as a basic type of secession. If property rights are clearly defined and recognised by all (key) agents, secession can be understood as a case of simple trade with the land. However, if the property rights are not defined or are not accepted, the so-called **predation model** can be used. Thus, for modelling the armed solution of secession, the Grossman and Kim's predator-prey model (Grossman and Kim 1995) is useful. Grossman-Kim's model is a two-agent model of the general equilibrium for one period. Each agent (prey and predator) uses its endowment to defend its property (for instance, for fortification), which reduces the wealth (endowment) of the agent, but only the predator allocates part of the endowment to gain the prey's property. Each agent also decides how much of the endowment should be used in defence and how much in attack. Predation is destructive and results in a solution where the predator gains less than the prey loses. Non-aggressive equilibrium occurs if the resources allocated to the predation are less effective than the defensive fortification of the prey or if the predation would be too destructive.

Using this initial setting of Grossman-Kim's model, we develop the basic secessionist model. Consider the state which contains the secessionist group. The full ownership of the land is required to secede (or to maintain the status quo). Suppose that part of the land is owned by pro-secessionists and part is owned by anti-secessionists who prefer the existing state. To achieve secession, however, the pro-secessionist can either buy the missing land in case the territorial rights are defined and accepted, or use armed power if the territorial rights are not defined or not accepted.

The formal model presumes land $T$ governed by state $R$, where territory $T_S, T_S \in T$ belongs, according to property rights, to the group $S$. Initially, state $R$ owns its own territory which it values at $w_R, w_R > 0$ as well as the territory of group $S$ which state $R$ values at $v_R, v_R > 0$. Secessionists $S$ are therefore not entitled to their property rights to territory $T_S$ which they value at $v_S, v_S \geq 0$.

First, assume that state $R$ wants to protect the indivisibility of the whole territory $T$ (including $T_S$) and that it is willing to buy from the secessionists $S$ the property rights to territory $T_S$ for price $p$ such that $v_S \leq p \leq v_R; p > 0$. In that case, state $R$ holds the property in the value of $w_r + v_R - p$, while secessionists gain price $p$.

However, it might also be possible, that state $R$ appreciates the property rights to the region $T_S$ less than the secessionists ($v_R < v_S$). In that case, price $p$, which is offered by state $R$ is lower than the price demanded by the secessionists and the trade is not affected. According to the conditions of this model, state $R$ recognise property rights of secessionists, which means it agrees with the secession. Thus, the state $R$ has a property of value $w_R$ while the new region $S$ has a property which it values at $v_S$ (see Table 1.2).

Second, assume that state $R$ wants to protect the indivisibility of the whole territory $T$. However, unlike the previous case, it does not recognise the property rights of the secessionists to territory $T_S$. If the secessionists declare independence, the situation results in armed (or diplomatic) conflict. Thus, to protect territory $T_S$, the secessionist allocates $\delta$ of their endowment. Those costs depreciate the value of territory $T_S$ regardless of who wins or loses. Hence, to conquer territory $T_S$, region $R$ needs to allocate endowment $\theta$. If the costs of predation are higher than the costs of defence ($\theta > \delta$), territory $T_S$ is conquered by region $R$. Region $R$ then has the wealth in the value of $w_R + v_R - \delta - \theta$ and the secessionists have wealth in the value of 0. Otherwise ($\theta < \delta$), territory $T_S$ remains in the hands of the secessionists. Region $R$, then, has wealth in the value of $w_R - \theta$, and secessionists have wealth in the value of $v_S - \delta$. The cost of defence cannot be higher than the value $v_S$ which territory $T_S$ has for the secessionists (therefore $\delta \leq v_S$). Similarly, the predatory costs cannot be higher than the value $v_R$ which territory $T_S$ has for predator $R(\theta \leq v_R)$.

If state $R$ appreciate region $T_S$ more than the secessionists ($v_R > v_S$), then the outputs (sorted by efficiency) are $v_1 > v_2 > v_3 > v_4$. Otherwise, if the secessionists appreciate region $R$ more than state $R$ ($v_R < v_S$), the effective order of the results is $v_2 > v_1 > v_4 > v_3$. In both cases, the system with recognised and accepted property rights (cases $v_1$ and $v_2$) is more efficient than the system with unrecognised or unaccepted property rights (cases $v_3$ and $v_4$).

*Table 1.2* Gains of the region $R$ and secessionist $S$

| | | | *Region* | | *Total wealth (R+S)* | *case* |
|---|---|---|---|---|---|---|
| | | | $R$ | $S$ | | |
| Property right | recognised and accepted | $R$ purchases property right from $S$ ($v_R \geq v_S$). | $w_R + v_R - p$ | $p \in \langle v_S; v_R \rangle$ | $w_R + v_R$ | $v_1$ |
| | | $R$ do not purchase property right from $S$ ($v_R < v_S$) $\rightarrow$ secession. | $w_R$ | $v_S > 0$ | $w_R + v_S$ | $v_2$ |
| | unrecognised/ unaccepted | Conflict won by $R(\theta > \delta)$. | $w_R + v_R - \delta - \theta$ | 0 | $w_R + v_R - \delta - \theta$ | $v_3$ |
| | | Conflict won by $S(\theta < \delta)$. | $w_R - \theta$ | $v_S - \delta$ | $w_R + v_S - \delta - \theta$ | $v_4$ |

Source: Author.

Region $R$ gains territory $T_S$ only if $\theta > \delta$, which equals to $v_R > v_S$. If this condition is not met, region $R$ will not fight for territory $T_S$. Secessionists, therefore, should demonstrate that they highly appreciate territory $T_S$.

Finally, consider the extreme case in which $\delta = v_S$ and $\theta = v_R$. If region $R$ wins the conflict ($\theta > \delta$), it gains $w_R + v_R - v_S - v_R$, while secessionists $S$ gains *0*. Otherwise, if secessionists protect their region $T_S$ successfully, region $R$ receives $w_R - v_R$ and region S gains $v_S - v_S = 0$. In both cases, secessionists might end up with the zero gain. Region $R$ win, if $w_R - v_S > w_R - v_R$ and, thus, $v_S < v_R \leftrightarrow \theta > \delta$. In the extreme case, secessionists always prefer recognition of the property rights to the conflict. However, region $R$ prefer recognition of the property rights only if

$$w_R + v_R - p > w_R + v_R - \delta - \theta \tag{1.4}$$

thus,

$$p < \delta + \theta \tag{1.5}$$

or, in the very extreme case,

$$p < v_R + v_S \tag{1.6}$$

However, this condition is always met if the regions are trading territory $T_S$ because

$$v_S \leq p \leq v_R \rightarrow p \leq v_R \tag{1.7}$$

and, thus, for $v_S \geq 0$ there is

$$p < v_R + v_S \tag{1.8}$$

In summary, secession is most effective (and least harmful) in case of trade between both regions. Trade requires recognition and enforcement of property rights. Armed conflict is a less effective solution for both regions.

*Prospect theory* as part of the young but progressive discipline in *Behavioural International Law and Economics* suggests that it is "far easier to prevent a state from taking something it does not already possess than to induce it to give something up" (Aaken 2012). In other words, there is such a situation when region $R$ values territory $T_S$ more when it faces the danger of secession than in the initial peaceful situation. It means that in the case of the secessionist threat, the value increases to $v_R' = v_R + \tau$, which makes the secession more costly and less attractive.

## 1.3 Practice of the secession

This subchapter is devoted to the practical features of the secessions. Firstly, the historic secessionist waves are summarised. Then the secessionist parties and movements of the recent EU are introduced. In the third section, the political attitudes toward the deeper European integration are discussed. Finally, the role of the pro-secessionist leaders as the potential elite is considered.

### *1.3.1 Secessionist waves in Europe*

Newly born states on the world map need to be recognised by the international community. Recognition is not just a formal diplomatic procedure as foreign governments tend to keep the status quo because of the existing relationships with the original country and its government (Wood 1981). Moreover, secessionist movements are less predictable than former governments. It might, then, be connected to the increasing instability in international relationships that are traditionally based on credibility and transparency. The most reluctant to recognise a new state tends to be governments which also face the secessionist tensions in their own country. Ten years after Kosovo declared its independence,[15] it was recognised by 111 member states of the United Nations (Talmon 2018); however, it was not recognised, for example, by Spain.[16] Spain's lack of recognition is clearly the result of its concerns about its secessionist movements. Moreover, the Spanish government wants to cut Kosovo from the plan of EU enlargement (Rettman 2018). According to foreign diplomats, the Spanish government informally asked Kosovo secessionist leaders not to proclaim their independence declaration until the Spanish general election (9 March 2008) to avoid its effect on the separatist movements in Spain (John 2008). Basque secessionist leaders immediately found similarities between Kosovo within Serbia and Basque within Spain; Catalan secessionists supported the Kosovar Declaration of Independence (Pouw 2016).

It is symptomatic that most of the modern European states were created by (often multiple) secessions. During the 19th to 21st century, there were more than 30 European secessions, a great deal of them resulting from the wars and the attempts to restore the former countries.

The first regular secession of the 19th century might be identified in Finland. The Finnish peninsula, which was (until the middle of the 12th century) "no man's land", and was influenced by Rome and the Byzantine Empire (Jussila et al. 1999:3), became part of the Swedish kingdom as the Grand Duchy of Finland. After the Finnish War (between Sweden and Russia), the eastern third of Sweden was annexed by Russia because of its strategic position. In 1809, Finland reached autonomy within the Russian Empire. The full Finnish independence occurred during the First World War, when it was proclaimed as a sovereign state in 1917 – curiously enough, by the People's Commissar responsible for national questions, Joseph Stalin (Ihalainen 2017:279).[17]

That declaration of independence was justified by the right to self-determination as well as by the claim that Russia "could not lose Finland because, actually, it was never our property. If we forcibly retained Finland, that would not mean that we had acquired it" (ibidem).

The Napoleonic Wars gave birth to two secessions. In 1814, Denmark, which lost the Napoleonic War, concluded the Treaty of Kiel with the United Kingdom of Great Britain and Ireland and the Kingdom of Sweden. Based on this treaty, Norway was ceded to Sweden. As the Denmark-Norway Union ceased to exist, Norwegians started to claim independence (within the Swedish kingdom) which was symbolised by the 17th May Constitution (Gammelgaard and Holmøyvik 2014:10–14). French defeat in the Napoleonic Wars led to the independence of Luxembourg. This was by the Treaty of Vienna; thus, Luxembourg was "attached to the new kingdom of the Netherlands by a personal union" (Putnam 1919:450). However, the United Kingdom of the Netherlands was an object of two secessions in the 19th century: the *Belgian War of Independence* (1830–1832) led to the foundation of sovereign Belgian monarchy, which was not recognised by the Netherland until 1839 (Bradford 2004:171); and Luxembourg became fully independent after the extinction of the male members of the House of Nassau in 1890 (Pearson 2014:70).

Three Balkan states seceded in the 19th and early 20th centuries from the Ottoman Empire. The Greek War of Independence resulted in the signing of the London Protocol from 1830, which made the Greek monarchy "the first of the newly formed nation states of Europe to win the full sovereignty and international recognition in the 19th century" (Ricks and Beaton 2013:1). The Romanian War of Independence led to the new sovereign Romanian state in 1877 (Jelavich and Jelavich 2012), and, finally, the Bulgarian independence on the Ottoman Empire was proclaimed in 1908 (Detrez 2014:248).

The First World War shattered European borders. The self-dissolution of the Austro-Hungarian Empire led to the rebirth of Poland[18] and the emergence of Austria as well as Hungary within a tighter territory. After the independence wars, all three Baltics states – Estonia, Latvia, and Lithuania – reached their independence after the fall of Tsarist Russia (Šleivyte 2009:117). The Great War also led to the emancipation of nations and their integration into new artificial unions. Balkan nations which used to be part of either the Byzantine Empire of the Austro-Hungarian Empire unified into the Kingdom of Serbs, Croats, and Slovenes (Fogelquist 2011). The Bohemian kingdom as the former part of Cisleithania and Slovakia as the former part of Transleithanian together with Carpatho-Ruthenia were unified into the Czechoslovak Republic (Perman 1962:8). There were only five states which did not change their borders after 1918: Netherlands, Luxembourg, Switzerland, Spain, and Portugal (Žídek 2009:65). Czechoslovak was then within three decades of three further secessions. In 1938, after the Munich Agreement, there was the irredentism of Sudetenland (Ambrosio 2001). Five months later (on the eve of the Nazi annexation of the rest of Bohemia and Moravia), Slovakia declared its independence (Felak 1995). On 15 March, independence was also declared by Carpatho-Ruthenia, just to be immediately occupied by Hungary, and in 1944–1946 by the Red Army.[19] On the 29th of June 1945, Carpatho-Ukraine was reunited "with its age old fatherland-Ukraine and is being incorporated in the Ukrainian SSR" (Harriman 1945). Post-war conflicts also resulted in the Irish War of Independence (1920–1921) and the creation of the Irish Free State based on The Anglo-Irish Treaty (Leeson 2016).

The Second World War was followed by a wave of decolonisation in the 1950s and 1960s,[20] which also led to two European secessions of Cyprus (1960) and Malta (1964) from the United Kingdom of Great Britain and Northern Ireland (Holland 2014).[21] On the contrary, the division of Germany into four military zones (1945) and the promulgation of the German Democratic Republic (1949) cannot be considered secession. For instance, O'Leary (2006) notes that "Political partitions should be carefully distinguished from secessions, decolonisations and disengagements", because they "involve a fresh cut, and, at least, [a] partially novel border, ripped through, at least, one national community's homeland".[22]

So far, the last secessionist wave among EU members occurred after the end of the Cold War. This wave has certain feathers in common with the wave which followed the First World War as it also covered the same Baltic and Balkan states and central Europe. Baltic states seceded without any other independence war, as their secession from the Soviet Union was legitimised by the independence

*Figure 1.2* Independence years of the recent European countries

Source: Author.

*Table 1.3* Independence referenda (1990–1991)

| *Country* | *Date* | *For independence (%)* | *Turnout (%)* |
|---|---|---|---|
| Slovenia | 23 December 1990 | 94.8 | 93.5 |
| Lithuania | 9 February 1991 | 93.2 | 84.7 |
| Estonia | 3 March 1991 | 78.4 | 82.9 |
| Latvia | 3 March 1991 | 74.9 | 87.6 |
| Croatia | 19 May 1991 | 93.2 | 83.6 |

Source: Roeder (2018:29). Own elaboration.

*Table 1.4* Secessionist pressures in the EU (2013–2015)

| | *Country* | *Region* | *Time* |
|---|---|---|---|
| Referendum | United Kingdom | Scotland | September 2014 |
| | Spain | Catalonia | November 2015 |
| | Belgium | Flanders | May 2014 |
| | Italy | Veneto | March 2014 |
| | France | Alsace | April 2013 |
| Election success | France | Corsica | December 2015 |
| | United Kingdom | Scotland | May 2015 |

Source: Own elaboration.

referendum, which was strongly in favour of the secession (Table 1.3). Croatia and Slovenia run referendum as well; nevertheless, they later underwent other wars on independence (Finlan 2004). Finally, in 1993, there was the dissolution of the Czechoslovak Republic into the two sovereign independent states of the Czech Republic and the Slovak Republic (Young 1994b).

The European continent at the end and beginning of the 20th and 21st centuries respectively has been the subject to two contradictory tendencies. On the one hand, member states of the EU lean towards deeper integration, which has resulted in a common economic, regional, or agricultural policy. On the other hand, we have witnessed an unprecedented growth of autonomous, secessionist, and separatist movements. On 18 September 2014, the Scottish independence referendum was held, and despite the majority being against independence, the Scottish National Party won 56 from 59 Scottish seats in the United Kingdom general election in 2015. The Scottish independence referendum was followed by an unofficial independence referendum in Catalonia, Spain, on 9 November 2014. Although the central government rejected the referendum (see Table 1.4), 81% of voters voted in favour of Catalonia's independence (with a turnout of 37%; see Gillespie and Gray 2015:117). Crepaz mentions the pro-autonomy support in the Veneto region of Italy where, in 2014, during an unofficial referendum, 89%

of voters were in favour of leaving Italy (Crepaz 2016:76). The Belgian federal elections in May 2014 were won by the Flemish independence party *Nieuw-Vlaamse Alliantie* (New Flemish Party, N-VA) whose main aim is the ultimate independence of Flanders (Thompson 2015:214). In Corsica, the French regional elections in December 2015 were won by the pro-independence political party, *Corsica Libera* (Lichfield 2015).

### *1.3.2 Secessionist parties and movements*

There were violent conflicts connected to separatism in 49 states within the 1946–2008 period (World Bank 2011:166). According to Griffiths, 403 distinct secessionist movements between 1816 and 2011 can be distinguished, with an average length of existence of about 11 years (Griffiths 2016:51). Among such secessionist movements, the secessionist political parties play crucial roles. The role of the party includes the representation of interests, formation of political elites and their recruitment, formulation of social goals and government policy, articulation and aggregation of interests, mobilisation and socialisation of the electorate, and organisation of governmental processes and institutional relationships (Heywood 2013:243). All these roles are substantial in secessionist regions.

Table 1.5 covers the secessionist parties in seven European countries,[23] which are represented in the regional or local parliaments. Most of them (14, which accounts for 56%) claims to be left-wing parties (L). Those parties prevail in Galicia, Catalonia, Scotland, Wales, or Corsica. The right-wing parties (R) are weaker, prevailing just in Flanders and represented in South Tyrol, Sardinia, as well as Basque. The rest of the parties declare that they are centrist (C). The highest

*Table 1.5* Dominant secessionist parties in the selected European countries

| *Country* | | | |
|---|---|---|---|
| *Regional representation* | | *Election Year* | |
| | *Abbrev.* | *Votes [%]* | *L/C/R* |
| *Belgium* | | | |
| *Flemish Parliament* | | *2014* | |
| Vlaams Belang | VB | 5.9 | R |
| New Flemish Alliance | NVA | 31.9 | R |
| *Total support* | | *37.8* | |
| *Finland* | | | |
| *Lagting (Parliament of Åland)* | | *2015* | |
| Future of Åland | AF | 7.4 | C |
| *Total support* | | *7.4* | |

(*Continued*)

*Table 1.5* (Continued)

| *Country* | | | |
|---|---|---|---|
| *Regional representation* | | *Election Year* | |
| | *Abbrev.* | *Votes [%]* | *L/C/R* |
| *France* | | | |
| *Corsican Assembly* | | *2015* | |
| Pè a Corsica | | 25.35 | L |
| *Total support* | | *25.35* | |
| *Italy* | | | |
| *Südtiroler Landtag* | | *2013* | |
| South Tyrolean People's Party | SVP | 45.7 | C |
| Die Freiheitlichen | dF | 17.9 | R |
| South Tyrolean Freedom | STF | 7.2 | R |
| *Total support* | | *70.8* | |
| *Regional Council of Sardinia* | | *2014* | |
| Party of Sardinians | PdS | 2.66 | L |
| Red Moors | RM | 2.63 | L |
| Independence Republic of Sardinia | iRS | 0.82 | L |
| Sardinian Reformers | RS | 6.02 | R |
| Sardinian Action Party | PSd'Az | 4.67 | L |
| Sardinian Democratic Union – Nationalist Project | UDS | 2.6 | R |
| *Total support* | | *19.4* | |
| *Council of the Valley* | | *2013* | |
| Valdostan Union | UV | 33.5 | C |
| Edelweiss | SA | 12.2 | C |
| Autonomist Federation | FA | 2.2 | L |
| Autonomy Liberty Participation Ecology | ALPE | 12.4 | L |
| *Total support* | | *60.3* | |
| *Spain* | | | |
| *Parliament of Galicia* | | *2012* | |
| Galician Alternative of the Left | AGE | 13.91 | L |
| Galician Nationalist Bloc | BNG | 10.11 | L |
| *Total support* | | *24.02* | |
| *Parliament of Catalonia* | | *2015* | |
| Together for Yes | IPA | 39.59 | L |
| Popular Unity Candidacy | CUP | 8.21 | L |
| *Total support* | | *47.8* | |

| | | | |
|---|---|---|---|
| *Basque Parliament* | | *2012* | |
| Basque Nationalist Party | EAJ | 34.16 | R |
| EH Bildu | EHB | 24.67 | L |
| *Total support* | | *58.83* | |
| *United Kingdom* | | | |
| *Scottish Parliament* | | *2016* | |
| Scottish National Party | SNP | 46.5 | L |
| *Total support* | | *46.5* | |
| *National Assembly for Wales* | | *2016* | |
| Plaid Cymru | PC | 20.5 | L |
| *Total support* | | *20.5* | |

Source: Author. Based on the Norwegian Centre for Research Data (2016), and party programmes.

total pro-secessionist support is revealed in the South Tyrol Parliament (Südtiroler Landtag), Italy, where it accounts for 70.8%, and in the Council of the Valley, as well as the Basque Parliament. However, the weakest representation has the secessionist movement in Finnish Åland.

### *1.3.3 Secessionist political parties and their attitude towards EU*

European integration, especially regarding economic integration, is a substantial economic secessionist factor. On the one hand, the *even, deeper integration* should lead to a diminishing of national differences. As Brubaker highlights, the EU is based on *post-nationalism* because the term *nation* begins to be considered as "suspicious, connected to intolerance, xenophobia, or militarism" (Brubaker 2004). As mentioned by Keating (2004), European integration is part of the *state transformation*, weakening the national state's competences, and loss of the state hegemony. The EU plays the role of the "third side" (Walker 2014) between the secessionist region and the rest of the country.

However, such *demystification of the state sovereignty* (a term used by Keating 2004) results in the creation of new structures within the national (secessionist) movements which try to find their new place within the EU. European economic integration provides the European secessionist regions with a protective umbrella. It allows the regions to concentrate more on the co-operation with other European regions than with the central government of their own countries. Independence within the EU is safer than independence outside the EU (Keating 2004). Such pro-secessionist tendencies are even promoted by EU organs such as the *Committee of the Regions*.

Committee of the Regions was created on the basis of the Maastricht Treaty as the advisory body. The Lisbon Treaty strengthened its role in 2009 (Walker 2014). Secessionist regions were, furthermore, supported by the administrative reform which established *The Nomenclature of Territorial Units for Statistics* (NUTS);

especially, the NUTS 2 regions (compare Baranyai 2013). These regions are of the highest importance, especially in terms of the redistribution of the European structural funds (Baranyai 2013; Walker 2014). This reform helped many regions such as Cornwall, England, appear on the European map (Deacon 2003).

As Calvet (n.d.) claims, modern secessionism highlights not only the borders and external sovereignty but also the so-called *cosmopolitan sovereignty* (Pogge 1992). Cosmopolitan sovereignty requires relationships with international organisations such as EU or OSN (Calvet n.d.). Keating (2004) goes even further when speaking about *post-sovereignty*, defining post-sovereignty as "the loss of the monopoly on the sovereignty".

From the EU point of view, secession is both desirable and undesirable. A disintegration of the national states strengthens the role of the EU. However, it can also trigger a disintegration of the supranational EU itself. This is possibly the reason the opinions of the European Commission on the secession develop. Walker (2014) shows that the former chairs, Barroso and Prodi, were against the Scottish secession, while Juncker is in his statements was less brusque.[24]

However, Alesina and Spolaore (1997) proved that the equilibrium number of countries is increasing with the amount of international economic integration. That is why Connolly (2013) postulates a *Paradox of separatism amid integration*. From the very nature of the Treaty of Rome, the EU led to an even deeper integration. It made independence more practical and desirable by the over-representation of small states in EU institutions (compare Connolly 2013; Baldwin and Wyplosz 2013). Furthermore, it did this by financial support to regions (such as the European Regional Development Fund), institutional support in Brussels (Committee of the Regions), para-diplomacy, subsidiarity, as well as the popular idea of *Europe of the Regions* which is being proclaimed since the Maastricht Treaty discussion (see Connolly 2013).

European integration under the EU umbrella weakens the national attributes. National border dissolution within the Schengen area, as well as the common European currency of euro, drag down the ties between the region and the national state. Furthermore, access to the European common market and protection under a latent safety umbrella reduces the costs and risks of separatism (Dvořáková and Ferrarová 2014). Keating (2002) argues that European integration has challenged state sovereignty.

Although many pro-secessionist movements are pro-European, the development has never been straightforward. For instance, Faroe Islands tend to express Eurosceptic opinions. Denmark joined the EU in 1973; nevertheless, the Faroe Islands maintain the neutrality of a *third country*, which enables them to stay outside the EU and have the permanent sovereign diplomatic representation in Brussels (Adler-Nissen 2014).

The great opportunity for small secessionist parties (called *ethnonationalist* parties by Deacon 2003) is presented not only in general elections but also in second order elections such as regional or European Parliament elections. As Keating (2004) mentions, direct elections by the European Parliament introduced in 1979 resulted in the creation of the *European Free Alliance* (EFA) in 1981. The EFA associates with regional secessionist parties. Since 1999, it formed the political group in the European Parliament together with the Greens (Watts 2008:160).

Moreover, the importance of secessionist parties is further enhanced by the structural funds, which, as Keating (2004:377) claims, are "a source of funding independent. . . .Member States" and "an arena for symbolic politics, in which regional politicians can claim to have established a funding link to Brussels".

The *supranationality* of the European [Political] Union, therefore, provides the secessionist regions with the opportunity of *paradiplomacy* (Walker 2014). Paradiplomacy, or parallel diplomacy, is considered as a "direct international activity by subnational actors supporting, complementing, correcting, [and] challenging the nation-states' diplomacy" (Tavares 2016). Due to this EU support, most of the secessionist movements are pro-European. However, Keating (2004) also mentions some Basque independence movements, Irish *Sinn Féin*, Gallic *Bloque Nacionalista Galego*, or the radical left groups in the French Bretagne and Occitania which are anti-European.

Based on political programmes and statements of the secessionist parties, most of the secessionist movements require their region to become an independent state within the EU (New Flemish Alliance 2016; Plaid Cymru 2016; Scottish National Party 2016). For instance, the Belgian *New Flemish Alliance* claims that its "final target is, indeed, an independent Flanders as a European Member State" and that the "currency, defence, migration, or internal market competencies must be transferred to the European level" (ibidem). Similarly, the *South Tyrolean People's Party* in Italy supports a "unified Europe of the Regions" (Südtiroler Volkspartei 2016). The Italian *Party of Sardinians* goes even further when it advocates "future United States of Europe" (Party of Sardinians 2016).

On the other hand, even pro-European secessionist parties such as the Welsh *Plaid Cymru* or the *Scottish National Party* called for EU reforms. The smallest group of secessionist parties is Eurosceptic. For instance, the Belgian party, *Vlaams Belang*, emphasises that it has a "critical attitude towards the EU with its bureaucracy and tendency to meddle where the sovereignty of the people should prevail" (Vlaams Belang 2016), and the Finnish party *Future of Åland* suggests that Åland should become a "sovereign, neutral, and demilitarized microstate in the ever growing and more and more respected European family of microstates" (Future of Åland 2016).

As was mentioned earlier, the European Parliament elections are, for secessionist parties, of the high importance, though their representation in Brussels and Strasbourg is not great. In the modern European Parliament (elected in 2014), the Belgian secessionist parties have five members (out of a total of 21), the Italians have six (out of 73), the Spanish have four (out of 54), and the British have three (out of 73). Neither Corsica nor Åland has its secessionist representation in the European Parliament (European Commission 2016).

### *1.3.4 Role of leaders*

> A genuine love for the nation and a desire for its flourishing inspires many nationalists in nations without states, especially in those cases where the nation feels culturally, politically, or economically oppressed by the state. Devoting one's life to the defence and enhancement of the specific character of one's own nation may act as a potent force.
>
> Guibernau (2003:17)

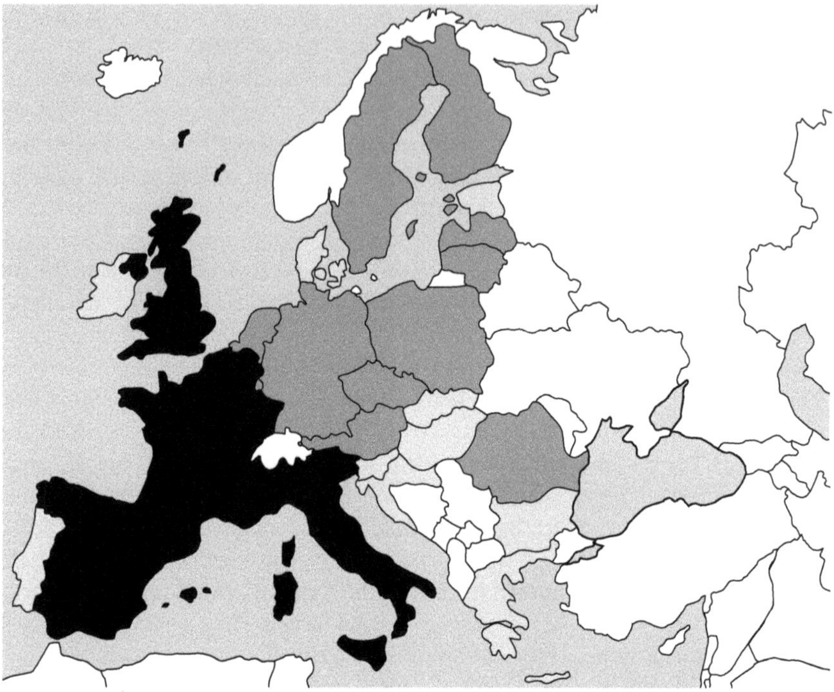

*Figure 1.3* Map of the European secessionist regions

Source: Author. The darker color mirrors the higher degree of secessionism in the country according to the number of regions.

Founders gain prominent places in the history of new states. As Doyle (2010) mentions, if the separatists succeed, cities, mountains, and state holiday are named after them. That was the fate of George Washington in the United States of America, the first Czechoslovak president Tomáš Garrigue Masaryk, and the commander of the Hungarian War of Independence, Gyulla Andrássy. If they fail, they are executed as traitors and rebels as a deterrent to warn others (for example, the Catalan revolutionary leader, Lluís Companys).

The so-called "Potential elite" (educated individuals, who would become leaders in case of a national movement success; Guibernau 2003:16), consists of those

- dissatisfied with the state's treatment of their community;
- excluded from the state's official elite because of their regional origin; and
- who prioritised their national allegiance to the integration within the state's official elite.

(ibidem)

Secessionist moods may attract so-called *political entrepreneurs* who can gain voter support thanks to independence demonstrations and uprisings (Wood 1981).

Charismatic leaders play an important role in peaceful and fast secessions (Young 1994a). According to Wood (1981), the role of leaders is even more important than the role of pro-secessionist ideologies (such as nationalism). The "secessionist entrepreneurs" create organisational structures for secession (Pavkovic and Radan 2013:178), and mobilise the people (Requejo Coll and Caminal i Badia 2011:193) using non-violent public propaganda, mass demonstrations, and civil disobedience (Wood 1981).

Secondly, most of the secessionist movements need elite and well-educated leaders who would be able to take the lead in international negotiations regarding the recognition of their country. Baranyai (2013) mentioned that the regionalism in Upper Silesia suffered from the lack of regional elites as the local political leaders always came from different Polish regions. Similarly, Deacon (2003) recalls that the leaders of the Cornish secessionist movements were mostly teachers and lower civil servants. Independence movement on the Faroe Islands was formed in 1888 by the young well-educated elites and university students (Adler-Nissen 2014). The Flanders independence movement was led by priests and other intellectuals (Vos 2002).

Hroch (1996) recognises three basic stages of the national movements:

1 *scholar interest*, which is comprised of the language, culture, history, as well as the habits studied by the enlightened scholars;
2 *national agitation*, that was promoted by the well-educated patriots; and
3 *mass movement*, in which thousands of citizens were mobilised.

A provocative view on the role of elites (intellectuals) is offered by Breuilly (1994), who depicts nationalist leaders as "unsuccessful professionals". They use nationalism merely as an opportunity to reach a more prestigious position in society. Intellectuals can be both the architects of the nationalist movement, as well as the formulators of the nationalist ideology, agitators, and mobilisers (Guibernau 2003:27).

Regions with successful secessionist movements have often provided their countries with numerous prime ministers. For instance, 15 Belgian prime ministers in 1946–2016 were born in Flanders, and 11 Italian prime ministers were born in one of the main secessionist regions. However, none of the Finnish prime ministers in 1917–2016 came from Åland. In 1958–2016, there was only one French prime minister from Corsica, and none of the Polish prime ministers in 1989–2016 came from Upper Silesia.[25] After the fall of Franco, there were just two Spanish prime ministers from the Spanish secessionist regions and from 1922 to 2016, only three British PMs from Wales and Scotland.

## 1.4 The reasons for secession

> The long-term history of country formation and separation has been influenced by the pattern of trade openness and economic integration and vice versa.
>
> (Alesina and Spolaore 2000)

On 27 October 2017, the parliament of Catalonia passed *The Catalan declaration of independence* by the 52% majority. This document "constituted the Catalan Republic, as an independent, sovereign, democratic, and social State under the rule of law" (Parlament de Catalunya 2017). The text of the declaration refers to the Catalan nation, language, culture, as well as the historical legitimacy, legal, and institutional traditions (ibidem). A unilateral declaration was annulled two weeks later, on 8 November by Spain's Constitutional Court.

A recent declaration is the fifth try to found the sovereign Catalan state. At least four centuries have seen the Catalans longing for freedom. The first Catalan republic was established in 1641 after the Catalan Revolt. Nevertheless, it lasted for merely six days (Guinot 2014:207). The second Catalan state followed in 1873 after the abdication of the King of Spain, Amadeus of Savoy (Balcells 1996:31). Other two Catalan republics were proclaimed in the 1930s. The so-called "Third Catalan Republic" (The Catalan Republic within the Iberian Federation), supported by the agreement of 98% plebiscites voters, lasted only four days in 1931 (Alland 2006:194). Finally, the Catalan State was proclaimed in 1934 only to survive for merely 24 hours (Blanch 2013:9).

As case of the Catalan clearly shows, secession is rarely the result of only one factor. Usually, it combines several different factors with nationalism being fundamentally principal to most of the secessions (Doyle 2010). Secessionist factors can be divided into two basic groups: romantic and economic (Rodríguez-Pose and Stermšek 2014). Similarly, Guibernau (2003:22) distinguishes *rational* and *emotional* arguments used by elites to "awaken the nation and generate a mass nationalist movement". Rational arguments mainly support economic factors of secession, while emotional arguments are connected to romantic factors (Table 1.6).

*Table 1.6* Economic and romantic factors

| | | *Arguments* | |
|---|---|---|---|
| | | *Rational* | *Emotional* |
| **Factors** | Economic | Retain regionally generated wealth<br>Higher quality of life<br>Fiscal justice<br>Discrete economy policy on the regional level | |
| | Romantic | Deepening of democracy due decentralisation and self-determination | Sense of continuity<br>Use of particular language<br>Sharing a common history<br>Sharing a common set of values<br>Art and artists<br>Folklore<br>Sport |

Source: Guibernau (2003) and Rodríguez-Pose and Stermšek (2014). Elaborated by the author.

Both classes of secessionist factors, however varied, are interconnected in one way: heterogeneity of preferences.

### *1.4.1 Romantic factors*

The traditional approach to secession had been based on assessing non-economic (meaning non-pecuniary) factors such as nationality, language, and religion. These factors were closely connected to *romantic nationalism*. Romantic nationalism has its roots in 18th and 19th century Romantic Movement, which was less oriented on previous rationalism and more on "irrational, emotional, ethnic, and religious factors" since the *human group identity* had been seen as a "function of the group's unique culture and history within a specific territory rather than of generic scientific, political, social, or economic development" (Hupchick 2002).

The uprising of the nation states at the beginning of the 19th century was closely connected to the "cultural, linguistic, and ethnic homogeneity of the groups that came together" (Alesina and Spolaore 2000:19). Similarly, according to Rodríguez-Pose and Stermšek (2014), secessionist movements want to preserve and promote the historical, cultural, language, and religious identity of the territory. The *right to self-determination* argument springs from the normative national principle that emphasises cultural and ethnic frontiers (Buchanan 1991b).

Secession had always been studied from the ethical point of view, especially in terms of the moral justification of the right to self-determination. The basic question addresses the very existence (or non-existence) of the right to founding a new independent state. An ethical point of view as presented by Buchanan (1991b) restricts such right, while according to Boykin (1998), the government may not prohibit secession by its legislation. There is widespread agreement that if secession is based on a referendum, then it is fully legitimate (Vaubel 2013), and if the central government ignores the citizen's decision, it loses its legitimacy (Wood 1981). Calvet (ND:17) suggests that the right to secession emphasises "democratic values rather than national values".

These normative solutions are somewhat weakened by the real legal system as it does not solve the common problem of secessionist-referendum prohibition. For instance, the Spanish Constitution does not allow any referendum on the regional level (Bieri 2014). However, the Supreme Court of Canada recognised secession rights in 1998 in a case agreed upon by all other Canadian regions (Vaubel 2013). Nevertheless, constitutions guaranteeing the right to secession are just rare. A prominent exception is represented by the Constitution of Principality of Lichtenstein from 2003. According to Article 4 (2), the individual communes have the right to secede from the State:

> A decision to initiate the secession procedure shall be taken by a majority of the citizens residing there who are entitled to vote. Secession shall be regulated by a law or, as the case may be, a treaty. In the latter event, a second ballot shall be held in the commune after the negotiations have been completed.

Thus, to conduct the secessionist referendum, the pro-secessionist ballot must satisfy the condition that it must be approved at least by two-thirds of the commune residents who are entitled to vote.

On the contrary, Catalonia in Spain does not have a right to run an official referendum on secession. As Calvet (ND:4), clearly, listed:

- Article 2 of the Spanish Constitution proclaims the indissolubility of the Spanish nation;
- Article 8 of the Spanish Constitution provides the Armed Forces with the duty to guarantee the territorial integrity of the State;
- Article 478 of the Spanish Criminal Code categorises secession on the same level of a rebellion offence; and
- The Constitutional Court decision STC 103/2008 (regarding Basque) states that "sovereignty lies in the Spanish people".

More spectacular is the question of *who* can secede. If the secession right exists, is it the right of the group of people (as supported by Buchanan 1991b), the nation, or individuals? The last approach, individual right to secession, was proposed by Mises (2004), who, in line with his methodological individualism, claimed that every citizen of every national unit could decide on his preferences in terms of nationality.

If such a right exists, there must be an agreement on the form of secession. While in Montenegro or Scotland, the independence referendum was used, the dissolution of the Czech and Slovak Federative Republic was based on the results of a general election in 1992 following negotiations between the political leaders. If it should be approved by referendum, the question of a majority vote and conditions of validity emerge.[26] Furthermore, if the new state needs to be recognised by the international community, it must be discussed.

An election threshold determines the stability of the status quo, which leads to a discussion regarding a higher threshold with respect to the aim of a secessionist referendum. For instance, Wellman (2010) suggests a kind of supermajority as the simple majority might lead to a result where 49.9% of citizens would be forced to live in a new state they do not want. Furthermore, Staal (2010) claims that majority voting leads to non-efficient results; democracy, especially, results in a "high" number of countries. On the contrary, according to Boykin (1998), secession should be judged by the same measure as any other constitutional change, which means that any additional restriction should not be applied. Vaubel (2013) sees the solution in the international legal framework, which would enforce keeping the agreed secessionist rules as well as protect the minority laws in the secessionist states.

Secessionism is closely connected to regionalisation – the designation of the division of the state into regions and the transfer of administrative and political responsibilities to those regions (Schrijver 2006:17). Such a regionalisation can be *top-down* (planned by the central government), or *bottom-up*, which, according to secessionist studies, is more important as it is affected by the regional identity as well as cultural and ethnic matters (Baranyai 2013).

Since the *United Nations General Assembly Resolution 1514: Declaration on the Granting of Independence to Colonial Countries and Peoples*, international law uses the term "right to self-determination"[27] (UN 1960). Traditionally, the roots of this approach are being sought in Woodrow Wilson's Fourteen Points Speech (Wilson 1918). However, President Wilson in his speech did not use term the "right to self-determination", and, except for Poland, he did not promote independence but only the autonomy of individual regions.[28]

Right to self-determination cannot be equated with the *right to secession*. While the international community has a certain understanding of the secession of former colonies and annexed areas (Buchanan 1999), secessionist movements are being tackled with clear disapproval. As Brilmayer mentioned, the "principle of self-determination, suggesting that every people has a right to its own nation-state, is contrary to [the] principle of international law, which upholds [the] territorial integrity of existing states" (Brilmayer 1991).

While the standard analysis deals with the ethical dimension of secession, there is a small and very heterogeneous group of scholars who highlight the concept of territorial principle in secessionist movements. According to Wellman (2010), the "primary question in a secessionist conflict concerns the territory contested". Self-determination in his point of view "necessarily involves a claim to territory". Knight (1985) developed the concept of *group territorial identity*, claiming that the "concept of self-determination is at once legal and geographical". Knight also defines territorial principal in terms of property rights since he regards territory as the "space to which identity is attached by a distinctive group who hold or covet that territory and who desire to have full control of it for the group's benefit" (Knight 1982). Brilmayer (1991) clearly states that "secessionist claims involve disputed claims to territory". Secession concerns the "relationship between people, states, and territory" where territory is the key factor. Therefore, secessionists need to "establish a claim to the territory" to be able to found the new secessionist state.

For the leaders of secessionist movements, it is easier to appeal to the citizens – their potential voters – through common history and religion to speak to them with a common language than to explain complex socioeconomic and geopolitical factors.

Even recent secessionist movements are based on this to shape their discourse and gain political support (Collier and Hoeffler 2002). According to Bieri (2014), autonomistic tendencies are supported by the effort to preserve common regional language and culture. However, secessionist tendencies in Catalonia or Flanders might also be supported by the history of oppression by the central government. Bieri recalls Franco's repression on the minority languages and regions in Spain as well as former Wallonia's dominance over Flanders (Bieri 2014).

Pföstl (ND:1–2) mentions that nationality can be based on *demos*, *ethnos*, or *language* (the so-called French model of a citizenship approach). Bilingualism might increase the probability of separation (Bolton and Roland 1995).

In this chapter, arguments for four main romantic secessionist factors are discussed theoretically: ethnicity, language, religion, and culture. Their reflections in the recent European secessionist tensions will be presented in Part 3.3.

### *Ethnicity*

> If borders can easily be changed, identity cannot.
>
> *Marco Brunazzo (The Guardian 2014)*

An important romantic factor is a nation as an entity with which individuals can identify and within which they maximise their utility functions. When France lost Alsace-Lorraine as the result of the Franco-Prussian War, the French philosopher Ernest Renan sought to define the nation. Brubaker (2004) claims that, currently, Renan's definition of a nation as an entity based on language, race, and culture is not the ethnocultural reality because modern values connect a nation with the solidarity of *the people* (ibidem). Max Weber considered a nation as *Wertbegriff*, the value concept which perceives a nation as "a category of practice, not a category of analysis" (Abbot 2007:38). Brubaker (2004) also advocates "nationalism" as it supports the redistributive social politics which need interclass solidarity.

A nation, in relation to secession, is connected with the so-called *stateless nations*, the "cultural communities sharing a common past, attached to a clearly demarcated territory, and wishing to decide upon their political future which lack a state of their own" (Guibernau 2003:4). Guibernau also recognises five dimensions of a nation:

1 psychological (consciousness of forming a group);
2 national;
3 territorial;
4 political; and
5 historical.

(ibidem)

According to Calvet, current stateless nations include Quebec, Scotland, and Catalonia, as well as Basque, Galicia, Bretagne, Corse, Wales, North Ireland, and South Tyrol of Alsace (Calvet ND).

A feeling of historic injustice may fuel the pro-secessionist tensions which reflect the "occupation" of the region.[29] For example the Faroese minister of trade and foreign affairs, Pould Michelsen (leader of the separatist *Progressive Party*), said in 2018: "We are not Danes, we will never be Danes, we can't be Danes, we are Faroese and that's it . . . we have to stand up for it and fight for it" (The Local 2018).

### *Language*

Language belongs to the key romantic secessionist factors. Nevertheless, language heterogeneity does not inevitably result in secessionist tensions. Boyle and Englebert (2008) noticed that separatist regions are "usually believed to be different from the rest of the country in terms of wealth, physical, or human capital, or natural resources endowment". Language stays for an important part of the human capital (compare Breton 1998; Pendakur and Pendakur 1998). Language was used to define the national culture, especially in the 19th century (Zwet 2015). In the Czech independence movement, Jungmann already identified the nation with the mother tongue (Patočka 1969). As Ernest Renant wrote in his pivotal contribution, *What is Nation*? (1882), "languages ask to be united, they do not force it".

Saideman (2001:27) suggests that the homogeneity and heterogeneity in language, religion, and ethnicity play a crucial role in receiving international support, which is necessary for the recognition of a new state. If states are "more likely to support actors with which important constituents share ethnic ties", the ethnic groups "are likely to define themselves by broader identities to maximise their domestic and international support" (Saideman 2001:28).

Language legislation might also heavily influence the economic condition of the country. Hechter claims that Quebec's language legislation promoting the usage of the French language led to an increase in Francophone owned companies share from 47% in 1961 to 61% in 1991 (Hechter 2017:xvii).

### ROLE OF EDUCATION

However, the knowledge of language is developed in schools where the substantial part of the individual as well as national human capital is built up. Moreover, the field of education is of the highest importance for secessionist movements and secessionist political parties. While typical European countries offload the education ministry to minor coalition parties (see Cabada 2006), secessionist parties in regional and local governments consider the education ministry as the key portfolio. For instance, according to the Basque government's minister of education, Cristina Uriarte, "the commitment to education is strongly linked to the national identity" as education is the key to keeping a Basque culture (Coughlan 2016). Similarly, Hauk and Ortega (2015) mention that schooling is used to create a common identity.

For the success of secessionist movements, the regions should also have a well-developed infrastructure, including universities (compare Deacon 2003; Mises 2004) and the high level of the human capital in general. Dorronsoro considers education to be a long-term investment, which needs the feeling of identity. This is why the accumulation of human capital supported in such regions as the Basque Country, where there was a suppression under Franco's dictatorship, enjoys strong public support of regional education (Coughlan 2016).

The effort to gain autonomy in education policy might also be motivated by the interregional migration in the countries with secessionist movements. If the secessionist region lacked high-quality education, the citizens moved to other parts of the country. Moreover, many of the secessionist regions in Europe promote teaching in their own language using their own curricula. If the citizen was educated just in the regional language (not knowing the language of e.g. the centrum), he or she would be tied to the region and would not assimilate with the central culture. (compare the concept of returns to the firm investment in human capital as developed, for instance, by Almeidam and Carneiro 2006).

### *Religion*

Religion significantly creates a border between Western (Catholic and Protestant) and Eastern (Orthodox and Muslim) worlds (Huntington 1997). This line can be observed in secessionist conflicts in Ukraine, as well as a latent decentralisation trend of Catholic Bavaria in relation to the rest of German Protestants. The successful secession in Sudan was among other (economic) factors also pushed by the religionist conflict between the Arabic North and Christian South of Sudan (Natsios and Abramowitz 2011).

Religion is an important unifying element within secessionist communities. As Griera mentions, "the first and foremost task in order to produce and reproduce nation-state in modern times was to homogenise cultural specificities . . . and to instil a sense of belonging to such communities" (Griera 2016:16). If there is an essential heterogeneity between the region and rest of the country, an affiliation to a different church might strengthen feelings of difference, exclusivity, as well as isolation. After all, all European wars had their roots in the confession of diversity (compare Griera 2016). The assistant bishop in Barcelona said in 2012 that the "[Catholic] Church must be at the side of the people" supporting the independence (Requejo and Nagel 2014:204). Similarly, Cardinal Martínez Sistach noted that "The Gospel neither provides arguments against the right to decide nor against independentism" (ibidem). However, the religion common to a secessionist region and the rest of the country might play the role of the unifying factor. The orientation of local church (such as on the archdiocese level) might, therefore, stress the Catholic (meaning universal, worldwide, and timeless) character of a religion, leading to the universality and unity of the state. The head of the Catholic Church, Pope Francis, did not support the secession, nor did he warn against independence movements when he said in 2014 in the Spanish newspaper: "The secession of a nation without a precedent of forced unity has to be taken with many tweezers and analyzed on a case by case basis" (San Martín 2017).

### *Culture*

The role of national identity might be demonstrated in the case of Alsace-Lorraine. The citizens of this region changed their citizenship four times in a century (1850 to 1950); their identity was, constantly shifting between German, French, and Alsatian (Kokaisl et al. 2013). Today, two-thirds of citizens identify themselves as Alsatian, less than one-third as French, and 6% as Europeans. However, according to Kokaisl et al. (2013), none of the respondents identified themselves with German, although all local traditions are held in the spirit of German culture. An inter-crossing of the cultural influence is also apparent in its economy; for instance, although the area is characterised by French-like wine, its viticulture is, nevertheless, run under the German methods.

The cultural heritage of secessionist regions also fosters cultural differences. For instance, the Catalans are proud of the works of Gaudi and its natives (Salvador Dalí or Joan Miró); Scottish cultural heritage covers Adam Smith, David

Livingstone, and David Hume; and Flemish culture is based on its Flemish school including Bruegel, Rubens, or van Dyck.

The heterogeneity of the romantic factors within one country might be curiously observed even in the sports field. Del Lago (as quoted by Kassimeris 2011:679) claims that Italian football culture is "a form of extended municipalism. The battle lines of the football 'ultras' are those of the ancient rivalries between regions and towns". Similarly, the UEFA membership responds to the state borders in most of the cases with several noteworthy exceptions: instead of the United Kingdom of Great Britain, there are four individual members – England, Scotland, Wales, and Northern Ireland. Furthermore, there is also membership for the Faroe Islands besides Denmark (UEFA 2019). Catalan nationalism is represented by the motto of FC Barcelona "more than a club". According to Berdún (2019:103), FC Barcelona "is key in advancing claims that Catalonia is a sovereign nation with the right to decide its political future". Guibernau also notices that FC Barcelona was "portrayed as a representative of the Catalan nation and exemplified resistance against the dictatorship" during Francoism (2004:22). However, the Flemish Football Association has not been recognised by UEFA (Dolan and Connolly 2017). Moreover, the extraordinary success of the Belgian national football team repeatedly led to the marginalisation of Flemish nationalism (Mudde 2014).

### *Intraregional heterogeneity*

The problem of heterogeneity in romantic factors might be demonstrated in the case of the Socialist Federal Republic of Yugoslavia, which was, according to the last census in 1981, extremely heterogeneous even in ethnicity (Figure 1.4).

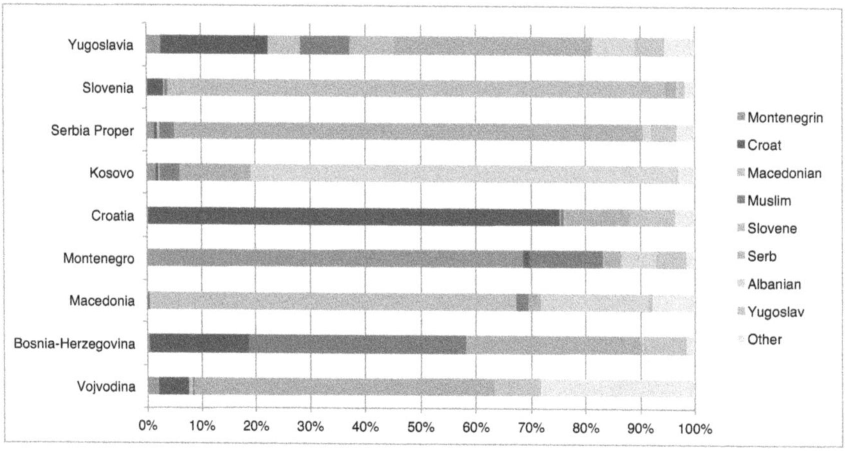


*Figure 1.4* Heterogeneity in ethnicity among the countries of the former The Socialist Federal Republic of Yugoslavia (in 1981)

Source: Szayna (2000). Author.

Ethnic heterogeneity, as measured by the Herfindahl-Hirschman Index[30] $HHI_{EE}$, was very high with $HHI_{EE} = 0.2$ (Figure 1.5). Slovenia was the most homogeneous part, and Bosnia and Herzegovina the most heterogeneous.

Even two decades after the secession of the Federal Republic of Yugoslavia and thus after the Yugoslav wars, individual countries are highly heterogeneous

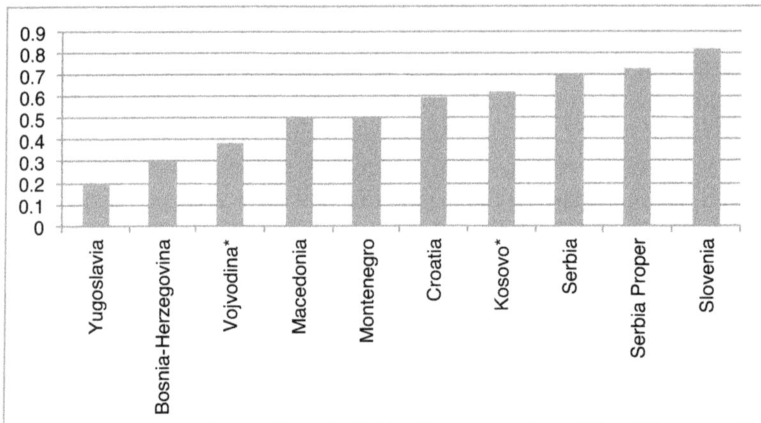


*Figure 1.5* Ethnical heterogeneity as measured by the Herfindhal-Hirschman Index in the former Socialist Federal Republic of Yugoslavia

Source: Szayna (2000). Author's calculation.

* Serbia comprises three regions: Serbia Proper, Kosovo, and Vojvodina.

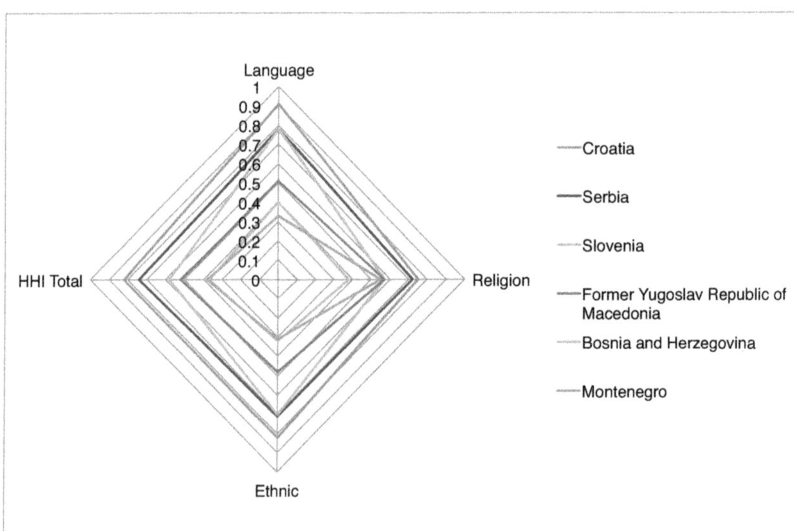


*Figure 1.6* Partial and total Herfindahl-Hirschman Index for the countries of the former Socialist Federal Republic of Yugoslavia

Source: EC (2019). Own calculation.

*Table 1.7* Herfindahl-Hirschman Index for the countries of former Federal Republic of Yugoslavia

| | | Croatia | Serbia | Slovenia | Former Yugoslav Republic of Macedonia | Bosnia and Herzegovina | Montenegro |
|---|---|---|---|---|---|---|---|
| HHI | Language | 0.91 | 0.78 | 0.78 | 0.51 | 0.40 | 0.33 |
| | Religion | 0.75 | 0.72 | 0.57 | 0.57 | 0.38 | 0.55 |
| | Ethnic | 0.82 | 0.71 | 0.70 | 0.48 | 0.32 | 0.31 |
| | Total | 0.82 | 0.74 | 0.68 | 0.52 | 0.37 | 0.38 |

Source: EC (2019). Own calculation.

in terms of language, religion, and ethnicity. The most heterogeneous is Montenegro, Bosna, and Herzegovina (Table 1.7). For instance, in Montenegro, 37% of residents speak Montenegrin and 43% Serbian; 72% are Orthodox Christians, 16% are Muslims, and 3% are Catholics. The population is divided between 45% of Montenegrins, 29% of Serbs, 12% of Bosnians, 5% of Albans, and 1% of Croats. However, the most homogeneous country is Croatia, where 95% of residents have Croatian as their mother tongue, 86% are Catholics and 90% Croats.

This pattern might be, at least in part, also observed in modern Spain. The most significant among the secessionist regions, Catalonia, is heterogeneous in terms of religion not only in the Spanish interregional comparison but also intraregional. Its religionist Herfindahl-Hirschman Index $HHI_{RR} = 0.43$ is, even, lower than Montenegro's and only slightly higher in comparison to Bosnian (Figure 1.5). Catalans also attend religious services significantly less often that rest of the Spanish. While 44% of Spanish attend religious services at least once a year, the same is true for 31% of Catalans.

### 1.4.2 *Economic factors*

> It is no coincidence that the first breakthrough for the party, at the regional election of 2009, coincided with the financial crisis and concomitant economic recession. The key message of the N-VA was that the Belgian state was unable to implement an efficient economic policy in the wake of the 2008 financial crisis. "Belgium does not work" was one of its slogans.
>
> (*Maddens 2017:57*)

While the romantic factors help to activate and formulate the electorate support, they might not be a sufficient condition for a successful secession. Collier and Hoeffler (2002), for example, state that romantic localism can be found worldwide. Nevertheless, successful secessionist movements are rarely viable on their own without the important support of economic factors. In other words, the romantic factors are "never sufficient for genuine secessionist movements to gain ground without . . . underlying economic impetus" (Rodríguez-Pose and Stermšek 2014:6).

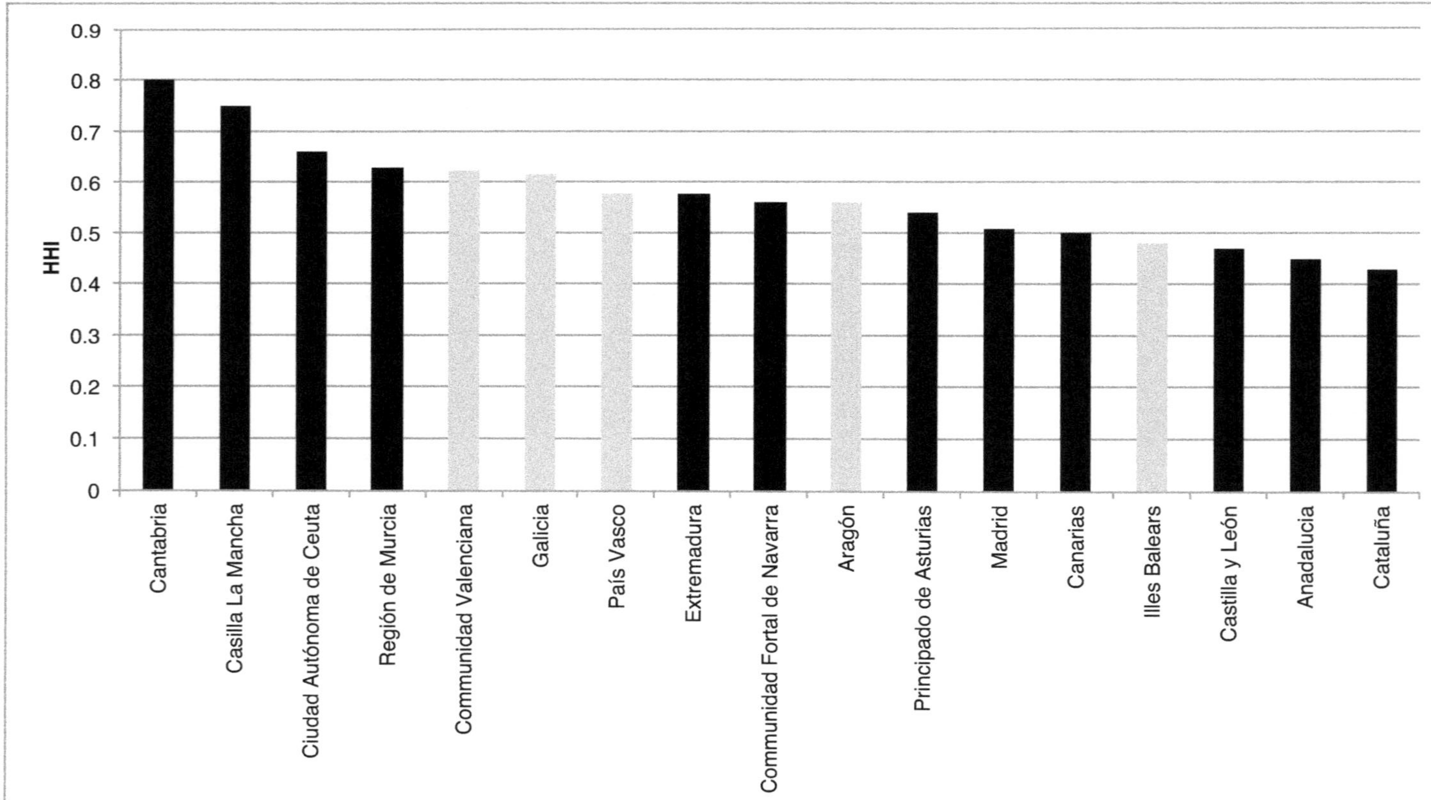


*Figure 1.7* Religionist Herfindahl-Hirschman Index for the Spanish regions

Source: GESIS (2018). Own calculation. Depicted in gray are the secessionist regions.

Wealth of the nation, approximated by the economic level, is the double-edged sword in discussion on the pro-secessionist factors. On the one hand, there is evidence for territories significantly poorer than the rest of their country which seek the secession; on the other hand, there is also evidence for the existence of significantly richer regions demanding their independence. Table 1.8 covers gross domestic product (GDP) level of 22 secessionist regions in the recent EU in comparison to the GDP level of the rest of their country. Twelve of them are poorer than the rest of the country (this difference is pronounced especially in case of Sicilia and Sardinia or Friesland), other ten are significantly richer (with South Tyrol having GDP level higher by nearly ½ in comparison to the rest of Italy, Basque ⅓ and Catalonia ¼ higher in comparison to the rest of Spain).

According to McHenry (2007), it is plausible that secessionist forces might appear due to the growth of economic inequality, which is the result of rapid economic development. On the contrary, the economically strong regions rich in raw materials (or the industrial regions) might seek for the disintegration because of the feeling of relative deprivation (McHenry 2007). For instance, the Basque Country, Catalonia, South Tyrol, Veneto, Flanders, and Scotland report lower unemployment as well as poverty rate than the rest of their countries.

*Table 1.8* GDP level in the secessionist region in comparison to the rest of the country

| *Country* | *Region* | *GDP level* | *GDP change* |
|---|---|---|---|
| Italy | **Sicilia** | **−11998** | **−41%** |
| Netherlands | Friesland | −13926 | −32% |
| Italy | Sardinia | −8121 | −28% |
| Czech Republic | Moravia | −4277 | −22% |
| France | Corsica | −6734 | −20% |
| France | Brittany | −5472 | −16% |
| Spain | Valencia | −3469 | −14% |
| France | Occitania | −4427 | −13% |
| Spain | Galicia | −2867 | −11% |
| United Kingdom | Scotland | −2942 | −8% |
| France | Alsace | −2676 | −8% |
| Croatia | Adriatic Croatia | −753 | −6% |
| Poland | Silesia | 454 | 4% |
| Spain | Balearic Islands | 1231 | 5% |
| Belgium | Flanders | 2590 | 7% |
| Finland | Åland | 6535 | 16% |
| Germany | Bavaria | 7708 | 20% |
| Italy | Aosta Valley | 6714 | 24% |
| Spain | Catalonia | 5953 | 25% |
| Italy | Trento | 7668 | 27% |
| Spain | Basque | 8286 | 34% |
| Italy | South Tyrol | 13921 | 49% |

Source: Eurostat. Own calculation.

Current social scientific researchers try to explain secessionism on the basis of economic factors using the concept of economic grievance and self-interest (Munoz and Tormos 2015, compare Rodríguez-Pose and Stermšek 2014). The basic assumption is based on the simple idea that wealthier regions tend to support sovereignty since, if they seceded, they have disposable resources. Their fiscal expenditures would decrease, and they could provide (effectively) more public goods because of the increase in preference homogeneity (Ibidem).

This was the case of the official reply by the Fiscal Commission Working Group to Scottish Government. The commission emphasised the benefits of the Scottish independence in economic terms when it claimed that "independent Scotland would perform better from an economic perspective" because "many countries of a comparable size and structure have used the full spectrum of policy levers to perform more successfully across a range of social and economic indicators in the long run" (Rodríguez-Pose and Stermšek 2014:3).

Typical economic factors as listed by Bookman (1993) are a region's

- share of national income;
- absolute level of development;
- trade with the rest of the country;
- capital flows with other regions; and
- fiscal autonomy.

Wealthier regions especially might use the secession threat to reduce the tax burden (Rodríguez-Pose and Stermšek 2014). Those factors together result in the importance of **economic integration**, which can accelerate secessionist tensions. Theoretically, economic integration should decrease the economic costs of secession as it allows newlyborn states to interact on the larger markets (Stegarescu 2009).

Generally, the economic aspects of secession might be divided into **microeconomic** and **macroeconomic** factors. Microeconomic factors are connected to the decision-making of individuals or households and might affect voter decision making in the case of a referendum. It is reflected by the individual utility function, which contains both the romantic factors as well as the macroeconomic factors. Optimisation of such a function is, therefore, determined also by how the decision-makers cope with uncertainty (for instance, if he or she is subject to status quo bias) and what his risk attitude is. The macroeconomic factors depend on the economic condition of a region, which is determined by the given factors as the geographical location (access to the sea, transport location, or landscape relief) as well as the endogenous factors which are results of the economic policy of the government. Economic policy affects secessionist tensions by both major sets of instruments: fiscal and monetary policy. Fiscal policy is, in terms of secession, connected especially to the canonical problem of fiscal decentralisation as described by Oates (1972) and Tiebout (1956), while monetary policy reflects the suitability of centrally set uniform interest rates for the whole country.

*Scarce resources*

> We are so far away from everything, we have a lot of everything, we don't need anything from anybody.
>
> Birgir Enni on the Faroese Islands (The Local 2018)

Geographic and topographic aspects play significant roles in the secessionism. Secessionist regions need clearly defined and detachable areas which are quite often determined by the geographical barrier. The geographical rule is incorporated (on the lower level), for instance, in the *Act* No *128/2000* Coll., on *Municipalities* (The *Municipal* Order, § 21) which require that "part of municipality which wants to be separated must have a separate cadastral area adjacent to at least two municipalities or one municipality and a foreign state and forming a coherent territorial unit". The same rule, though not incorporated in international law, is applicable also on the level of states. A typical example of such a natural geographical border defining a secessionist region is an island: examples include Ålands or Faroe Islands, Sardinia, and Sicily or Corsica. Similarly, all recent secessionist regions in the EU find themselves on the edge of existing states. The key requirement is not to endanger the military defence of the original country (Wood 1981), which would not be ensured if the new state was an enclave (such as in Lesotho in the middle of the South African Republic). A potential problem is connected with the Flemish secession since, after a "successful secession", the Brussels region would be an enclave disconnected from Wallonia. Territorial integrity is also the reason the diaspora makes the new emergency state much more difficult. Negotiation on a new state is complex, for instance, in the case of Kurds who live in jurisdictions of Iraq, Iran, and Turkey (Ibidem).

Further geographical aspects of secessions are connected to the convenient location and access to the sea. Serbia lost, after the secession of Montenegro, direct access to the Adriatic Sea; Montenegro also lost its access to the river Danube (Huszka 2013: 130). The geographical location of the region is also connected to the location of the scarce resources, which are usually not uniformly distributed over the entire country (Collier et al. 2003:78). Moreover, possession of land abundant with natural resources might help the region to finance the secessionist movements (together with donations from diasporas and subventions from hostile governments; see Collier and Hoeffler 2004).

Within four decades (from 1960 to 1999), Collier and Hoeffler identified 47 civil wars. According to their results, civil wars tend to have a secessionist character if the country exports scarce resources (Vaubel 2013). The crucial natural resource which plays leading roles in the secessionist conflicts is oil. Oil was the focus of the 22-year long civil war in Sudan, which was ended in 2011 after the referendum which led to the birth of South Sudan as a new country on the map of Africa (compare Natsios and Abramowitz 2011).[31]

In 1967, oil and natural gas were discovered in the North Sea (Sobel 1975). From the very beginning, oil was more pronounced as a pro-independence factor than gas because it has always been more profitable for Scotland (Scottish

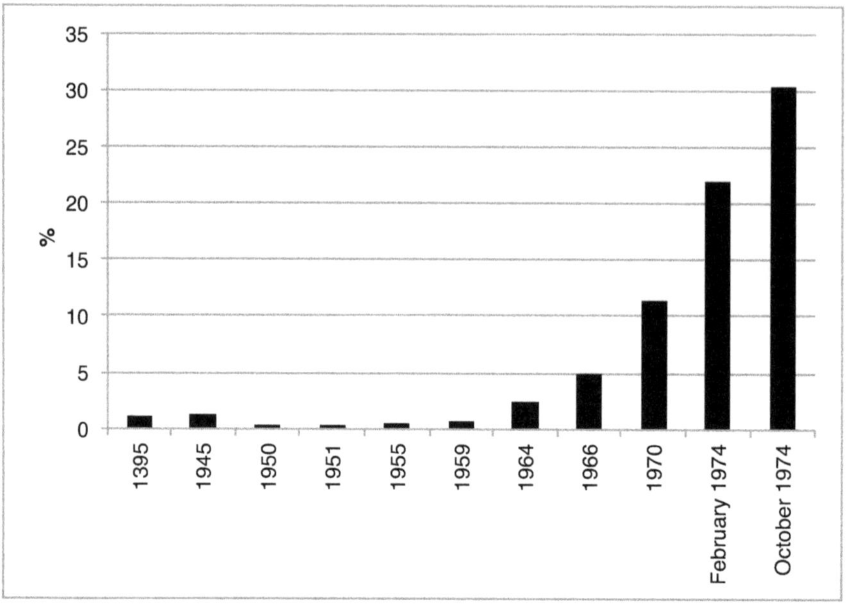


*Figure 1.8* SNP results in United Kingdom General Elections (1934–1974)
Source: Camp (2014). Own.

Government 2014:42). However, in 1972, oil became the most important theme of the election campaign (Smout 1992).

The Scottish National party has been leading the Scottish independence force. Founded in 1934, it received merely 1.1% of Scottish votes in the General election of 1935 (Camp 2014); the results were not better until the 1960s (see Figure 1.8).

By 1970, the SNP succeeded in Northeast Scotland, where the oil industry was concentrated. The "oil card" helped win Robert D. McIntyre[32] the by-elections in Stirling and Falkirk (16th September 1971; Smout 1992). One year later, this success motivated the SNP to run a campaign with the motto "It's Scotland's Oil". This became a symbol of the Scottish independence effort (Levy 1990; Pittock 2001).[33] Nevertheless, Pittock claims that oil on its own could not have been the crucial factor of the SNP success as the oil returns were lower than expected.[34] In autumn of 1971, the first oil crisis burned out which fostered the political importance of the "Scottish oil".

The campaign was based on the idea that the Scottish oil belongs to the Scots and it should be mined in favour of the Scots, not the United Kingdom or Europe.[35] In line with this conviction, SNP sent its delegation into the OPEC structures in 1971. According to OPEC estimates, Scotland could be on the same level of importance as Kuwait, Venezuela, or Libya with a potential stock of 150 million tons. The first conflict between Scotland and the rest of the United Kingdom concerned the volume of oil mining. Scottish representatives wanted their country to become an exporter, which would mine merely 80 million tons per year (to keep the oil prices high), while the rest of the United Kingdom proposed a quick and large extraction to decrease the prices (Cappon 1973:424).

In 1973, oil prices quadrupled due to the oil crisis (World Bank 2003:60). One year later, the British government asked Professor Gavin McCrone to elaborate a report on the effect of oil on the secession. According to McCrone's report, the discovery of oil in the North Sea fundamentally changed the framework of the discussion about the economic consequences of nationalism. It shifted the SNP proclamation from romantic factors to real economic factors. McCrone correctly estimated that the oil stocks in Scotland would be much higher, which might turn the "Scottish pound" into a reserve currency such as the Swiss franc. These conclusions, which supported the secession, encouraged the British government to classify the McCrone Report as "secret". It was only published in 2005.

### *Fiscal policy*

Secession is not necessarily the ultimate goal of secessionist groups. It can be seen as an instrument. According to Rosůlek (2014:36), one dimension of secession is the so-called *vanity secession* (a term used by Norman 1998). Vanity secession is a strategy where an interest group (such as *Lega Nord* in Italy) blackmails the government with the threat of secession to gain an economic profit. Similarly, Boykin (1998), Gradstein (2004), Vaubel (2013), and Rodríguez-Pose and Stermšek (2014) mention that secessionist threats can be used as a way of gaining better taxation conditions.

The study by Sebastian (2011) is crucial for explaining vanity secession on the grounds of bargaining as it discusses whether the implementation of a unilateral divorce law for Egyptian women alters their bargaining position within the household. According to Sebastian, the existence of divorce laws contributes to changes in income allocation between a husband and wife and greater autonomy of woman in marriage.

In our case, the subject of bargaining is the fiscal transfers between regions. It is for this reason that it is the richer regions that seek greater autonomy from the (poorer) rest of the country than vice versa. Mustafa claims that these secessionist tendencies are promoted if the richer regions feel that they contribute more through the formal or informal equalization mechanism to central government revenues than they benefit from it (Mustafa 2015:15).

Based on these presumptions, the following theoretical hypothesis can be formulated:

> The threat of secession enables the secessionist region to gain (a higher degree of) autonomy.

The secession phenomenon is closely related to fiscal federalism. As Panizza (1998) showed, the central government can prevent secession thanks to the decentralisation.

At least, since Tiebout's canonical paper (1956) was published, it is clear that the heterogeneity of the region's preferences might be solved by decentralisation. Nevertheless, some of the regions do not accept mere decentralisation but require (from their point of view) a more effective secession. Such *fiscal appeasement* (Sorens 2016) is then meaningful from the political point of view if the central government considers secession as the real threat. However, this policy can also undermine governmental ability to fight secession in the long run (ibidem).

Fiscal decentralisation in countries with secessionist regions is, therefore, a double-edged sword. On the one hand, it can quieten the secessionist region, which is satisfied with a higher level of fiscal autonomy and higher revenues, though the fiscal reasons for the secession can be lost. This, presumably, might be the case of Scotland after the Scottish independence referendum. Although a slight majority was against independence, the threat of secession led former Prime Minister David Cameron to promise Scotland a higher level of fiscal autonomy. Since April 2016, there is a new *Scottish rate of income tax* which makes Scotland the EU's most powerful subnational state (The Economist 2016). On the other hand, fiscal decentralisation might give more power to the local government. For instance, the tax autonomy provides the region with a potential instrument for financing future real secessions as was the case of Yugoslavia or the Soviet Union in the early 1990s (Sorens 2016).

Fiscal autonomy can also result in *fiscal profligacy* (Clayes and Martire 2015) when the regions' expenditures increase because of soft budget constraints. Nevertheless, some countries prevent fiscal profligacy by the analogy of European Stability and Growth Pact. For instance, Italian regions are subjects to the *Domestic Stability Pact* (Giuriato and Gastaldi 2009) and Spanish regions should follow the new Article 135 of the Spanish Constitution. According to this article, *the Autonomous Communities shall not incur a structural deficit that exceeds the standard established by the EU* (Fabbrini 2016).

However, other secessionist regions are not bound by similar rules. For instance, the Finnish Government according to the Åland Self-Government Act (Suksi 2011:169) cannot intervene in Åland's spending or budgetary process (except for providing equal social conditions for all citizens). Similarly, German *Länder* (individual federal states) were allowed to increase their expenditures without increasing their revenues, which could result in increased regional debt (Rodríguez-Pose and Gill 2005).

### *Monetary policy*

As Young (1998:42) mentions, "having a separate currency and an independent monetary policy allows governments to adopt a distinct stance of inflation" and, ideally, "different regions will have different monetary-policy (and Exchange rate) needs, and this can cause regional tensions". A typical example of such monetary-fuelled tensions is Ontario in Canada.

The unsustainability of a centrally driven monetary policy for all regions was discussed in the 19th century United States. Edward Kellog saw the solution in free banking based on the decentralized non-interest currency (Kuzminski in Miller and Williams 2013:51). In such a free banking system, without the central bank, secessionist tensions should not be accelerated by a uniform monetary policy.

While there might be a certain degree of fiscal decentralisation, monetary decentralisation is very rare. It was observed, for instance, in China at the end of the 1980s when the local governments received *greater control over state bank branches* (OECD 1998:121). In the former Socialist Federal Republic of Yugoslavia as well, it had *eight central banks at the level of republics and provinces* (Mates 2011:2). The National Bank of Yugoslavia together with eight national banks created a uniform central banking system, and the board of governors comprised the governors of eight national banks (Green and Petrick 2002:107). The suitability of one centrally driven monetary policy for a country with a secessionist region might be studied through the very same means as the suitability of a common currency for the monetary union. The question is the same: do secessionist regions together with the rest of the country form the optimal currency union?

Binner et al. (2018) tested if Scotland and the rest of the United Kingdom meet the microeconomic foundations of an optimal currency area. According to the findings, the modern United Kingdom of Great Britain might be seen as the optimal currency union in the broadest sense. However, their findings are seriously weakened by the fact that the authors could not use a time series for the Scottish inflation rate. Furthermore, using banking data, Chaudhry et al. doubt the optimality of the British "Pound" union.

A specific example is the case of Scotland. Since the Bank Charter Act of 1844, the banks in the United Kingdom lost the right to issue banknotes – except for the Scottish commercial banks. Currently, three Scottish banks are issuing their own banknotes: Bank of Scotland, the Royal Bank of Scotland, and Clydesdale Bank, even though they are under the supervision of the Bank of England (Herger 2019:13).

## *Economic integration*

Economic integration is widely seen as the trigger of the emerging secessionist wave in the EU. Roots can be found in the administrative reform which established the Nomenclature of Territorial Units for Statistics (NUTS).

The costs of secession are higher in the case of new trade barriers, which lead to smaller inner markets. Nevertheless, this disadvantage might be mitigated, or even entirely removed, if there is free trade. Initial inefficiency of secession may then change into efficiency if it takes place within the economic integration (compare Alesina and Spolaore 1997).[36]

Small states also express a higher degree of preference homogeneity and, therefore, fewer conflicts of interests. They do not need large bureaucratic systems, and their political costs are, therefore, lower. However, larger states are supposed to have lower unit costs on the non-rival public good, and their tax system is supposed to be more effective (Alesina et al. 1997; Rodríguez-Pose and Stermšek 2014).

Economic integration allows the secessionist state to profit from the economies of scale of the larger market in combination with the flexibility of the smaller state. An advantage of the smaller state, according to Becker (1994), is in the recent increase in the integrated world. Due to the division of labour, they can specialise only in a few commodities in such a narrow niche that is not in the interest of large economies. Moreover, those commodities are often not subject to the barriers in a trade as they do not compete with the big players. Nevertheless, Alesina et al. (2000) also mention that, even in the absence of any explicit barriers of trade, there will always be implicit trade barriers resulting from cultural, linguistic, legal differences, and business practices.

Using data from the United Nations Conference on Trade and Development (UNCTAD), Becker's hypotheses can be easily tested. If there was a higher degree of specialisation in smaller states, the concentration index of production should acquire higher values. The concentration index for the *j*-th country is calculated as the standard Herfindahl-Hirschmann Index $H_j$:

$$H_j = \frac{\sqrt{\sum_{i=1}^{n}\left(\frac{x_{ij}}{X_j}\right)^2} - \sqrt{\frac{1}{n}}}{1-\sqrt{\frac{1}{n}}} \tag{1.9}$$

where $x_{ij}$ is the value of export for country *j* and product *p* with $X_j = \sum_{i=1}^{n} x_{ij}$, and *n* represents the number of products according to the Standard International Trade Classification (SITC) Revision.[37] If the country exported just one product $H_j = 1$, and if it exports "all products", it converges to 0.

Thus, to estimate the differences between the production trade structure of the *j-th* country and rest of the world, diversification index $S_j$ is used:

$$S_j = \frac{\sum_i \left|h_{ij} - h_i\right|}{2} \tag{1.10}$$

where $h_{ij}$ represents the share of product *i* in total exports or imports of country *j* and $h_i$ is the share of product *i* in total world exports or imports. The greater the divergence is, the closer $S_j$ is to the value of 1.[38]

The UNCTAD data for 34 European countries (in 2016) were used. Given the aim of this study, we expect higher values of both the concentration index and the diversification index for smaller states than for larger states. Both indices are highly correlated with the Pearson correlation coefficient $\rho = 0.89$ as we would expect. The correlation between population (as an approximation of country size) and concentration is in line with Becker's hypothesis of a negative and significant $\rho (\rho = -0.35)$. However, the correlation between population and diversification is higher ($\rho = -0.58$). The smallest European states with a population of less than

*Table 1.9* Concentration and Diversification indices according to the country size

| *Population* | *Concentration Index* | *Diversification Index* | *N* |
|---|---|---|---|
| (0; 3) | 0.27 | 0.59 | 11 |
| (3; 10) | 0.16 | 0.50 | 10 |
| > **10** | 0.10 | 0.37 | 13 |

Source: UNCTAD. Own calculation.

three million have the highest concentration as well as diversification index. The largest (with a population higher than 10 million citizens), nonetheless, show the lowest values of both indices (see Table 1.9). Those results are consistent with Becker's hypotheses.[39]

Deeper international integration leads to a higher optimal number of countries than would be suitable in a world with a lower integration degree (Alesina and Spolaore 1997). Cox (1995) mentions that the motivation of Baltic states, states of the former Yugoslavia, or Czechoslovakia to split would be lower if they could have expected only the economic isolation instead of the economic integration. Separatist tendencies in the Canadian Francophone province, Québec, accelerated after the *North American Free Trade Agreement* (NAFTA) was established (Stegarescu 2009). On the contrary, the era of political integration was accompanied by an increase in trade barriers (Alesina et al. 2000). The Unification of Germany occurred after the Franco-Prussian War, which was also followed by increasing tariffs in Germany (Allen 2004). While the customs union (*Zollverein*) between German states supported the economic growth of the new state, industrial interests forced Chancellor Otto von Bismarck to promote external protectionism (Brown 2003). Similarly, during the Great Depression's collapse in international trade, only two new states (Iraq and Saudi Arabia) emerged on the world map.

Figure 1.9 depicts a simultaneous increase in the number of countries (according to data published by *The World Factbook, CIA*) and the degree of international economic integration (DGI). This indicator was estimated by Arribas et al. (2006) using the degree of openness, GDP, and, finally, the total connection between 59 countries representing 96.7% of world trade (ibidem). Correlation between both variables is positive and very significant (Pearson correlation coefficient $\rho = 0.92$).[40]

Within the EU, secessionism is supported by the motto "Europe of Regions". For instance, the European Committee of the Regions gives voice to the particular interests of individual regions. The principle of subsidiarity (Article 5(3) of the Treaty on EU) provided regions with a higher degree of competence. Moreover, the voting weights of smaller countries are higher. In the last three decades, the fiscal decentralisation, as well as the tax autonomy of regions within the Organisation for Economic Co-operation and Development, increased. This led to a decrease in the role of the central government (Stegarescu 2009). Furthermore, the role of regions increased because of the administrative regionalisation forced by the EU which established *Nomenclature of Units for Territorial Statistics* (NUTS) (Baranyai 2013).

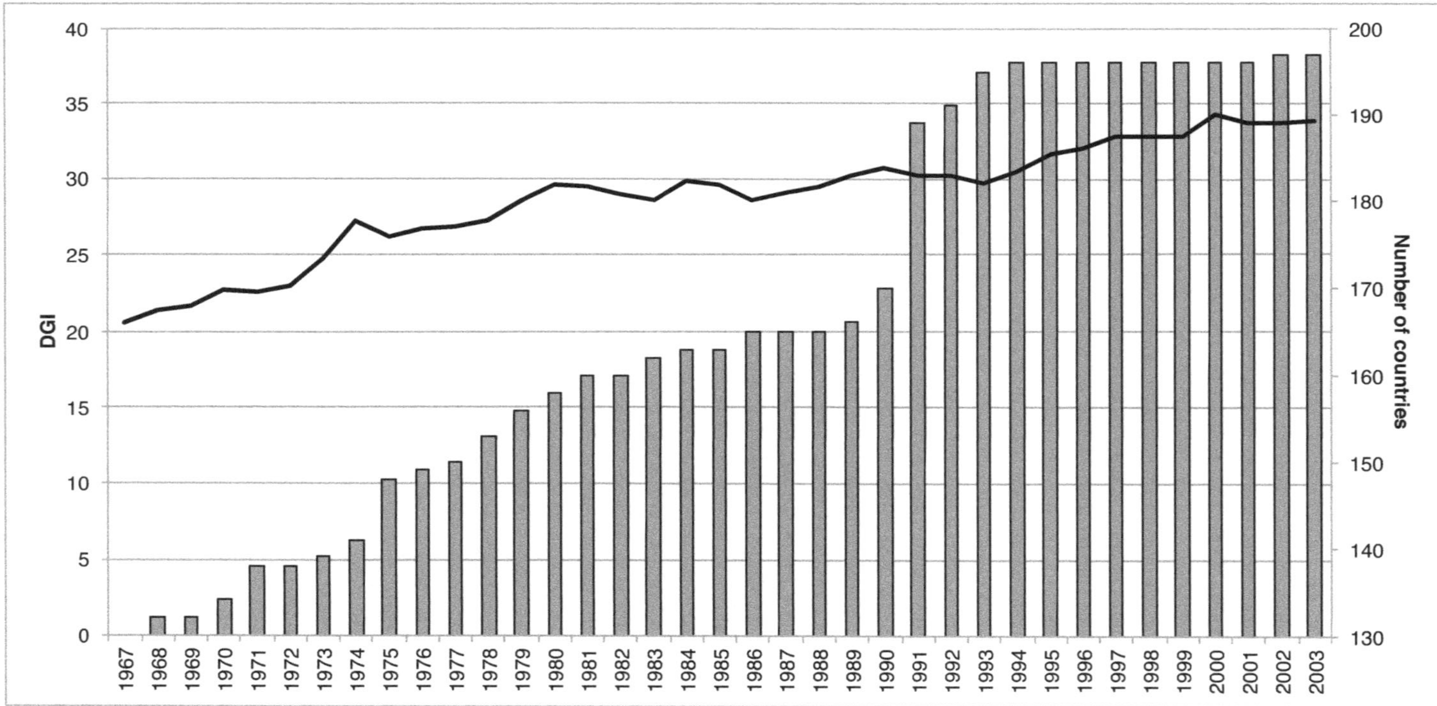


*Figure 1.9* Degree of international economic integration (DGI) and number of countries (1967–2003)

Source: The World Factbook (2018) and Arribas et al. (2006). Own construction.

International and supranational integration decrease costs of secession and make them, therefore, easier to deal with. At the same time, they do not support separatist movements and tensions explicitly. The United Nations (UN) recognises the right to self-determination (Buchanan 1991b), but it does not recognise the right to secede. Newly born states cease to be UN members; they formally have to submit new applications for membership (Vaubel 2013). Article 50 of the Lisbon Treaty explicitly allows the withdrawal from the EU as an inner secession within the European integration. Nevertheless, the Union leaders have been staunch opponents of the secession within the member states. The former President of the European Commission (EC), José Manuel Barroso, claimed that a "new state, if it wants to join the EU, has to apply to become a member like any state" and that the EU's membership procedure is "a procedure of international law" (Connolly 2013:84). Similar attitudes were presented by the other former EC President, Romano Prodi, in 2004; European Commissioner Reding towards Catalonia in 2012; and the former President of the European Council, Van Rompuy, toward Scotland.

### *Risk attitude*

In a referendum, economic subjects are thought to behave as risk-averse (Hobolt 2006:627). Secession leads to a significant change in the status quo, which means that pro-secessionists might either be less risk-averse people (alternatively, slightly more risk-loving), or those who expect a significant increase in their utility. Sorens claims that risk aversion makes secession difficult in established democracies as "some voters will vote against secession even when the expected net benefits are positive, because they are more concerned about avoiding the worst possible outcomes" (Sorens 2012:85).

Risk aversion can be estimated in several ways.[41] Thus, employing a questionnaire survey, there are two basic possibilities: The Dohmen measure or the reservation price of lottery, which is based on self-estimation. Respondents answer simple questions as follows:

> How do you see yourself? Are you generally a person who is fully prepared to take risks or do you try to avoid taking risks? Please tick a box on the scale, where the value 0 means "not at all willing to take risks" and the value 10 means "very willing to take risks".
>
> (Kemayou 2016:82)

The Dohmen measure is, however, too subjective and suffers from the lack of incentive compatibility. Incentive compatibility is not fully solved by our approach, which is based on the subjective decision about the reservation price of lottery.

In the question *Q4* (see further subchapter 2.2), the respondents were asked what their reservation price for a lottery ticket would be if the probability of winning a lottery jackpot of €1,000 is 10%. The expected value of such lottery (which is a *measure of the average payoff the lottery generate*; see Besanko and Braeutigam 2010:643) is calculated as

$$EV = \rho \times W + (1-\rho) \times 0 = 0.1 \times €1000 + (1-0.1) \times €0 = €100$$

and variance of the outcomes of the lottery is

$$\sigma^2 = 0.1 \times (1000-100)^2 + 0.9 \times (0-100)^2 = 90000$$

A risk-neutral person would pay €100.[42]

*Discount rate*

Discount rates reflect the time preferences of economic subjects, which also includes one's ability to defer immediate pleasure in exchange for higher future profit. Homo economicus prefers (*ceteris paribus*) €100 today to €100 in one year. He is willing to wait for this amount only when he receives some bonus payment. Such a bonus payment is, therefore, the difference between future value $FV$ and present value $PV$:

$$FV = PV + bonus \tag{1.11}$$

Discount factor $DF$ is the ratio of present and future value

$$DF = \frac{PV}{FV} \tag{1.12}$$

and the discount rate is calculated as

$$r = \frac{1}{DF} - 1 \tag{1.13}$$

Secession is thought to be connected to certain economic sacrifices in the first period after the new state emerges, which might be followed by better economic conditions in the later period. It is, therefore, reasonable to expect that secessionists have a lower discount rate as they are more patient and can endure discomfort. As Young (2013) mentions: "Secessionists would need to have a very low discount rate to accept independence under these assumptions,[43] or else they would have to place a high value on non-material benefits".

## 1.5 Solutions of secession in the economic theory

Secession is the complex mixture of numerous factors which took shape with completely different intensity in each and every particular case. Nevertheless, the economic science enables us to have theoretical discussions on the potential ways of solution. The *Law & Economics* makes it possible to study secession as the problem of property rights. Science of the *Public finances* contributes to the potential solution with the theory of fiscal decentralism. This brief outline certainly does not have ambition to suggest the universal solution of any secessionist problem. The goal of this chapter is more modest: to identify the potential space for the economic science even in the conflict, which had been for centuries evaluated as purely non-economic.

### *1.5.1 Secession and the property rights*

This approach brings into focus property rights and the resulting territorial claims. Pipes (2008) quotes Harrington, who claims that each government is an expression of property rights. The proprietor who holds a majority of the land determines the nature of government. Similarly, according to the *physiocrats*, the landowners should govern the country as they are the ones who own their homeland[44] (ibidem). In short, the landowner has the freedom to dispose of it, and he can decide if his part of the land (and, therefore, part of the country) should secede or should stay a part of the existing state.

Consider the schematic in Figure 1.4. On the left side, there is a homogenous division of the land of country *R*. Landowners E, F, G, and H (depicted in grey) want to secede and found their new country *S*. Landowners A, B, C, and D are satisfied with the existing country *R*. If the territorial property rights are clearly defined and recognised by all the citizens (A, B . . . and H), the land can be easily divided into two subsequent states. A problem arises in the case where citizens A, B, C, and D do not recognise the property rights of owners E, F, G, and H and consider their land as part of the whole indivisible country. In that case, diplomatic, economic, or even armed conflicts may erupt.

On the right side of Figure 1.4, the land distribution between the pro-secessionist and anti-secessionist landowners is heterogeneous. Pro-secessionist landowners A, D, E and H do not have common borders; thus, they cannot easily claim their lands as the new country *S*. However, if the territorial property rights are well-defined, it is possible to exchange, for instance, land A for land F and land D for land G to receive the homogenous area. If the landowner D values his land more than land G, he could be paid compensation.

Such purchases of land for state formation were not rare in history. Even the borders of the Czech lands were often formed not only by conquests or marriages but also by purchases and sales. For instance, *Brandenburg*, which was part of the Czech lands since 1373, was sold by King of Bohemia Sigismund of Luxemburg in 1415 to the House of Hohenzollern for 400,000 florins (Vokáč 2006), which made Brandenburg a part of Germany (currently being one of the sixteen federal states). Similarly, the former Czech *Duchy of Siewierz* was sold by Duke Wenceslaus I of Cieszyn to Zbigniev Olesnicki, the Bishop of Kraków, in 1443 for 6,000 groschen (Žáček 2004). It has been part of Poland, with short breaks, until now.

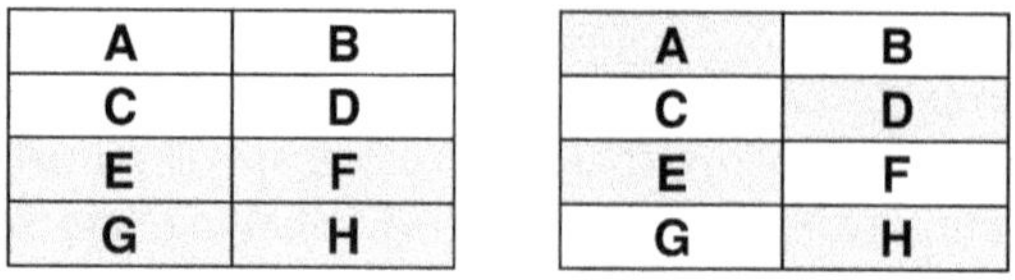


*Figure 1.10* Division of property
Source: Lipovská (2017).

The real problem lies precisely in the recognition of the territorial claims. Brilmayer (1991) states that such claims usually have historical origins. The land in question used to belong to the secessionist group, which lost it in favour of the existing state "by some unjustifiable historic event". Pipes (2008) recalls the historic way of property rights recognition. The so-called *seisin* (seizin) postulated that a land belongs to the man or nation who proved that he (or his ancestors) dwelt and cultivated on it for a longer period than other interested parties.

### *1.5.2 Fiscal decentralism*

As can be seen here, secession has significant economic aspects, which have been, for most of the time, excluded from serious economic research. For instance, Pigou did not consider these real movements as economic; he claimed that an "exclusively economic interpretation of war would be to neglect evident truths" (1921:17–18).

It is widely recognised that pro-secessionist tensions should be most vivid in the most advanced regions as they are the net payers to the state's budget. There are several reasons for such an opinion. First, secession is connected to substantial risks, which cannot be easily undergone by weaker and poorer regions (Zipfel 2015). This is supported by Munoz and Tormos (2015), who argue that for the richer regions, there will be larger (financial) resources available even after the secession as they will not have to face the fiscal imbalances towards the central state budget. Second, newly born states should express higher degrees of homogeneity preferences, which should result in more effective distribution of public goods. Third, Alesina (2000) shows that it is especially the fiscal policy which accelerates secessionist tensions. For instance, the *Fiscal Commission Working Group* mentions in its report on the Scottish Independence that the independence can support the full usage of the Scottish economic potential. This can be illustrated by the increase in Scottish secessionist pressures after the Yom-kippur war when the British government claimed 90% of the additional profit from the Scottish oil reserves (Rodríguez-Pose and Stermšek 2014). Furthermore, the economic crisis provoked the Catalan secessionist motto "Spain robs us!" (ibidem).

Economic factors, then, led some authors to deny the *right to secession* because of missing fiscal transfers from the former secessionist regions (Berkowitz as quoted by Graziosi 1997; Vaubel 2013). According to Buchanan, secessionists should compensate for the rest of the state, which lost wealth and investments on the secessionist's territory (Boykin 1998). However, Vaubel (2013) opines that the taxpayers from the secessionist regions probably subsidised infrastructure of other regions, not vice versa.

Traditional secession theorists further claim that voters support secessionists movements only if they expect their personal utility to increase. According to this theory, secession should be supported by middle-class voters, professionals (ISCO Group 2 Classification such as medical doctors, teachers, or legal professionals), and employees in the private sector, as these groups are relatively independent of the central government. On the contrary, agricultural and industrial workers, whose income depend on the integrated national market, economies of scale, and state support would be against secessionist tendencies (Rodríguez-Pose and Stermšek 2014; Wood 1981; Munoz and Tormos 2015).

The political calculation is provided not only by rational voters who compare marginal utility and marginal costs but also by the whole regions. Young (1994a) mentions that if the secessionist regions reach high economic levels when staying on their own than being part of a political union, secession might be proper. Nevertheless, there might also occur the so-called *negative independence dividend*, which is connected with war costs and international sanctions as in the case of the former Yugoslavia (Rodríguez-Pose and Stermšek 2014), exclusion from the political union (Stegarescu 2009), and new economic barriers between a new state and the rest of the former country (such as barrier of trades and new currency). The interconnected dependence between citizens of new and former regions as well as the formation of a coalition may burden the act of secession with additional costs. The so-called *internal negotiation* mitigates the secessionist tendencies in France, Italy, and Spain, for instance, where the regional pro-secessionist support is fragmented between several parties. Such parties are, on the one hand, connected with a common goal; on the other hand, their political competitiveness does not allow their cooperation which results in their relative weakness regarding the aim of secessionist negotiations. This reflects Koffka's phrase on Gestaltism: "The whole is something else than the sum of its parts" (Koffka 1935:176) as the same number of votes divided between more parties or movements has a lower political impact:

$$w(N) > \sum_{i=1}^{V} w_i(n_i); \sum_{i=1}^{V} n_i = N \tag{1.14}$$

where $w(N)$ is the impact of one political "block" consisted of $N$ voters, and $w_i(n_i)$ is the impact of the $i-th$ political party comprised $n_i$ voters.

Secession might be costly and, therefore, also undesirable for industrial traders. As Pigou (1921:19) mentioned, in the world of tariffs and trade barriers, it is proper for traders if they "see as large a part of the world as possible controlled by their own government".

## Summary

Secession as the permanent intentional separation of the territory and inhabitants from the existing state and its government is conducted to found an independent sovereign state. As a typical conflict based on the heterogeneity of preferences, it is studied by the PEC. Apart from its macroeconomic aspects, it also has a microeconomic dimension because the secessionist conflicts might be analysed by optimising the standard utility function.

Most of the European states were created by some form of secession. The recent European secessionism is exceptionally robust in Spain (Catalonia), Belgium (Flanders), the United Kingdom of Great Britain, and Northern Ireland (Scotland). While politology, law, and moral philosophy deal with the right to secession, further economic contributions within the PEC deal with the recognition of the property rights to the territory. Finally, secession as a kind of disintegration is closely connected to economic as well as political integration within the EU because it makes the national state less important for the economic well-being of its regions.

Collier and Hoeffler (2002) claim that "the fragile and recent cause of romantic nationalism could, thus, be allied to the robust and ancient cause of economic self-interest" and that "there are literally hundreds of romantic secessionist groups – probably most areas of the earth are subject to the claims of one or more of them. However, the mere existence of such a group does not help us to understand those few secessionist movements that, by their violence or electoral support, have become serious political phenomena.

Two types of secessionist factors are recognised: romantic (based on emotional arguments) and economic (based on rational arguments). Romantic factors are connected to romantic nationalism and include ethnicity, language, religion, and culture. They have been discussed since the beginning of the 19th century, and they can also influence the country's economic condition.

There is a shift from romantic factors toward economic factors in the last decades. As Maddens mentions regarding modern Flanders in Belgium: "The linguistic issue is still important in Flemish nationalist discourse, more specifically the language legislation in Brussels and its periphery. But the main focus is now on economic issues" (Maddens 2017:57). The romantic factors, with their microeconomic dimension, are not sufficient, and the role of macroeconomic factors increase. Among the crucial economic factors, there should be a recognised distribution of scarce resources (especially, crude oil and natural gas), fiscal and monetary policy, the degree of economic integration, as well as the individual risk attitude and discount rate. The discovery of oil has strongly affected the development of Scottish secessionist movements, at least, since the election in 1972. Fiscal policy also has a *vanity* dimension as the threat of potential secession enables the region to gain a higher degree of autonomy without a real secession. Monetary policy might be a secessionist factor, especially in the case of divergence between required interest rates in individual regions as approximated by the Taylor rule. Secessionist tensions are also promoted by economic integration leading to a common market, as the small homogeneous states are more viable under the umbrella of integration units. Small states have highly concentrated production with low diversification.

Lastly, the secessionist tensions might also be affected on the microeconomic level. If voters are risk-averse, they might vote against the secession even if it could, potentially, increase their utility function. Similarly, the pro-secessionists are expected to have a significantly lower discount rate in comparison with the rest of the population.

Table 1.10 summarises the main hypothesis based on the theory behind the romantic and economic factors of secession.

*Table 1.10* Main hypotheses

| | | | | |
|---|---|---|---|---|
| Factors | Romantic | Language | R1 | There is linguistic frontline between the secessionist region and the rest of the country. |
| | | | R2 | The linguistic preferences are manifested by the media selection. |
| | | Culture and history | R3 | The lower heterogeneity in terms of cultural as well as political preferences is connected to the higher economic level. |
| | | | R4 | Secessionists feel closer to their region than to the country as whole. |
| | | | R5 | There is path dependency in institutions. |
| | | Religion | R6 | Heterogeneity in religion is connected to the secessionist tendencies. |
| | | | R7 | Believers tend to be more pro-secessionist than unbelievers. |
| | | Intraregional heterogeneity | R8 | Heterogeneity in political opinions is connected to the secessionist tendencies. |
| | Economic | GDP | E1 | There is higher support for secession in regions with better economic conditions. |
| | | | E2 | There is higher support for secession if the citizens are more optimistic on their economic development. |
| | | Scarce resources | E3 | There is a strong relationship between potential wealth from scarce resources and support for secession. |
| | | | E4 | Pro-secessionist more often feel exploitation from the central government. |
| | | Fiscal policy | E5 | Secessionists want exclusive responsibility for taxation. |
| | | | E6 | The better the condition of region is, the more the respondents want the tax decentralisation. |
| | | | E7 | There as feeling of grievance in the secessionist region. |
| | | Economic integration | E8 | Pro-secessionist support EU integration. |
| | | Risk attitude | E9 | The dependence between risk attitude and willingness to vote for secession. |
| | | Discount rate | E10 | Discount rate of pro-secessionists is lower than for anti-secessionists. |
| | | Infrastructure | E11 | The higher the educational infrastructure, the higher the support for secession. |

## Notes

1 UCDP distinguishes *state-based* conflict, where at least one of the armed parties is a state government, and *non-state conflicts* organised, for instance, by rebel and communal groups (Melander et al. 2016).
2 Peace economics can be defined as an "economic study and design of political, economic, and cultural institutions, their interrelations, and their policies to prevent, mitigate, or resolve any type of latent or actual destructive conflict within and between societies" (Brauer and Caruso 2013:151–152).
3 Defence economics focuses on the *economic aspects of managing the defence sector*, including *military Research and Development, procurement, the defence industry, military manpower, game theory used to devise strategies in the nuclear arms race, and the alliance theory* (Brauer and Caruso 2013:150).
4 He also mentioned the interdependence of economic and war interests:

> An Offensive Forreign War is caused by many, and those very various, secret, personal distastes coloured – with publick pretences; of which we can say nothing, but that the common encouragement unto them particularly here in England is a false opinion, that our Countrey is full peopled, or that if we wanted more Territory, we could take it with less charge from our neighbours, then purchase it from the Americans; and a mistake, that the greatness and glory of a Prince lyeth rather in the extent of his Territory, then in the number, art, and industry of his people, well united and governed. And moreover, that it is more glorious to take from others by fraud or rapine, then to gain ones self out of the bowels of the Earth and Sea.
>
> Defensive Wars are caused from unpreparedness of the offended State for War, as when defective Stores are served into the Magazines by corrupt Officers at the rate of good; when Armies are falsly Mustered; when Souldiers are either Tenants or Servants to their Commanders, or else persons, who for their Crimes or Debts, want protection from Justice; when the Officers are ignorant of their business, and absent from their Commands; and withal afraid to punish, because unwilling to pay. Wherefore, to be alwayes in a posture of War at home, is the cheapest way to keep off War from abroad.
>
> (Petty 1662)

5 RAND (Research and Development) Corporation was founded in 1948 as the US-based think-tank interconnecting military planning, research, and development. More than 20 Nobel Prize economic winners worked for or co-operated with Rand, including Kenneth J. Arrow, Robert J. Aumann, Gary S. Becker, Ronald H. Coase, Gerard Debreu, Peter A. Diamond, James Heckmann, Leonid Hurwicz, Tjalling Ch. Koopmans, Harry M. Markowitz, John F. Nash, Edmund S. Phelps, Paul A. Samuelson, Thomas Schelling, Theodore W. Schultz, Lloys S. Shapley, William F. Sharpe, Herbert A. Simon, Vernon L. Smith, Robert M. Solow, James Tobin, William S. Vickrey, and Oliver Williamson (RAND 2018). This list of Nobel Prize winners among the RAND´s staff is not self-serving: it illustrates the long-term and very close interconnection between economic research and conflicts.
6 The political economy of conflict can be classified as a subdiscipline of the Analysis of Collective Decision Making (JEL code D74) and International Political Economy (JEL code F51). Secessions themselves have their own JEL code H77.
7 Weber, also, referred also to Trotsky who, supposedly, says at Brest-Litovsk: "Every state is founded on force" (ibidem). This is fully in line with our attitudes toward self-determination and secession as the subject of the PEC.
8 A useful overview of the various approaches to the definition of the state is listed in Heywood (2013), Chapter 3 (pp. 56–79).

9 In the *Corpus of Contemporary American English*, the frequency of "separatism" is 421 (in years 1990–2017), while the frequency of "secession" is 936. Similarly, according to the *Oxford English Dictionary*, the frequency of the word "secession" is in Band 5 (1–9.9 used per million words), while "separatism" is in Band 4 (0.1–0.99 used per million words). On the contrary, in the *Czech national corpus*, the word "separatismus" (separatism) is eighteen times more frequently used than "secese" (political secession).

10 Compare Althusius (1614):

> One of the estates, or one part of the realm, can abandon the remaining body to which it belonged and choose for itself a separate ruler or a new form of commonwealth when the public and manifest welfare of this entire part altogether requires it, or when fundamental laws of the country are not observed by the magistrate but are obstinately and outrageously violated, or when the true worship and disclosed command of God clearly require and demand that this be done. And then this part of the realm can defend by force and arms its new form and status against the other parts of the realm from which it withdrew. Thus, the Israelites broke loose from the house and imperium of David and founded their own realm. . . . Thus also subjects can withdraw their support from a magistrate who does not defend them when he should, and can justly have recourse to another prince and submit themselves to him. Or if a magistrate refuses to administer justice, they can resist him and refuse to pay taxes.

11 Secessions can be severally classified. For instance, Buchanan (1991a:327) distinguishes secession as follows: (i.) individual vs group: according to Tomz, there was no significant case of individual secession in the century. Despite this fact, such a classification is meaningful, as there is a wide discussion on whether the "right to secession" should be applied as an individual or a group right (Tomz 1994:12).; (ii.) minority vs majority: minority secession is thought to be the secession of a social-demographic minority, while majority secession is the exclusion of the majority by the minority (Coakley 2003:267); (iii.) central vs peripheral: after the central secession, the rest of the country is not the convex set (so-called "hole of the donut", Buchanan 1991a:327). (iv.) national vs local: local secession occurs when the region secedes from another region of the state. Buchanan mentions the secession of West Virginia out of a part of Virginia (1991a:327).

12 Even today the "secession" in the United States is closely connected to this historic reminiscence. According to the Google trends statistics, the most frequent connotations of the "Secession" among the American internet users are "confederate states" and "Confederacy". "Secession" is also most often searched in the South Carolina, Arkansas, and Texas.

13

> Physically speaking, we cannot separate. We cannot remove our respective sections from each other, nor build an impassable wall between them. A husband and wife may be divorced and go out of the presence and beyond the reach of each other; but the different parts of our country cannot do this. They cannot but remain face to face, and intercourse, either amicable or hostile, must continue between them. Is it possible, then, to make that intercourse more advantageous or more satisfactory after separation than before? Can aliens make treaties easier than friends can make laws? Can treaties be more faithfully enforced between aliens than laws can among friends? Suppose you go to war, you cannot fight always; and when, after much loss on both sides, an no gain on either, you cease fighting, the identical old questions as to terms of intercourse are again upon you.
>
> Abraham Lincoln in his First Inaugural Address (1861)

14 This subchapter is based on the study by Lipovská (2017).

15 February 2008–2018.

16 The first state which recognised Kosovo was Costa Rica on 17 February 2018. The break-through in the recognition process was a decision by the United States of America on 18 September. So far, the last one has been the government of Barbados on the 15 February 2018.

17 In response to the application of the Finnish Government for recognition of the independence of the Finnish Republic, the Council of People's Commissars, in full conformity with the principle of the right of nations to self-determination, resolves to recommend to the Central Executive Committee:

> a) to recognise the state independence of the Finnish Republic; and
> b) to set up, in agreement with the Finnish Government, a special commission (composed of representatives of both sides) to elaborate the practical measures necessitated by the secession of Finland from Russia.
>
> (Stalin 1953:23–25)

18 Poland was after the so-called *Third Partition* in 1794, divided between Russia, Germany, and Austria.

19 This irredentism made it impossible to "restore the Czechoslovakia within its pre-Munich frontiers".

20 The so-called *Year of Africa* was the result of decolonisation as a very specific form of secession (Griffiths 2016:103).

21 Maltesian secession was preceded by the Maltese constitutional referendum on 21 September 1964. Citizens approved the independence by 54.5% votes with a 79.7% turnover (Miller et al. 2013).

22 O'Leary (2006) further mentions the Partitions of Poland in 1772, 1793, and 1795; partitions of Ireland (1920); Hungary (1920); Kurdistan (1920–1923); and Cyprus (1974) as clear examples.

23 For detail information on the selection see the following chapter.

24 It might be explained by the particular interests of both chairs. The Scottish independence would not be desirable for Spain and Italy as their countries of origin, because it could trigger a ripple effect resulting in the success of secessionist movements in Spain as well as in Italy. (Author would like to thank for bright notion to prof. assitent Libor Žídek.)

25 After the dissolution of the Austro-Hungarian Empire in 1918, most political leaders of the new nation-states were the former members of the Austrian (or Hungarian) Parliament. For instance, from the ten interwar Czechoslovak prime ministers, five were former MPs (Masaryk, Kramář, Tusar, Udržal and Hodža). Similarly, the last Austrian Parliament had experienced leaders from Poland (such as Daszyński, Dembiński, Głąbiński, and Moraczewski), Italy (De Gasperi), Yugoslavia (Čingrija, Korošec, Laginja), short-lived West Ukrainian People´s Republic (Holubovyč, Levyckij), and Austria (Renner, Dinghofer).

26 Let country *C* consist of the secessionist region *S* and the rest of the country *R*. There are, in fact, three forms of independence referendums:

> 1 A referendum exclusively in region *S;* independence may occur if more than 50% of voters from this region vote for the secession.
> 2 A referendum in the whole country *C*; independence may occur if more than 50% of voters from the whole country vote for the secession (regardless of whether the majority was from region *S* or *R*).
> 3 A referendum simultaneously in region *S* and *R*; independence may occur if more than 50% of voters from region *R* and at the same time more than 50% of voters from region *S* vote for the secession.

Each of this type of referendum has a different impact on the total utility in country *C* and regions *S* or *R*. Nevertheless, virtually only type is widely used: the first one.

27 Careful attention should be paid to the fact that the Declaration deals with the right of *people* to self-determination, but not with the right of *nations* to self-determination.
28 "The peoples of Austria-Hungary, whose place among the nations we wish to see safeguarded and assured, should be accorded the freest opportunity to autonomous development" (Point X).
29 The fight for a higher degree of autonomy dates back to the 19th century. When in 1946, the separatists won the election, the Faroese parliament was dissolved from the Copenhagen centrum (The Local 2018).
30 Composition of the Index is clarified in subchapter 2.4 in detail.
31 In the 2011 Southern Sudanese self-determination referendum, 98.83% of voters voted for separation (with a turnout in many locations tending to be 100%; Arnold and LeRiche 2013:23).
32 McIntyre was the first ever SNP PM elected (on the 13th April 1945).
33 Sample from the campaign:

> It's HIS Oil, so why . . .
>
> - are 40,000 Scots kids on part-time education? And why is there only 1 job for every 5 school-leavers?
> - are there so few jobs for Scots? Why do we have the worst unemployment rate in industrial Europe?
> - are many Scotswomen in substandard houses? Why do we have 97.5% of the UK's most deprived areas?
> - are many Scots old folk cold and undernourished? Why do 5,000 die of hypothermia every year?
>
> If you want it, demand it! Scotland's oil. Time to go for self-government.
> England expects Scotland's oil. Time to go for self-government.

It might be seen as a romantic approach towards the economic factors.

34 Thanks to the campaign´s success, the term "oil weapon" was used not only for the Arabic countries but also for Scotland (Cappon 1973).
35 Currently, Scottish oil production stays for 96% of total United Kingdom production (Scottish Government 2018).
36 Montesquieu summarised the question of an optimal country size in 1748 (Book IX:1): "If a republic be small, it is destroyed by a foreign force; if it be large, it is ruined by an internal imperfection". However, a *small* state does not mean a *weak* state as Gligorov reminds us (see Rodríguez-Pose and Stermšek 2014). Ancient Greek philosophers preferred small city-states as the sovereign institutions which allowed their citizens to directly take part in the decision-making process (Bolton et al. 1996). Plato (1961:357) set the optimal nation size to 5,040 families: "Let us assume that there are – as a suitable number – 5,040 men, to be land-holders and to defend their plots; and let the land and houses be likewise divided into the same number of parts – the man and his allotment forming together one division". As Jowett (2008), in his translation, notes, Plato wrote his Laws under the influences of the Pythagorean school. An advantage of number 5040 lies in being 7!, which allowed its divisibility by all numbers smaller than 12 (except for 11) and have a total of 60 divisors.
37 The explanation is taken from the UNCTAD Summary of Concentration Index: http://unctadstat.unctad.org/wds/TableViewer/summary.aspx.
38 Ibidem.
39 Data on population and values for both the Concentration and Diversification indices are presented in Appendix B.
40 To roughly estimate the relationship between economic integration and the number of countries on the world map, we decided to use an indicator based on the *fixed* number

of countries. Clearly, the more countries exist, the higher the degree of integration and international trade we (ceteris paribus) can observe.

41 The main approaches are summarised in Holt and Laury (2002), Deng et al. (2010), Hartog et al. (2002), Grable and Lytton (2003), Guillemette et al. (2015), Kuzniak et al. (2015), and Roszkowski and Grable (2005).

42 For more details, see subchapter 3.1.2.

43 By "these assumptions", Young means not only the direct loss from secession, but also the opportunity costs of secession: "It would take about 30 years for GDP to reach what it would have been as a region, and a much longer period of time – about 50 years – to recover all the lost output" (Young 2013).

44 This idea of property rights is already embedded in the etymology: the Latin phrase for "homeland" is *patrie*, while patrimony is *patrimonie*. Similarly, even in the Czech language, *vlast* (patrie) has common etymological roots with *vlastnictví* (patrimonie): *vlast* is developed from *government* and *power*, while *vlastnictví* means "something that belongs to someone's dominion" – compare Rejzek (2015).

# 2 Methodology and data

This chapter is dedicated to the empirical part of our research: our original *Survey on autonomist and pro-independence movements* (SAPIM). First, the methodology, including the statistical and econometric methods used for our analysis, is briefly described. In the second subchapter, data are introduced. The focus group and questionnaire are introduced in detail, and the respondents are briefly described. Finally, the secondary data sources which were used for better understanding of the secession in its fullness are introduced.

## 2.1 Methodology

In this section, the statistics and econometric methods used are briefly described. Standard descriptive statistics such as the arithmetic and geometric mean, standard deviation, variance, frequency, and Pearson coefficient of correlation were used to describe the data. Furthermore, the standard non-parametric Chi-squared test, t-test, Analysis of Variance, and linear regression were used. Heterogeneity of preferences was approximated by the Herfindahl-Hirschman index, and for utility function estimation, Factor Analysis was used.

### *Chi-squared test*

The relationship between the categorical data is tested using the non-parametric test of independence. The Pearson independence $\chi^2$ statistic tests the null hypothesis of identical proportions (Budíková et al. 2010),

$$H_0: \theta_k = \theta_{k\cdot}$$

versus the alternative hypothesis,

$$H_1: \theta_k \neq \theta_k$$

Thus, to test these hypotheses, the *Pearson statistic* for the dataset of size $n$ is used (Cramér 1946:281):

$$\varphi^2 = \sum_{j,k} \frac{\left(p_{jk} - p_{j.}p_{.k}\right)^2}{p_{j.}p_{.k}} \tag{2.1}$$

where $p$ is a simultaneous probability estimated by the relative frequencies.

Asymptotic distribution of the Pearson statistic is then realised by the Pearson distribution with degrees of freedom determined by the number of rows $r$ and columns $s$ of the contingency table (Budíková et al. 2010).

$$\varphi^2 \sim \chi^2\left((r-1)(s-1)\right) \tag{2.2}$$

The strength of the independence between categorical variables can be measured by the *Cramer's V:*

$$V = \sqrt{\frac{\varphi^2}{n(m-1)}}; m = \min(r,s), 0 \leq V \leq 1 \tag{2.3}$$

Given the aim of our analysis, we use criteria of strength listed in Table 2.1.

### *Analysis of variance (ANOVA)*

The analysis of variance (ANOVA) was used, for instance, to test the relationship between attitudes towards secession and willingness to take part in the lottery. The model

$$x_{ij} = \mu + \alpha_i + \varepsilon_{ij}, i = 1,\ldots,r; j = 1,\ldots,n, \varepsilon \sim N\left(0;\sigma^2\right)$$

*Table 2.1* Strength of Cramer's V

| *Cramer's V* | *Independence* |
|---|---|
| (0, 0.1) | Insignificant |
| $\langle 0.1, 0.3)$ | Weak |
| $\langle 0.3, 0.7)$ | Moderate |
| $\langle \mathbf{0.7,1} \rangle$ | Strong |

Source: Budíkova et al. (2010:214). Author.

was estimated to calculate the test statistic

$$F_A = \frac{\frac{S_A}{f_A}}{\frac{S_E}{f_E}} \tag{2.4}$$

where $S_E$ being the error sum of squares with $f_E = n - r$ degree of freedoms, and $S_A$ is the model sum of squares with $f_A = r - 1$ degree of freedoms.

If the null hypothesis is valid, the test statistic is realised with the Fisher distribution.

$$F_A \sim F(r-1, n-r)$$

The equality of variance was tested using the Levene's test. Scheffé's method was used to conduct the posthoc test.

***Two sample t-test***

The two-sample t-test is used to compare the two means. The Null hypothesis,

$$H_0\colon \mu_1 = \mu_2$$

is tested with the alternative hypothesis,

$$H_1\colon \mu_1 \neq \mu_2$$

using the test criterion,

$$t = \frac{m_1 - m_2}{\frac{(n_1 - 1)s_1^2 + (n_2 - 1)s_2^2}{n_1 + n_2 - 2} \times \sqrt{\frac{1}{n_1} + \frac{1}{n_2}}} \tag{2.5}$$

where $n_i$ is the sample size, $m_i$ is the arithmetic mean, and $s_i$ is the standard deviation of the $i - th$ sample. The null hypothesis is rejected on the level of significance of 5% if the p-value is lower than 0.05 (Budíková et al. 2010).

***Linear regression***

The Standard Ordinary Least Squares (OLS) model,

$$y_i = \beta_1 + \beta_2 x_{2i} + \ldots + \beta_k x_{ki} + \varepsilon_i; i = 1, \ldots, n \tag{2.6}$$

where

$$\varepsilon \sim N\left(0, \sigma^2 I\right)$$

is estimated using the standard diagnostic tests (Heij et al. 2004).

### *Herfindahl-Hirschman Index*

Heterogeneity of preferences can be approximated by measuring diversity in one country. Pastiurko et al. (2011) claim there is a link between the economic success of a country and its cultural homogeneity. Thus, to estimate homogeneity, they use an index of linguistic, ethnic, and religionist fractionalisation. Their index is the Rae index,[1] as they compute it as one minus the Herfindahl-Hirschman Index.

In this study, we prefer the Herfindahl-Hirschman Index to the Rae Index for its simple, direct interpretation. Hirschman developed the Herfindahl-Hirschman Index (HHI) in 1945, and it is used to calculate concentration if it is a function of unequal distribution and fewness (Hirschman 1964). The Hirschman original index was computed as

$$HI = \sqrt{\sum \left(\frac{x_i}{x}\right)^2} \tag{2.7}$$

where $x_i$ is the value of a country's trade in commodity $i$ and $x$ is its total trade.

Regarding the study aim, we use a recent version of this formula, modified by Herfindahl in 1950:

$$HHI = \sum s_i^2 \tag{2.8}$$

The HHI ranges from 0, if there is total heterogeneity, to 1, in case all subjects are the same.

We compute religious $HHI_{RR}$ as the sum of squares of the individual religion shares in each country. In the same way, the linguistic $HHI_{LL}$ and ethnic $HHI_{EE}$ were computed. Thus, to compare the total diversification of each country in all three variables, we use the composed $HHI_{Total}$, which is calculated as the geometric mean:

$$HHI_{Total} = \sqrt[3]{HHI_{RR} \times HHI_{LL} \times HHI_{EE}} \tag{2.9}$$

### *Cluster analysis*

Cluster analysis enables us to classify the data. Given the research aim, the *k-Means Clustering* method was used. K-Means Clustering minimises variability within the cluster and maximises variability between clusters (TIBCO Software Inc. 2017).

The Euclidian distance $d_{ih}$ of an observation $i$ from cluster $k$ is computed as:

$$d_{ih} = \sqrt{\frac{1}{N}\sum_{j=1}^{N}\left(X_{ij} - \bar{X}_j^k\right)^2} \tag{2.10}$$

The aim of the analysis is to minimise objective function

$$J = \sum_{h=1}^{k}\sum_{i=1}^{n} u_{i,h}, d_{i,h}^2 \tag{2.11}$$

if conditions

$$\sum_{h=1}^{k} u_{i,h} = 1, i = 1\ldots n, \sum_{i=1}^{n} u_{i,h} > 0, h = 1\ldots k \tag{2.12}$$

are met, where $u_{i,h} = 1$ means the assignment of object vector to the cluster (Řezanková 2014).

### *Cobb Douglas function*

Researchers who do not consider secessionist conflicts being the economics problem argue that the macroeconomic aspects play just a marginal role in decision-making of the citizens – especially in comparison to the romantic factors (e. g. Huszka 2013). Weights of both the romantic and economic factors might be with caution estimated using the two-dimensional Cobb-Douglas function. Cobb-Douglas function

$$u(R, E) = A \times R^{\alpha} E^{1-\alpha} \tag{2.13}$$

is considered to be "*a convenient parametric form*" because it has only two parameters (Varian 2000:181).

To estimate the Cobb-Douglas function, we need vector $R$ of romantic factors and vector $E$ of economic factors. Those vectors are computed using the multivariate factor analysis as an "interdependence technique whose primary purpose is to define the underlying structure among the variables in the analysis" (Hair et al. 2013:97) and it make available to reduce number of variables.

Let's have $n$ vectors $x_1, x_2 \dots x_n$, which are thought to have two underlying factors $F_1$ and $F_2$.[2] To run the R-type factor analysis, the correlation matrix based on the correlations among variables is estimated as the multicollinearity is desirable. Using the factor loadings based on the orthogonal (VARIMAX) rotation and Principal components extraction method, the new factors are estimated.

To estimate the utility function

$$u(R,E) = A \times R^{\alpha} E^{1-\alpha} \tag{2.14}$$

using the OLS method, the vectors are normalised so as all their elements were non-negative (compare Field 2013:203; LeBlanc 2004:218):

if romantic and economic factors are given by vectors $R$, $E$

$$R = \begin{bmatrix} r_1 & \dots & r_n \end{bmatrix},\ E = \begin{bmatrix} e_1 & \dots & e_n \end{bmatrix}$$

utility

$$u = \begin{bmatrix} u_1 & \dots & u_n \end{bmatrix}$$

is vector of willingness to pay (Q1.1)
and constant

$$A = \begin{bmatrix} 1 & \dots & 1 \end{bmatrix}$$

then

$$\bar{r} = \min(R), \bar{e} = \min(E)$$
$$k = \min\{\bar{r}; \bar{e}\}$$

and consequently the transformed vectors are computed as

$$\hat{R} = \begin{bmatrix} r_1 + k & \dots & r_n + k \end{bmatrix},\ \hat{E} = \begin{bmatrix} e_1 + k & \dots & e_n + k \end{bmatrix}$$
$$\hat{u} = \begin{bmatrix} u_1 + k & \dots & u_n + k \end{bmatrix},\ \beta_0 = \begin{bmatrix} 1 + k & \dots & 1 + k \end{bmatrix}$$

The Cobb-Douglas function

$$\hat{u} = \beta_0 \times \hat{R}^{\beta_1} \times \hat{E}^{\beta_2} \tag{2.15}$$

is then transformed to the logarithmic form

$$\log \hat{u} = \log \beta_0 + \beta_1 \times \log \hat{R} + \beta_2 \times \log \hat{E} \tag{2.16}$$

and estimated using the OLS model with restriction

$$\beta_1 + \beta_2 = 1 \tag{2.17}$$

Finally, the constant $l\_\beta_0$ needs to be re-transformed as

$$\beta_0 = e^{l\_\beta_0} \tag{2.18}$$

## 2.2 Data

Originality of our research is derived from the original data collected among the members of the secessionist parties and movements. This Survey on autonomist and pro-independence movements (SAPIM) is introduced in the first part of this section. The second part is devoted to the brief survey data description. Nevertheless, the sample survey cannot cover all aspects of secessionist and anti-secessionist tensions in time and space. In the third subchapter, the other data sources are therefore described.

### *2.2.1 A survey on autonomist and pro-independence movements*

There are three possible focus groups which could be addressed:

a) citizens living in the secessionist region (or, as the subgroup, all citizens of the region who have active voting rights within the region);
b) pro-secession voters; and
c) pro-secession institutional actors (especially political parties and movements).

The first potential focus group (*all* citizens or voters) would cover not only the pro-secessionists but also the anti-secessionists who could serve as the control group. However, such a focus group would be faced with two challenges. First, each respondent's identification with the secessionist goals would be unclear; even the citizen, who would, in a referendum, vote against the secession, might declare his pro-secessionists values, springing from his current mood or actual dissatisfaction with a particular decision of the central government.[3]

This second obstacle would persist even if the second potential focus group was chosen. Moreover, it would not be possible to identify pro-secession voters with the highest accuracy: some of them would not be motivated to tell the truth on their voting preferences. Additionally, a regional secessionist referendum has been recently conducted in just two European regions: Scotland in 2014 and Catalonia in 2017.

The most appropriate, concerning our research, was therefore the third group covering members of the secessionist parties and movements. These respondents sharply reveal their secessionist preferences by their active membership. Paying membership fees and declaring one's self as a party or movement member distinguish wholehearted secessionists from latent secessionists who are not willing to suffer any sacrifice connected to the active support of the secession because they might simply be indifferent to the utility of status quo and the potential (uncertain) utility of sovereign post-secession state. This group of respondents is also well-organised and easily achievable via the political parties' structures.

Instead of addressing particular secessionist parties and movement among the EU, we used the existing infrastructure of the European Free Alliance (EFA) which is "an umbrella organisation that gathers 45 progressive nationalists, regionalist, and autonomist parties throughout the EU, representing stateless nations, regions, and traditional minorities in Europe" (EFA 2018).[4] Since the first European election (1979), EFA is represented in the European Parliament, and since 2004 it has a status of a European political party (ibidem).

The questionnaire was distributed as an online form to members of 34 parties and movements who are part of the European Free Alliance. Data were collected between 21 June 2018, when respondents received mails with an invitation to the survey, and 1 August 2018, when the data collection was closed. Additionally, one reminder was sent to all respondents on 27 July 2018.

### *Questionnaire*[5]

With respect to the research aim, an original anonymous questionnaire was constructed. Questions were divided into three sections:

1 identification of respondent;
2 secessionist attitudes; and
3 economic attitudes.

The first section covers background information. The usual basic demographic questions deal with the age, sex (male or female), place of residence, and highest achieved education (primary, lower secondary, upper secondary, tertiary with a bachelor's degree, and tertiary with master's degree or higher). Furthermore, respondents were asked for their job description and their current status in terms of the labour market (a public sector employee, a private sector employee, self-employed, unemployed, student, parental leave, retirement). Questions related to romantic factors close the first section: religious denomination, language knowledge (including the mother tongue), and type of media followed by respondents (regional, national, or international).

The second section deals with the secessionist attitudes of respondents. First, they should decide whether they prefer the independence of their region as a separate sovereign state, autonomy of the region within the existing country, unitary state with the central government, or a federation (*Qs1*). Subsequent questions asked for the reasons for supporting independence (*Qs1a*), and the form of government in the new potential state (*Qs1b*) – these questions were answered just in case the respondent called for independence. Two other questions examine respondent's attitudes toward the EU by asking whether one would like the new independent state to become EU member states (*Qs2*) and whether one would vote for EU membership of the existing country. The final questions deal with the political self-identification of respondents with the region and the country (*Qs4*) and one's trust in the regional, national, and European political institutions (*Qs5*). The five-step scale inspired by Hierro (2015) was used for self-identification. While Hierro asked if respondents identified themselves as "primarily Spanish", "more Catalan than Spanish", or "Only Catalan", we asked respondents if they identified only with their region, more with their region than the country, with their region as well as with their country, with their country more than with their region, and, finally, only with their country. Trust in the political institutions was found using the standard Eurobarometer question *Trust in National and International Institutions* (GESIS 2018). Questions *Qs1*, *Qs1a*, *Qs2* and *Qs5* were answered using the *Likert scale* (Kotler and Keller 2007). Respondents could choose among these options: "definitely yes, rather yes, yes, rather no, no, and definitely no".

The last part of the questionnaire focused explicitly on economic questions. The first two questions deal with the willingness to accept and the willingness to pay. Respondents were asked what maximum monthly contribution they would be willing to pay as a special tax related to the costs of independence (*Q1.1*), and what minimum monthly benefit they would like to receive to continue living in the current country instead of the newly independent state (*Q1.2*). Two further questions deal with subjectively assessing of the regional, national, and EU economy condition (*Q2*), as well as a subjective perception of living standard change in case of a successful secession (*Q3*), using the five-level Likert scale. The willingness to take risk is approximated by the simple example (*Q4*): if the probability of winning a lottery jackpot of €1000 was 10%, how much euro would the respondent be willing to pay for a lottery ticket? Thus, to estimate the personal discount rate, we described a simple situation to the respondents (*Q5*): you could be given €100 today or €100 plus bonus a year later. How high would the bonus have to be for you to be willing to choose the latter option?

Fiscal decentralisation is connected to the division of power between the central and regional government. Respondents were, therefore, asked to decide on the field (education, taxation, healthcare, foreign affairs, safety, European policy, and social policy) in which power should be handed exclusively to the central government, what an exclusive jurisdiction of regional government should be, and which tasks should be shared by both degrees of power (*Q6*).

It is supposed that some circumstances are more favourable for a successful secession. Respondents, therefore, chose the circumstances under which they would support the emergence of a new state (*Q7*). They could also choose among a sufficient amount of universities in the region, excellent infrastructure (such as motorways or railways), good political representation, the Prime minister or other central government leading politicians coming from the region, a high living standard, and, finally, a serious economic crisis. The last question (*Q8*) focused on the *greed and grievance* phenomenon. Respondents were asked if they agree with three statements: a) tax contributions to the central budget are higher than the amounts they receive back; b) at the national level, they could decide on public expenditures better than the central government decides; c) the central government has disproportionally high profits from regional resources (including oil or raw materials). Both questions *Q7* and *Q8* were replied using the five-level Likert scale.

Based on the responses, new additional categorical variables were introduced.

The dummy variable, *secession*, takes on a value of 1 if a respondent wants *independence of region as a separate sovereign state* ($Qs1a = 1$) and a value of 0 (if respondents prefer autonomy, unitary state, or federation). If the variable, *secession*, takes on the value of 1, the label "secessionist" or "pro-secessionist" is used in the subsequent text. If it takes on the value of 0, we call the respondent "anti-secessionist" even if his secessionist attitudes might be connected to a call for a higher degree of autonomy.

The variable, *Trust*, reflects the total satisfaction of respondents with institutions in general (covering regional, national, and supranational institutions):

$$Trust = \sum_{i=1}^{5} Q_s 5.i; Trust \in \{5,6\ldots25\} \tag{2.19}$$

Similarly, the variable, *Satisfaction*, reflects the respondent's total satisfaction with the economic situation in the region, country, and EU:

$$Satisfaction = \sum_{i=1}^{3} Q_s 2.i; Trust \in \{3\ldots15\} \tag{2.20}$$

*Table 2.2* Categories of variable *Trust*

| Trust *category* | | Trust *value* |
|---|---|---|
| 1 | definitely trust | 5–9 |
| 2 | rather trust | 10–14 |
| 3 | neither trust nor not trust | 15–19 |
| 4 | rather not trust | 20–24 |
| 5 | definitely not trust | 25 |

Source: Author.

*Table 2.3* Categories of variable *Satisfaction*

| Satisfaction *category* | | Satisfaction *value* |
|---|---|---|
| 1 | Good | 3–8 |
| 2 | neither good nor bad | 9–11 |
| 3 | Bad | 12–15 |

Source: Author.

As for the romantic factors, we need to evaluate whether the respondent's mother tongue and his religion are in accordance with the prevailing language and religion of the country. Two new variables – *religion* and *mother tongue* – are therefore introduced.

Respondents were classified into four categories according to their match with the "country" religion (Table 2.4). For instance, if the Czech respondent claimed he is Catholic, the match in his denomination with the Czech population is 27.1 as according to the Eurobarometer there are 27.1% Catholics among the Czech citizens (see Table 2.5). Regarding the research aim, it would be convenient to use data for the rest of the country (without the secessionist region). However, such data was not available.

*Table 2.4* Religions structure

| | *Catholic* | *Orthodox* | *Protestant* | *Non-believer/ Agnostic/Atheist* | *Other* |
|---|---|---|---|---|---|
| Czech Republic | 27.1 | 0.2 | 1 | 64.4 | 7.3 |
| Germany | 31.1 | 0.9 | 33.1 | 23.5 | 11.4 |
| Netherlands | 21.9 | 1.9 | 17.8 | 48.8 | 9.6 |
| Greece | 0.4 | 92.9 | 0.1 | 3.5 | 3.1 |
| Italy | 77.8 | 4.9 | 0.6 | 10 | 6.7 |
| Austria | 66.5 | 2.2 | 7.2 | 16 | 8.1 |
| Hungary | 60.3 | 1.1 | 5.1 | 20.7 | 12.8 |
| Belgium | 52.9 | 1.6 | 2.1 | 18.6 | 24.8 |
| France | 47.8 | 0.6 | 1.8 | 40.4 | 9.4 |
| Sweden | 1.6 | 0.9 | 36.5 | 50 | 11 |
| Luxembourg | 64.8 | 3.5 | 3.6 | 21.5 | 6.6 |
| Poland | 90.7 | 0.2 | 2 | 5.8 | 1.3 |
| Spain | 64.2 | 1.4 | 0.8 | 27.9 | 5.7 |
| Denmark | 1.2 | 2.2 | 60 | 27.9 | 8.7 |
| Finland | 0.1 | 2 | 69.7 | 19.2 | 9 |
| United Kingdom | 33.3 | 1.3 | 42.4 | 10 | 13 |
| Croatia | 84.2 | 2.3 | 0.2 | 10.2 | 3.1 |

Source: Eurobarometer 83.4, Author.

*Table 2.5* Categories of variable *Religion*

| Religion *category* | | Religion |
|---|---|---|
| 1 | Same | (50;100⟩ |
| 2 | Similar | (20;50⟩ |
| 3 | Distinct | (10;20⟩ |
| 4 | Different | (0;10⟩ |

Source: Author.

The binary variable, *mother tongue*, takes on the value of 1 if respondent's mother tongue is also the main language of the country and the value of 0 if it is a minor language (Table 2.6 summarises the percentage of the population speaking the main languages).

The binary variable, *university*, takes on the value of 1 if a respondent achieved tertiary education (either a bachelor's degree or a master's degree and higher) and value of 0 if he reached primary or secondary (lower or higher) education. Similarly, the binary variable, *teacher*, takes on the value of 1 if a respondent works as a teacher.

The variable, *white*, takes on the value of 1 if the respondent works in a white-collar job and value of 0 if he works in a blue-collar job. Jobs, as described by the respondents, were classified manually to the categories of the International Standard Classification of Occupation (ISCO). We used the approach of the Organisation for Economic Co-operation and Development which divides ISCO categories into four groups as Table 2.7 shows.

*Table 2.6* Mother tongue

| *Country* | *Main language* |
|---|---|
| Czech Republic | Czech (98%) |
| Germany | German (87%) |
| Netherlands | Dutch (94%) |
| Greece | Greek (99%) |
| Italy | Italian (97%) |
| Austria | German (93%) |
| Hungary | Hungarian (99%) |
| Belgium | Dutch (94%)<br>French (38%)<br>Germany (0.4%) |
| France | French (93%) |
| Sweden | Swedish (93%) |
| Luxembourg | Luxembourgish (52%)<br>French (16%)<br>German (2%) |
| Poland | Polish (95%) |
| Spain | Spanish (82%)<br>Catalan (8%)<br>Galician (5%)<br>Basque (1%) |
| Denmark | Danish (87%) |
| Finland | Finish (94%)<br>Swedish (5%) |
| United Kingdom | English (88%) |
| Croatia* | Croatian (95%) |

Source: Eurobarometer 386 (2012).

* Croatia was not an EU member in 2012; thus, it was not included in the Eurobarometer 386. Data for Croatia were taken from the dataset World Atlas.

*Table 2.7* White- and blue-collar workers

| | | ISCO-08 Category | |
|---|---|---|---|
| White-collar | White-collar high skill | 1 | Managers |
| | | 2 | Professional |
| | | 3 | Technicians |
| | White-collar low skill | 4 | Clerical support workers |
| | | 5 | Service and sales workers |
| Blue-collar | Blue-collar high skill | 6 | Skilled agricultural, forestry and fishery workers |
| | | 7 | Craft and related trades workers |
| | Blue-collar low skill | 8 | Plant and machine operators, and assemblers |
| | | 9 | Elementary occupations |

Source: OECD (1998) and ILO (2008). Author.

The multinomial variable, *Risk*, takes values of 1–3 according to the respondent's risk attitudes. For calculation, answers on question *Q4* were used.[6] Consider a nondegenerate lottery $L$ and a degenerated lottery $\tilde{L}$, where $L$ is a simple lottery consisting of outcome probabilities $L = (p_1 \dots p_N), p_N \geq 0, \sum_{n=1}^{N} p_n = 1$, and $\tilde{L}$ is a degenerated lottery which yields only one consequence with probability 1 and probabilities of all other consequences are 0. Thus, the respondent is

a) strictly risk-averse, if for any lottery $l$ he finds $\tilde{z}_l \geq l$; which means $\tilde{L} > L$;
b) risk-neutral, if $\tilde{L} \sim L$; and
c) risk loving, if $\tilde{L} < L$

(see Mas-Collel et al. 1995).

In our case, the probability of winning the lottery is $p = 0.10$, and the expected value of lottery ticket is therefore

$$EV = 0.1 \times 1000 + 0.9 \times 0 = 100$$

Considering the primitive utility function $u(c) = c$, the respondent is

- risk-averse (the variable *Risk* takes on a value of 1) if he would be willing to have a lottery ticket of any amount $P \in \langle 0;100)$;
- risk-neutral (the variable *Risk* takes on a value of 2) if he would be willing to have a lottery ticket of a specific amount $P = 100$; and
- risk loving (variable *Risk* takes on a value of 3) if he would be willing to have a lottery ticket of any amount $P > 100$.

However, the choice of the utility function is, undoubtedly, questionable since it anticipates personal attitudes toward risk. Furthermore, the utility function and decision-making under risk depend, also, on the original wealth level (Bernoulli [1954]), and consumers tend to consider it underweight with fewer probable outcomes (Kahneman and Tversky 1979). Unfortunately, we were not able to use the Bernoulli utility function or S-shaped utility function as data on the original wealth level were not available.

Regarding the research aim, the precise expected utility is not as crucial as any basic monotonous utility function (for instance, the risk-averse function $u(c) = \sqrt{c}$ or risk-loving utility function $u(c) = c^2$) to keep the order of the risk preferences and change the magnitude of the risk.

Data available from the questionnaire are mostly categorical and are either nominal (such as *Sex* or *Education level*) or ordinal (respondent answers using the scale, such as *How much do you trust the European Commission*); only a few variables are quantitative (see Table 2.8).

*Table 2.8* List of categorical and quantitative variables used in survey

| *Categorical* | | | | *Quantitative* | |
|---|---|---|---|---|---|
| *Nominal* | | *Ordinal* | | | |
| Qi2 | Sex | Qi4 | Education | Qi1 | Age |
| Qi3 | Place of residence | Qi8 | Local language | Q1.1 | Independence Tax |
| Qi5 | Employment | Qi9 | Media | Q1.2 | Independence Benefit |
| Qi5a | Current state | Qs2 | EU membership | Q4 | Risk Attitude |
| Qi6 | Religious denomination | Qs3 | Referendum of EU exit | Q5 | Discounting future |
| Qi7 | Languages | Qs4 | identification with region | | |
| Qs1 | Future of country | Qs5.1 | Trust to European Commission | | |
| Qs1a | Independence vote | Qs5.2 | Trust to European Parliament | | |
| Qs1b | Form of government | Qs5.3 | Trust to national government | | |
| Q6 | Sharing of the powers | Qs5.4 | Trust to regional authorities | | |
| Q7 | Support of secession | Qs5.5 | Trust to local council | | |
| | Secession | | Economic situation | | |
| | Religion | Q2.1 | in region | | |
| | Language | Q2.2 | in country | | |
| | Mother Tongue | Q2.3 | in EU | | |
| | University | Q3.1 | in newly independent country | | |
| | Teacher | Q3.2 | in the rest of former country | | |
| | White | Q3.3 | in family | | |
| | Risk | Q8 | Reasons for secession | | |
| | | | Trust | | |
| | | | Satisfaction | | |

Source: Author.

### 2.2.2 *Survey description*

In total, 590 responses were collected. However, 24 respondents were excluded because of missing regional information or the incompleteness of replies. The dataset used to satisfy the aim of our research consisted of 566 fully answered questionnaires. Most of the respondents came from Italy (57.2%), especially the South Tyrol autonomous province (91.7% of the Italian answers), Belgium (9.9%; all answers were from Flanders), and Germany (9.9%; most of the answers were from Bayern). There were also single responses for regions such as Åland or Southern Denmark (Table 2.9).

*Basic description of the dataset*

The questionnaire was available in six languages: apart from Czech (5.1% of filled forms), respondents could choose German (71.6% of forms), English (12.9%), Italian (4.4%), Spanish (4.2%), and French (1.6%).

*Table 2.9* Countries and regions

| *Country* | *respondent* | | *NUTS 2* | | *Capital* | *respondent* | |
|---|---|---|---|---|---|---|---|
| | *N* | *%* | | | | *N* | *%* |
| IT | 324 | 57.2 | ITD1 | South Tyrol | Bolzano | 298 | 92.0 |
| | | | ITD4 | Friuli-Venezia-Giulia | Trieste | 11 | 3.4 |
| | | | ITD2 | Trento | Trento | 5 | 1.5 |
| | | | ITC4 | Lombardy | Milan | 4 | 1.2 |
| | | | ITD3 | Veneto | Venice | 2 | 0.6 |
| | | | ITD5 | Emilia-Romagna | Bologna | 2 | 0.6 |
| | | | ITF2 | Molise | Campobasso | 1 | 0.3 |
| | | | ITG2 | Sardegna (Sardinia) | Sagliari | 1 | 0.3 |
| DE | 56 | 9.9 | DE2 | Bavaria | Munich | 21 | 37.5 |
| | | | DE40B | Oberspreewald-Lausitz | Senftenberg | 8 | 14.3 |
| | | | DE11 | Stuttgart | Stuttgart | 6 | 10.7 |
| | | | DE3 | Berlin | Berlin | 4 | 7.1 |
| | | | DEA | Nordrhein-Westfalen | Düsseldorf | 4 | 7.1 |
| | | | DED2 | Dresden | Dresden | 3 | 5.4 |
| | | | DE7 | Hessen | Wiesbaden | 2 | 3.6 |
| | | | DE9 | Niedersachsen | Hannover | 2 | 3.6 |
| | | | DEB | Rheinland-Pfalz | Mainz | 2 | 3.6 |
| | | | DE4 | Brandenburg | Potsdam | 1 | 1.8 |
| | | | DEB3C | Bad Dürkheim | Bad Dürkheim | 1 | 1.8 |
| | | | DEF | Schleswig-Holstein | Kiel | 1 | 1.8 |
| | | | DEG | Thüringen | Erfurt | 1 | 1.8 |

(*Continued*)

*Table 2.9* (Continued)

| *Country* | *respondent* | | *NUTS 2* | | *Capital* | *respondent* | |
|---|---|---|---|---|---|---|---|
| | *N* | *%* | | | | *N* | *%* |
| BE | 56 | 9.9 | BE2 | Flanders | Brussels | 56 | 100.0 |
| AT | 44 | 7.8 | AT33 | Tyrol | Innsbruck | 22 | 50.0 |
| | | | AT32 | Salzburg | Salzburg | 7 | 15.9 |
| | | | AT13 | Vienna | Vienna | 4 | 9.1 |
| | | | AT12 | Lower Austria | Sank Pölten | 3 | 6.8 |
| | | | AT31 | Upper Austria | Linz | 3 | 6.8 |
| | | | AT34 | Vorarlberg | Bregent | 2 | 4.5 |
| | | | AT1 | *Eastern Austria* | *missing data* | 1 | 2.3 |
| | | | AT11 | Burgenland | Eisenstadt | 1 | 2.3 |
| | | | AT22 | Styria | Graz | 1 | 2.3 |
| CZ | 29 | 5.1 | CZ06 | Southeast | Brno | 14 | 48.3 |
| | | | CZ06–08 | Moravia | Brno | 4 | 13.8 |
| | | | CZ07 | Central Moravia | Olomouc | 10 | 34.5 |
| | | | CZ08 | Moravian-Silesian | Opava | 1 | 3.4 |
| ES | 26 | 4.6 | ES52 | Valencian Community | Valencia | 16 | 61.5 |
| | | | ES21 | Basque Community | Vitoria-Gasteiz | 3 | 11.5 |
| | | | ES51 | Catalonia | Barcelona | 3 | 11.5 |
| | | | ES53 | Balearic Islands | Palma de Mallorca | 3 | 11.5 |
| FR | 10 | 1.8 | FRM0 | Corsica | Ajaccio | 5 | 50.0 |
| | | | FR4 | *EST* | *missing data* | 2 | 20.0 |
| | | | FRH0 | Brittany | Rennes | 2 | 20.0 |
| | | | FRF1 | Alsace | Strasbourg | 1 | 10.0 |
| NL | 8 | 1.4 | NL12 | Friesland | Leeuwarden | 6 | 75.0 |
| | | | NL22 | Gelderland | Arnhem | 1 | 12.5 |
| | | | NL42 | Limburg | Maastricht | 1 | 12.5 |
| UK | 4 | 0.7 | UKL | Wales | Cardiff | 2 | 50.0 |
| | | | UKK30 | Cornwall and Isles of Scilly | Truro | 1 | 25.0 |
| | | | UKM | Scotland | Edinburgh | 1 | 25.0 |
| PL | 2 | 0.4 | PL22 | Slaskie | Katowice | 2 | 100.0 |
| GR | 1 | 0.2 | GR122 | Thessaloniki | Thessaloniki | 1 | 100.0 |
| HU | 1 | 0.2 | HU23 | Southern Transdanubia | Pécs | 1 | 100.0 |
| SE | 1 | 0.2 | SE22 | *Sydsverige* | *Malmö* | 1 | 100.0 |
| LU | 1 | 0.2 | LAU1 | Luxembourg | Luxembourg | 1 | 100.0 |
| DK | 1 | 0.2 | DK03 | Southern Denmark | Vejle | 1 | 100.0 |
| FI | 1 | 0.2 | FI20 | Åland | Mariehamn | 1 | 100.0 |
| HR | 1 | 0.2 | HR03 | Adriatic Croatia | *Rijeka* | 1 | 100.0 |
| Total | 566 | 100.0 | | | | | |

Source: SAPIM.

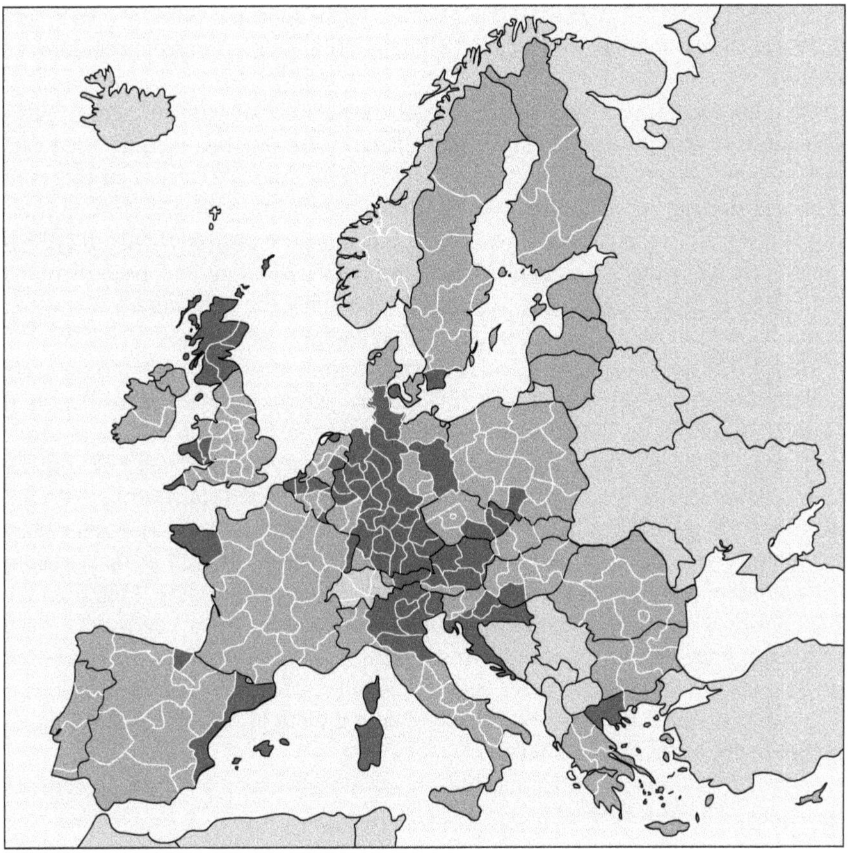

*Figure 2.1* Respondents distribution among the EU regions
Source: Author.

## 2.3 Other data sources

Apart from the original data from the survey secondary data sources were used. There are high-quality institutional data provided by: Eurostat, OECD, or national institutions. Eurostat, as well as national statistical agencies, provide data on the *nomenclature of territorial units*. The Kingdom of Spain is divided into 19 NUTS 2 units (Comunidades y ciudades autonómas). It is useful for the aim of our analysis that these NUTS 2 units coincide with the potentially secessionist regions in Spain.

For each of these regions, data on the elections results are available. We focused on the 2016 general election (Ministerio del Interior 2017). Twelve political parties were elected to the *Cortes Generales* on 26 June 2016. Four of them also run for the seats regarding the whole country. Election gains for the four nationwide parties were aggregated to the variable, *Nationwide Parties*, in each of the NUTS

2 regions. Similarly, election gains for all relevant regional parties were summed into the variable, *Local Parties*. Data on the gross domestic product (GDP) and GDP per capita (p.c.) as well as the total population were used from the Eurostat dataset.

Religion represents a very sensitive factor, especially since inhabitants of post-communist countries hesitate to reveal their faith. Despite this fact, we used data provided by *Centro de Investigaciones Sociológicas* (2015) to recognise shares of main religions in recent Europe. Apart from Catholicism, which is still the leading religion in European countries, we included protestants (covering all protestants churches), other Christians (such as Orthodox), Muslims and, because of the United Kingdom, Hindus. The last group represents the unaffiliated. European countries are not homogeneous in terms of language.

Data on the results of general and regional elections as well as voter turnout were collected from the *European Election Database* (Norwegian Centre for Research Data 2016). Data on the regional distribution of the European structural funds were used from the DG Regional Policy *Data for Research* dataset (European Commission 2016). Regional economic and demographical statistics by NUTS 2 classification were taken from the Eurostat database (Eurostat 2016). Finally, data on citizens' satisfaction with current economic situations as well as their trust in their political representation on the regional and national level were taken from the *Flash Eurobarometer 427* and *Flash Eurobarometer 472*. A survey for the Flash Eurobarometer 427 was conducted from the 3rd to 23rd of September 2015, based on fieldwork at the NUTS 2 level. Similarly, a survey for the Flash Eurobarometer 472 was conducted from the 10th of October to the 6th of November 2018, based on fieldwork at the NUTS 2 level.

Table 2.10 summarises four questions selected from a total of 17 Eurobarometer questions, which were used in our research.

The amounts in questions *Q1.1*, *Q1.2*, *Q4* and *Q5* were converted using the Purchasing Power Parity. Unfortunately, there were no actual data available on the regional level. However, at least the national comparison as published by OECD (2019) is sufficient for the research aim.

The Purchasing Power Parity estimated by OECD (2019) is published in national currency units ($E_N^{PPP}$) in US dollars. Such exchange rates need to be converted to euro currency ($E_N^{€}$) using the exchange rate $E_{€} = 0.728\, EUR / USD$:

$$E_N^{€} = \frac{E_N^{PPP}}{E_{€}} \tag{2.21}$$

The coefficient $\psi$ in converting the national currencies to the euro currency in the Purchasing Power Parity is calculated as

$$\psi = \frac{E_N}{E_N^{€}} \tag{2.22}$$

*Table 2.10* Questions used from the Flash Eurobarometer 427

| *Code* | *Question* | *Answers [%]* |
|---|---|---|
| Q1.1 | How would you judge the current situation in the quality of life in your region? | Total 'Good' = Very good + Rather good<br>Total 'Bad' = Rather bad + Very bad<br>Don't Know/No Answer |
| Q1.2 | How would you judge the current situation in the situation of the economy in your region? | |
| Q4 | I would like to ask you a question about how much trust you have in the European Union. Could you please tell me if you tend to trust it or tend not to trust it? | Tend to trust<br>Tend not to trust<br>Don't Know/No Answer |
| Q5 | From the following political representatives, which ones are best placed to explain you how European policies impact your day-to-day life? | Members of the European Commission.<br>Your (NATIONALITY) political representatives.<br>Your regional or local political representatives. |

Source: Eurostat (2015), author.

*Table 2.11* Questions used from the Flash Eurobarometer 472

| *Code* | *Question* | *Answers [%]* |
|---|---|---|
| Q1.1 | How would you judge the current situation in the quality of life in your region? | Total 'Good' = Very good + Rather good<br>Total 'Bad' = Rather bad + Very bad<br>Don't Know/No Answer |
| Q1.2 | How would you judge the current situation in the situation of the economy in your region? | |
| QD8 | I would like to ask you a question about how much trust you have in the European Union. Could you please tell me if you tend to trust it or tend not to trust it? | Tend to trust<br>Tend not to trust<br>Don't Know/No Answer |
| QD8 | Could you please tell me if you tend to trust the (NATIONALITY) government or tend not to trust it? | |
| Q3 | What do you think are the two most important issues facing (OUR REGION) at the moment? (MAX. 2 ANSWERS) | Immigration/ Crime/ Economic situation/ Unemployment/ People and/or business going away from the region/ The educational system/ The environment/ Healthcare system/ Other |

Source: Eurostat (2019), author.

Finally, the amounts $A_i$ are, for the aim of questions *Q1.1*, *Q1.2*, *Q4* and *Q5*, converted to amounts

$$A_i^{PPP} = A_i \times \psi \tag{2.23}$$

*Table 2.12* Conversion of the national currencies to the euro currency in the Purchasing Power Parity

| *Country* | $E_N^{PPP}$ | $E_N^{€}$ | $E_N$ | $\psi$ |
|---|---|---|---|---|
| AUS | 1.44 | 1.98 | 1.00 | 0.51 |
| BEL | 0.78 | 1.07 | 1.00 | 0.93 |
| CZE | 12.5 | 17.20 | 25.83 | 1.50 |
| DNK | 6.95 | 9.55 | 7.53 | 0.78 |
| FIN | 0.87 | 1.20 | 1.00 | 0.83 |
| FRA | 0.77 | 1.07 | 1.00 | 0.94 |
| DEU | 0.75 | 1.04 | 1.00 | 0.97 |
| GRC | 0.58 | 0.81 | 1.00 | 1.24 |
| HUN | 136.07 | 186.88 | 322.74 | 1.73 |
| ITA | 0.69 | 0.96 | 1.00 | 1.05 |
| LUX | 0.86 | 1.18 | 1.00 | 0.85 |
| NLD | 0.79 | 1.09 | 1.00 | 0.92 |
| POL | 1.75 | 2.40 | 4.29 | 1.78 |
| ESP | 0.64 | 0.88 | 1.00 | 1.14 |
| SWE | 8.86 | 12.16 | 10.28 | 0.84 |
| GBR | 0.69 | 0.95 | 0.89 | 0.95 |
| EA19 | 0.73 | 1.00 | 1.00 | 1.00 |
| HRV | 3.37 | 4.63 | 7.40 | 1.60 |

Source: OECD (2019) and Eurostat (2019). Own calculation.

An overview of the main data sources used is listed in Appendix D.

The last, unconventional and novel source of data is available due to the web-based tool Google Trends. This service provides researchers with data on the development of searching for the key words among time (since 2004) as well as among the regions all over the world. It is based on the Search Volume Index (SVI) which "measures how many times a keyword has been submitted to the Google search engine (Narita and Yin 2018). Google also provides application *Google Correlate* which "finds search patterns which correspondent with real-world trends" (Google 2019). Data are available for the time span from the 2004 to the first quarter of 2017 with weekly and monthly frequency.

Google Trends data are gradually being used for the scientific purposes; for example, for estimating the spread of influenza. However, as Mohebbi et al. mention the Google Trends data are connected also to some weaknesses:

1 underlying cause of search behavior can never be known;
2 data does not represent a random sample of the population; and
3 several subgroups are underrepresented.

(Mohebi et al. 2011:4)

Other weaknesses might consist in the spurious correlation due to the two parallel phenomena: for example, for the Czech mutation of the Google Correlate the term correlated to "Donald Trump" is, beside terms correlated to the US president, also the chocolate bar "Toblerone" with $\rho = 0.84$. However, this correlation was concentrated just to one week: on 8 November 2016, the main Czech servers published an article about "changing shape" of the chocolate bar Toblerone which "gets more gappy". Search for this news reached its peak on 9 November, exactly in the days of the US presidential election in November the correlation coefficient rocketed to the 0.99, while in 2015 it was $\rho = -0-17$. The Google Trends and Google Correlate data therefore should be used cautiously, not mechanically, and together with the other data sources.

The statistical software, Dell Statistica (data analysis software system) version 13.2, and econometric software, Gretl 1.9.14, were used for the data processing.

## Summary

The empirical part of our research is based on an original survey of members of secessionist parties and movements from 34 different political subjects in 17 European countries. The final dataset consists of 566 respondents, most of them being residents in South Tyrol (Italy) and Flanders (Belgium). The questionnaire consists of questions regarding the demography of respondents, secessionist attitudes, and economic attitudes. Additional data were used, especially to illustrate differences between the secessionist regions and the rest of their country. It was also used to describe their macroeconomic conditions, political preferences, and convert the pecuniary data according to the Purchasing Power Parity.

Standard descriptive statistics, as well as advanced statistical and econometrical methods, were used. Apart from the Chi-squared test, ANOVA, two sample t-test, linear regression, cluster analysis, and the HHI of diversity were calculated.

Among the respondents, males were more than females, respondents with higher education were more than those with lower education, and believers were more than those without denomination. More than three-quarters of the respondents call for total independence and sovereignty of their region, and most of them also identify themselves only with their region, not with their country. This is connected to a higher trust in the local and regional political institutions in comparison to the low degree of trust in the national government. Most of the respondents are also optimistic about regional economic conditions and their prospect while they are not satisfied with their country economy. While most of the policies – especially education, taxation, and social policy – should be conducted exclusively by the regional government, the European policy and foreign affairs could be shared between both the regional and central government. Respondents would promote the secession especially if the region had a good political representation. Finally, they support the greed and grievance theory as they seem to believe their regions to be exploited by the central governments.

## Notes

1 Rae index $RIF = 1 - \sum seat - share_i^2$; Rae (1967).
2 It is recommended to have at least five variables for each proposed factor (Hair et al. 2013:100).
3 Furthermore, the direct address of relevant and reliable statistical sample in regions of 17 European countries would require close co-operation with social research agencies which would make the research too expensive.
4 The list of members is attached in Appendix C.
5 The English version of the questionnaire is attached in Appendix A.
6 The probability of winning a lottery jackpot of €1,000 is 10%. How much euro would you be willing to pay for a lottery ticket?

# 3 Romantic and economic factors

## Empirical results

This chapter introduces detailed results of the survey, especially regarding respondent attitudes towards the secession. The first subchapter is devoted to simple statistical description of the respondents. The next chapter deals with the romantic factors in terms of the informal as well as formal institutions. It focuses on the heterogeneity in language, religion, and ethnicity, but it deals also with the culture and education. Thanks to our original SAPIM data, the impact of religiosity or relations to the teachership are studied. The formal institutions are studied mainly using the secondary data to analyse the heterogeneity in the political preferences. Final chapter deals with the economic factors. Macroeconomic factors cover the economic level and economic performance of region, role of scarce resources, impact of fiscal position in terms of the fiscal decentralisation, and the economic integration. The microeconomic factors are on the contrary devoted to the decision-making of the individual economic subject – homo economicus – especially to his risk attitudes and discount rate.

### 3.1 Description of the respondents

In this section, the survey respondents are described. The average age of respondents – members of the secessionist party – is 44.5 years. Males prevail significantly (84% in comparison to 16% female), which is in line with the significant female underrepresentation in political parties. For instance, according to Sundström and Stockemer (2015), there were nearly 25% of locally elected women in 29 European countries in the 2007–2013 period. Similarly, Coffé and Bolzendahl found that "women's odds of participation in political parties are 32.8% less than men's" (Coffé and Bolzendahl 2010).

Most of the respondents achieved higher degrees of education. Nearly 40% hold at least a Bachelor's degree. However, less than 6% achieved only primary education. It is in line with the professional structure of respondents as 83% of all economically active party members were classified as white collar and 17% as blue collar. Three-quarters of respondents are economically active, with most of them (53%) being private sector employees. Among the economically non-active, the retirees prevailed.

Three-quarters of respondents declared themselves as believers (90% of them being Catholics), 18% have no denomination, and the rest of them were unwilling to answer the question.

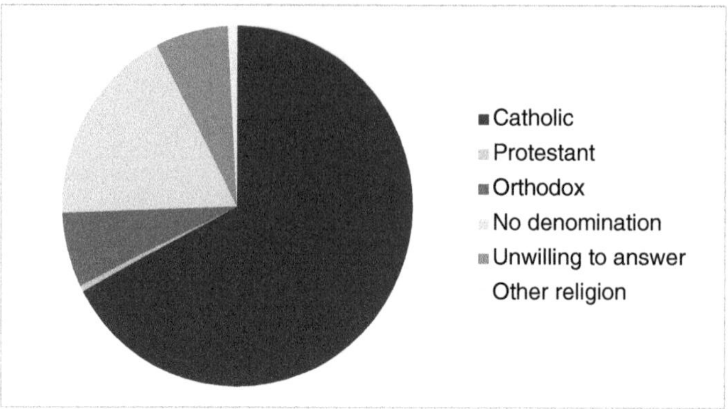


*Figure 3.1* Respondents according to their religion
Source: SAPIM, own calculation.

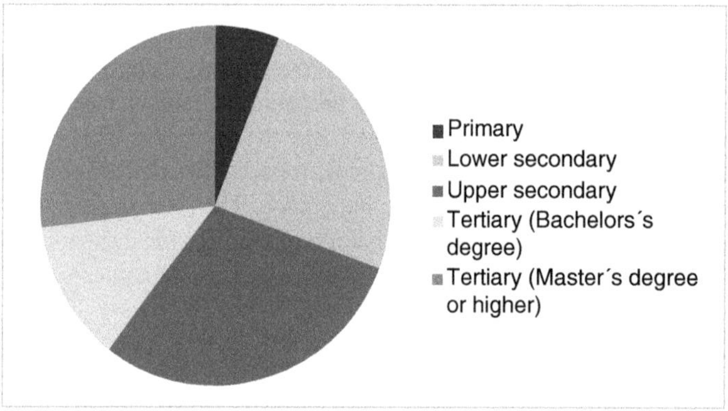


*Figure 3.2* Respondents according to their education level
Source: SAPIM, own calculation.

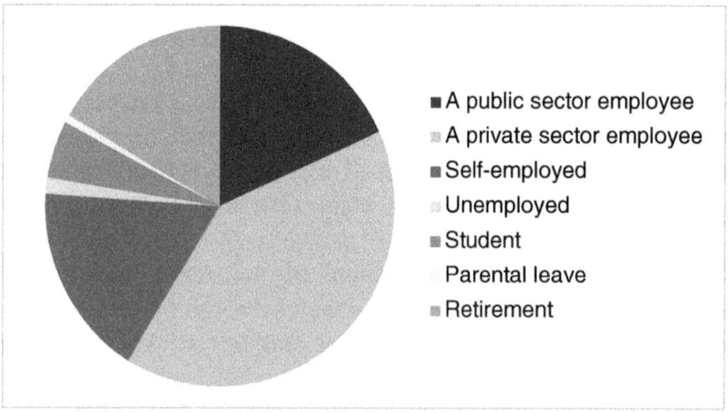


*Figure 3.3* Respondents according to their current state
Source: SAPIM, own calculation.

Most of the respondents (95%) follow[1] the regional media. Nevertheless, slightly more of them follow the international media (83%) in comparison to the national media (80%).[2] Moreover, three-quarters of respondents closely follow the regional, national, as well as international media simultaneously (Figure 3.4).

Nearly 78% of respondents said that, if they had to decide on the future of their country, they would opt for the independence of their region as a separate sovereign state; 13% prefer autonomy within the existing country; 7%, federation; and 2%, a unitary state with the central government. Most of those who would vote for independence want the sovereign state. Nevertheless, 5% of those "exit-voters" merely want to express their dissatisfaction with the recent government without really preferring the secession; 13% do not want secession but want to use the pro-secessionist vote in a referendum as the mean to obtain autonomy for their region; and 10% call for the restoration of the former historical arrangement.[3]

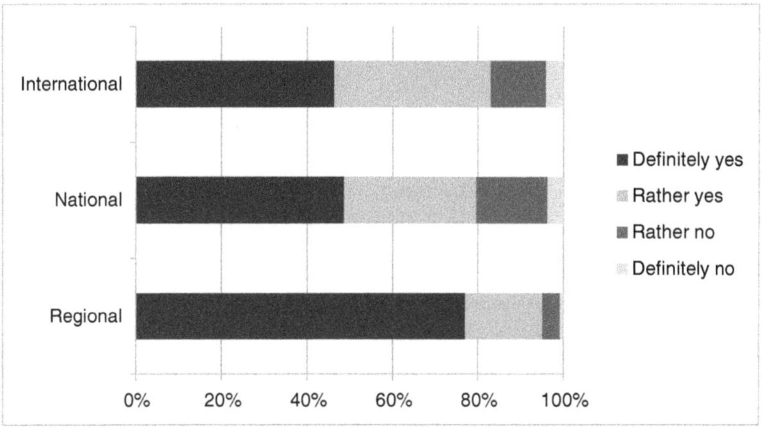


*Figure 3.4* Media which the respondents follow
Source: SAPIM, own calculation.

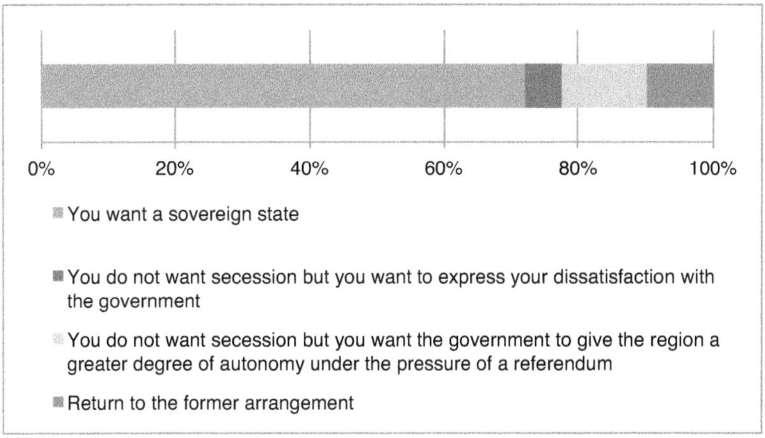


*Figure 3.5* Why would the respondents vote for independence of their region?
Source: SAPIM, own calculation.

Those who would want the independent state prefer a republic (94%) to a monarchy. In total, 62% of respondents claim that if their region became a new independent state, they would like it to be an EU member state. However, one fifth would prefer it not to be a member of the EU. Moreover, if there were a referendum on their existing country's membership of the EU, 40% of respondents would vote for exit and 45% against exit (the rest, 15%, do not know).

Most of the respondents politically identify themselves only with their region (60%); only 7.4% identify more with their country or only with their country.

Respondents trust, chiefly, in their local councils (more than 63% do trust) and regional authorities (42%). However, their trust in the national government is very low (70% of respondents do not trust them), even lower than the trust in institutions of the EU.

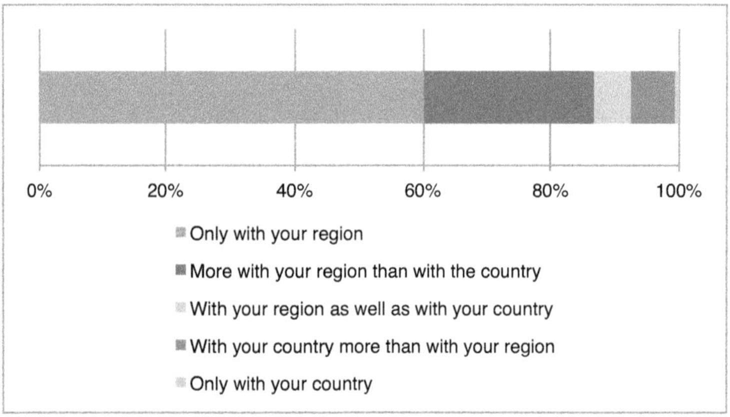


*Figure 3.6* Do the respondents identify with their region or with their country?
Source: SAPIM, own calculation.

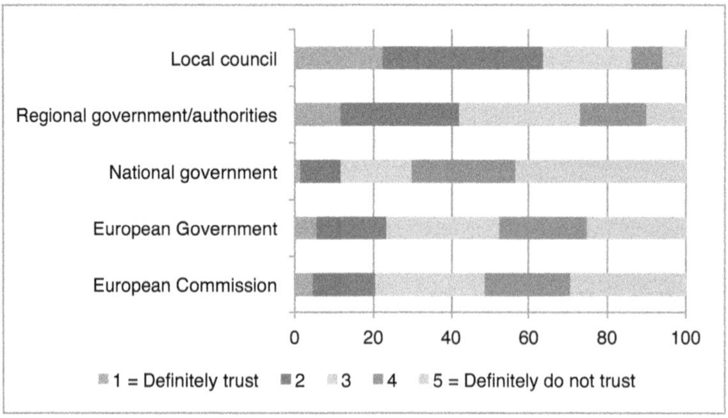


*Figure 3.7* Trust to the institutions
Source: SAPIM, own calculation.

Most of the respondents assess the current economic situation in their region as good or very good (76.5%). However, more than two-fifths assess the economic situation of their country as bad or even very bad. The economic condition of the EU is assessed slightly better in comparison to the country. However, it is significantly worse in comparison to the region (Figure 3.8).

More than 86% of respondents believe that in the case of their region's independence, the living standards of the newly independent country would increase. On the other hand, nearly one-third of respondents claim the living standards of the rest of the former country would decrease, and, according to nearly 46% of them, it would not change. Meanwhile, 80% of respondents expect an increase in living standards with respect to families in the case of a secession.

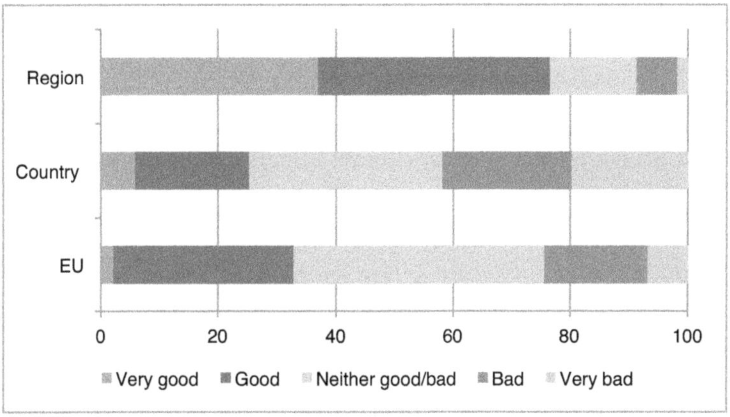


*Figure 3.8* Assessment of the economic situation

Source: SAPIM, own calculation.

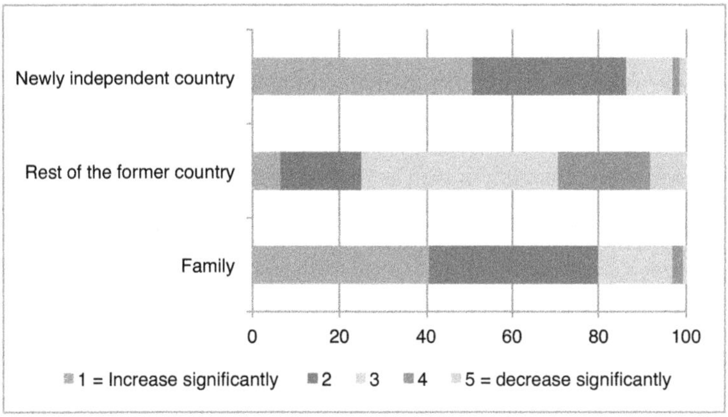


*Figure 3.9* How would the living standards change in case of the region's independence?

Source: SAPIM, own calculation.

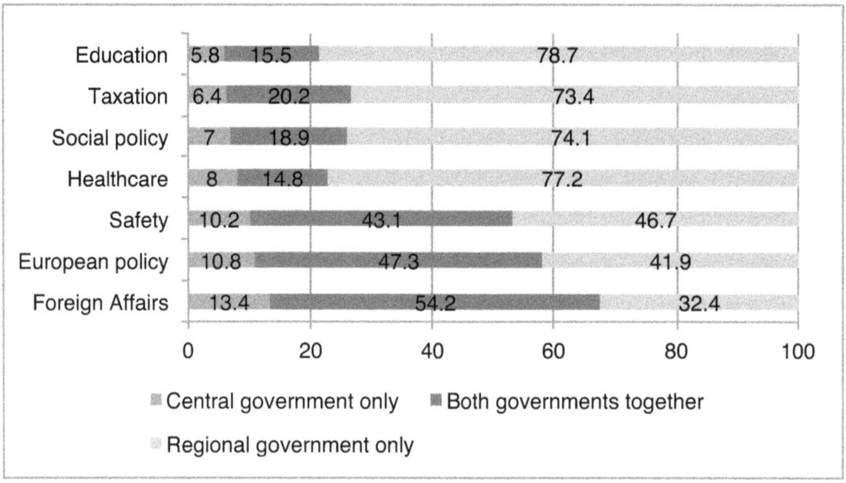


*Figure 3.10* Sharing the powers between central and regional government
Source: SAPIM, own calculation.

If the region were to remain part of the current state, most of the respondents would prefer if education, taxation, social policy, and health care were managed only by the regional government. However, in the case of foreign affairs, European policy, and safety, the respondents agree with sharing powers between the central and regional government or even exclusive management by the central government.

Such attitudes to the sharing of powers are in line with the recent division of policies in secessionist regions. The Åland Parliament (Lagting) is autonomous in the field of healthcare, environment, education, culture, police, traffic, and local administrations. However, the foreign affairs, judiciary, fiscal policies, and customs duties are in the hands of the Finnish parliament where the Ålands are represented by one member (compare Dudáková 2008). Similarly, the Faroe Islands seek to take control of all policies including migration affairs except for defence policy and parts of foreign, monetary, and judicial policies (The Local 2018). South Tyrolean autonomy covers the economy, social policy, culture, environment, mining, agriculture, tourism, as well as traffic (Pföstl ND).

The most important criterion under which the respondents would support the secession of their region would be good political representation. However, three times fewer respondents found, as the most important criterium, the recent experience of the regional politics on the national level (Figure 3.11).[4]

Nearly nine out of 10 respondents think that their tax contributions to the central budget are higher than amounts their region receives back. The same proportion thinks that, at the national level, they could decide on public expenditures better than the central government decides. Finally, more than 80% agree that the central government has disproportionally high profits from their resources (including oil and raw materials).

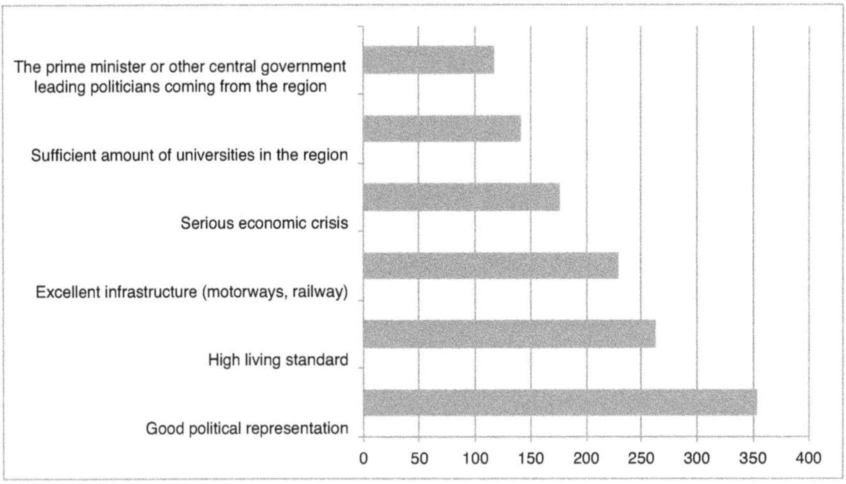


*Figure 3.11* Circumstances under which the respondents would rather support secession
Source: SAPIM, own calculation.

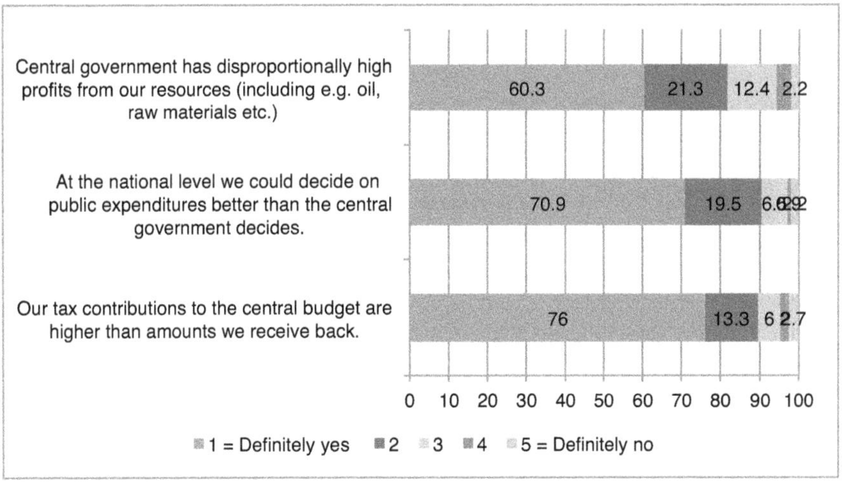


*Figure 3.12* Agreement with the “greed and grievance” statements
Source: SAPIM, own calculation.

## 3.2 Romantic factors

In this section, the impact of the romantic factors on secessionist attitudes is analysed. As we have seen, the romantic factors are closely connected to the institutions. This chapter is therefore divided into two larger parts: the first one is devoted to the informal institutions including religion, language, and ethnicity, as well as the impact of culture, education, and media. The second part, devoted to the formal institutions, covers the heterogeneity in the political preferences as the aggregate of the heterogeneous interests rooted in the romantic factors.

### *3.2.1 Informal institutions*

Heterogeneity of the secessionist regions might be measured using the three crucial romantic factors – religion, language, and ethnicity – as they can be easily quantified. The first part of this section is therefore devoted to the estimates of the heterogeneity in the romantic factors trinity using the Herfindahl-Hirschman index (HHI). It includes also the case study of the Spanish secessionist regions based on the secondary data. In the next section the cultural factors connected to language as well as education are studied: attitudes of the teachers who call for decentralisation, impact of the educational infrastructure in the secessionist regions, and role of the media. Last but not least, data from our original SAPIM survey were used to study the differences in pro-secessionist attitudes between the believers and unbelievers.

*Religious and linguistic heterogeneity among the European countries*

Cluster analysis based on Religious and Linguistic HHI reveals that the most fragile European countries (according to these two factors) are Spain, Belgium, and Luxembourg. The Composed HHI* is weakest (and the heterogeneity is, therefore, the greatest) for Luxembourg (HHI* = 0.41) and Belgium (0.45). However, HHI* is also significantly small for Germany (0.47) and Latvia (0.41), especially, because of the high religious heterogeneity. This group also includes the United Kingdom, the Netherlands, and Estonia. Moreover, HHI* is close to 1 and signals a great degree of homogeneity for Malta, Portugal, and Greece.

Religious HHI shows the greatest degree of heterogeneity among Spanish regions in Melilla (HHI = 0.36), Basque Country (0.42), and Catalonia (0.43), while the greatest homogeneity is observed in Murcia (0.74), Canary Islands (0.72), and Aragón (0.69).

Data on language homogeneity are not readily available for Spanish regions. The main official language is Castilian Spanish. However, especially in regions, Galician, Catalan, Euskera (Basque), Aragonese, and Asturian are also spoken (Europe Review 2003:305). Nevertheless, we were able to find, at least estimates for Catalonia. In Catalonia, about 17% of the population speak, as their first language, Catalan, 7% speak Galician, 2%, Basque, and 0.01%, Aranese. The rest of the Catalans speak Castilian Spanish as their first language. The heterogeneity of Catalan in terms of language is therefore higher in comparison to the rest of Spain (HHI = 0.53 in comparison to 0.64).

The linguistic border among regions might be depicted using the Google Trends search data. The simple phrase "Merry Christmas" was used as a key word because it differs among the regional languages (see Table 3.1), it is widely used, and there was enough search within years 2004–2019.

In all Spanish secessionist regions, the Spanish phrase "*Feliz Navidad*" is the most frequent. Nevertheless, the second search is more variable: 25% of searches

*Table 3.1* Merry Christmas in different regional languages

| *Country* | *Region* | *"Merry Christmas"* |
|---|---|---|
| Spain | Basque | "Eguberri on" |
| | Galego | "Bo Nadal" |
| | Catalan | "Bon Nadal" |
| | Spanish | "Feliz Navidad" |
| Belgium/Italy | Dutch | "Vrolijk kerstfeest" |
| | French | "Joyeux Noël" |
| | German | "Frohe Weihnachten" |
| Italy | Italian | "Buon Natale" |

Source: Author.

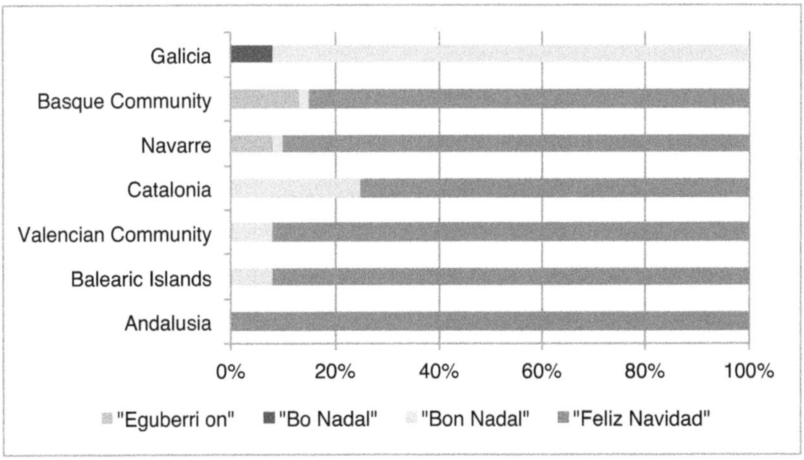


*Figure 3.13* Search for the phrase "Merry Christmas" in national languages (Spain)
Source: Google Trends. Author.

in Catalonia are in Catalan (*Bon Nadal*), as well as 8% in the Balearic Islands and Valencian community. Similarly, 13% of searches in the Basque community and 8% in Navarre are in Basque (*Eguberri on*), and 8% in Galicia is in Galego (*Bo Nadal*). On the other hand, in other regions (here represented by Andalusia, Figure 3.13), the only language used is Spanish.

While Spanish seems to be dominant among the Google searches in Spain, the linguistic frontier is much sharper in Belgium (Figure 3.14 and 3.15). Dutch (*Crolijk kerfstfeest*) is dominant in Flanders (66% of the search for "Merry Christmas" key word within the Flemish search), and French equivalent *Joyeux Noël* is dominant both in Wallonia (76%) and in Brussels (64%). German reamains for about one-fifth within all three regions. Finally, in Trentino-Alto Adige/South Tyrol 22% of searches are for the German phrase *Frohe Weihnachten* while 78% for Italian *Buon Natale.*

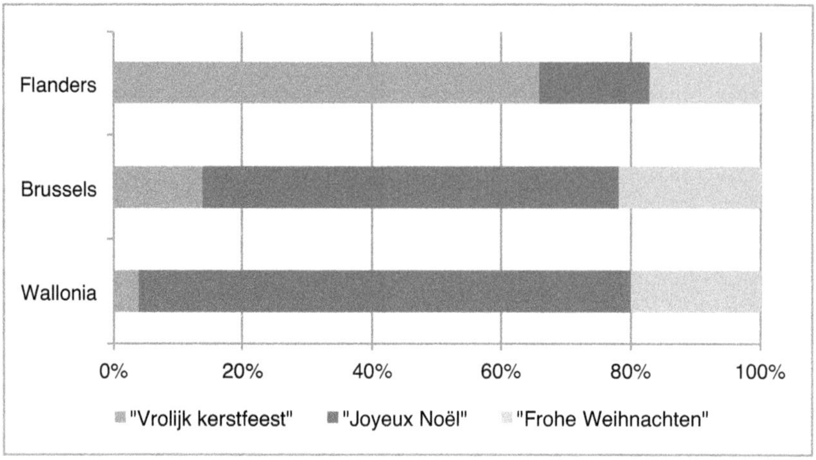


*Figure 3.14* Search for the phrase "Merry Christmas" in national languages (Belgium)
Source: Google Trends. Author.

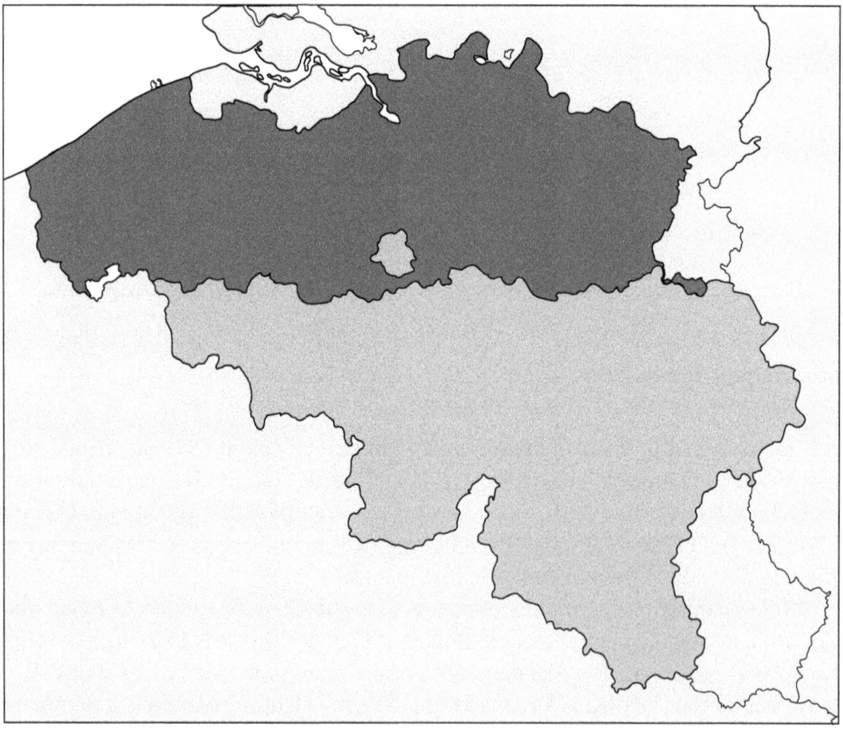

*Figure 3.15* Map of search for the phrase "Merry Christmas" in national languages (Belgium)
Source: Google Trends. Author. Dark = Dutsch, light = French.

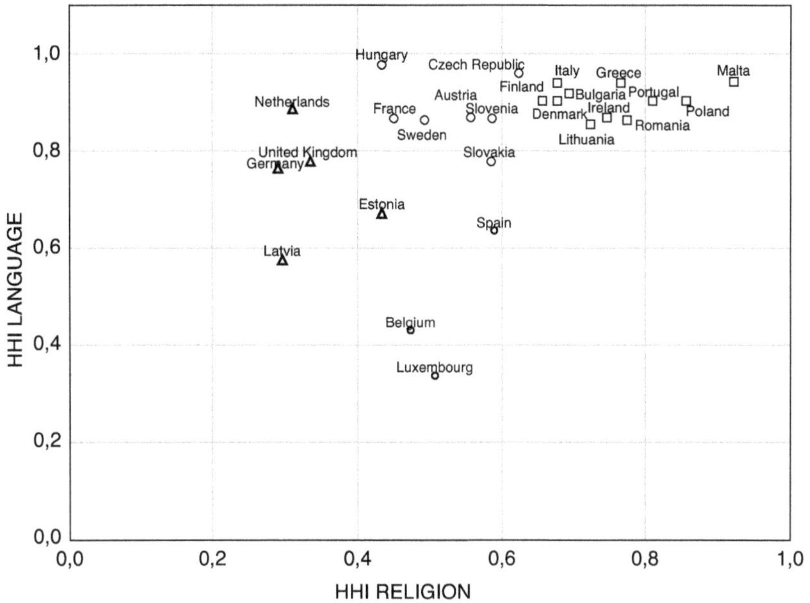


*Figure 3.16* Cluster analysis of the HHI linguistic and religionist index in the EU countries

Source: Author.

According to the cluster analysis, the most fragile countries with respect to cultural heterogeneity represented by religion and language are those which have secessionist regions. According to Alesina (2003), larger countries are supposed to be less homogeneous than smaller countries. When we approximate the size of the country by the number of inhabitants, we observe a mild negative correlation between the size of the country and HHI* (Pearson coefficient = – 0.2). It means that smaller countries are more homogeneous in terms of religion and language. However, this relationship is far from perfect. For instance, Luxembourg, with merely 0.5 million of inhabitants, is a very heterogeneous country (however, it is without any serious secessionist tensions), while Poland, with 39 million of inhabitants, is very homogeneous (HHI* = 0.89).

Pastiurko et al. (2011) showed that the cultural homogeneity of a country goes hand in hand with its economic success. This hypothesis was confirmed even by our research. The correlation between the index of heterogeneity and GDP p.c. in Spanish regions is negative and very strong (Pearson coefficient of correlation = – 0.78). The lower heterogeneity in terms of cultural as well as political preferences is, therefore, connected to the higher economic level.

According to the Religious HHI, the greatest secessionist tensions should be observed in Basque Country and Catalonia. Melilla is an interesting case of Spanish towns in North Africa. It has been part of Spain since the 16th century, and we can find an interesting mixture of Christian as well as Islam religions which stays behind in heterogeneity.

Our results suggest that the most fragile Spanish regions with secessionist potential are Catalonia, the Basque country, and Navarra. All of them also show the largest GDP per capita. While Catalonia and the Basque country are well known for their secessionist tensions, Navarra has not been widely discussed. Nevertheless, its secessionist potential should not be neglected. The former Kingdom of Navarre is today an autonomous community of Spain with full responsibility for its education, social services, housing, and collecting taxes. It has its own parliament and president who was elected for the Basque nationalist coalition to incorporate Navarra into the Basque country after the referendum.

### *Teachers in secessionist regions*

A survey among members of pro-independence parties covered 30 teachers from nine countries. This dataset size is on the lower bound of datasets needed for running basic statistic tests which allow us to compare attitudes of teachers and non-teachers.

There was a considerably higher rate of females among the teachers than among the non-teachers (43% in comparison to 16%). The average rate of respondents is significantly higher (49 years in comparison to 42.5 years among non-teachers).

Opinions on the European integration; reasons for secession; and personal characteristics such as religion, language, and confidence to the institutions do not differ significantly among the respondents (teachers as well as non-teachers). Nevertheless, there is a considerable difference in opinion about living standards after the potential independence of the region. Teachers, as well as those in the rest of the former country, seem to be less optimistic about the development of a newly independent country. Similar opinions can be seen in the case of the expected living standard of families (Table 3.2).

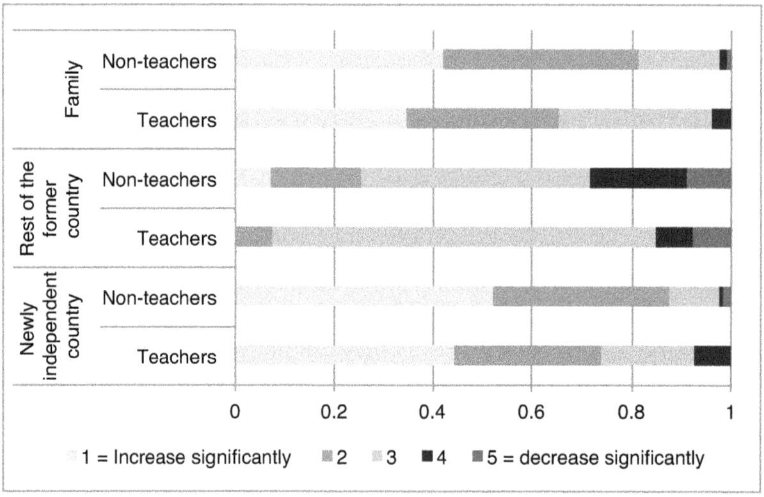


*Figure 3.17* Teachers' opinions on the development of the newly independent country, rest of the former country, and their families

Source: SAPIM, own calculation.

*Table 3.2* Results of $\chi^2$ test

| | *Pearson* | *p-value* | *Cramer's V* |
|---|---|---|---|
| Newly independent country | 10.75 | 0.03 | 0.15 |
| Rest of the former country | 10.17 | 0.04 | 0.15 |
| Family | 4.85 | 0.30 | 0.10 |

Source: Own calculation.

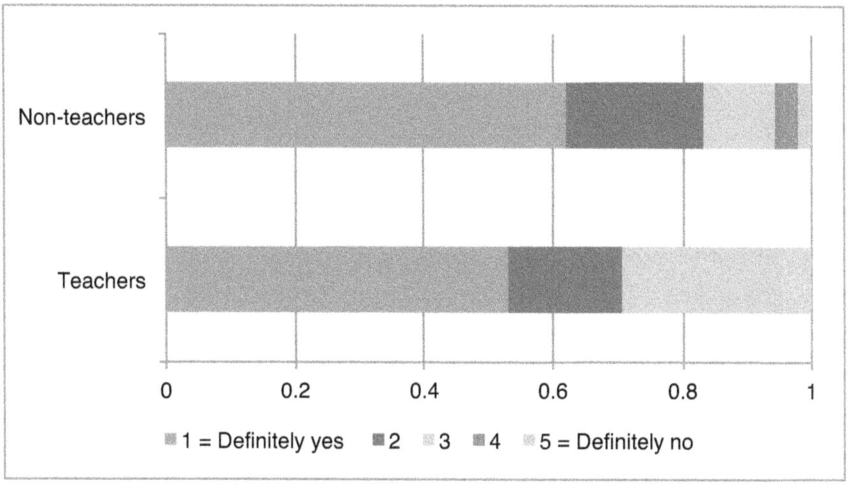


*Figure 3.18* Does the central government have disproportionally high profits from our resources? Teachers' opinions.

Source: SAPIM, own calculation.

*Pearson* $\chi^2 = 8.45$, *p-value = 0.076 and Cramer's V = 0.14.*

Teachers are also less convinced that the central government has disproportionally high profits from regional resources (71% of teachers in comparison to 83% of non-teachers).

*Higher educational infrastructure in the region*

A higher educational infrastructure does not influence the support of secession. Neither the pro-secessionists nor the anti-secessionists find the existence of a "sufficient amount of universities in the region" as the crucial factor which would move them to support the secession (75% of respondents in both groups consider it as an unimportant factor).

This might be explained by the fact that strongly secessionist regions are considerably rich on higher educational infrastructure. In Flanders, there are five universities and eleven university colleges, three of which achieve the highest ranking among higher educational institutions in Belgium. Considerably successful are also universities from the secessionist regions in Spain or the United Kingdom.[5]

However, the existence of universities in the secessionist region is considered to be a crucial pro-secessionist argument for tertiary educated respondents (34%) than respondents with a lower level of education (22%). Similarly, the "university factor" is more important for white-collar workers (25%) than for blue-collar workers (16%). Lastly, respondents who claim that educational policy should be exclusively in the hands of the regional (not central) governments find the presence of universities in region as an important secessionist factor than those who prefer sharing the educational policy between the central and regional government or, even, those who call for full control of the central government (see Figure 3.19).

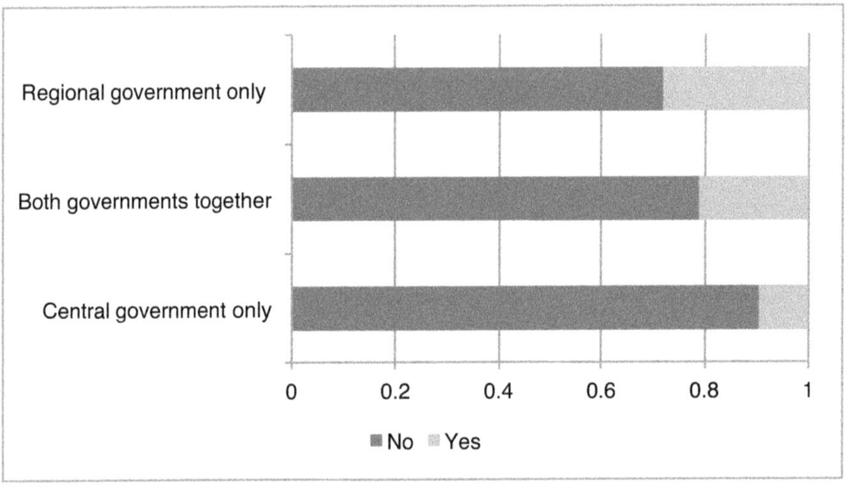


*Figure 3.19* Support of secession in case of the sufficient amount of universities in the region according to the attitudes towards the sharing of the power between then central and regional government

Source: SAPIM, own calculation.

*Table 3.3* Results of $\chi^2$ test

| | *Pearson* | *p-value* | *Cramer's V* |
|---|---|---|---|
| Secession | 0.036 | 0.849 | 0.008 |
| University degree | 9.504 | 0.00205 | 0.129 |
| Blue-/white-collar | 3.323 | 0.068 | 0.084 |
| Sharing the power | 6.495 | 0.0389 | 0.109 |

Source: Own calculation.

*Media*

Media are of the crucial importance in terms of spreading the pro-secessionists ideas and sentiments. They form the public opinions and moods and can influence the decision-makers. The structure of media followed by the members of the secessionist parties can therefore anticipate if their goal is really the secession or rather decentralisation.

The respondents who support the full independence of their region and follow national media are significantly less than those who are against secession (76% in comparison to 80%). However, they follow considerably more international media (88% in comparison to 78% of respondents). Moreover, there is no difference in the category of *regional* media (Figure 3.20).

These results are in line with the opinion-barometer for Catalonia (CEO 2018). Most of the Catalan respondents get news about politic from television (75%),

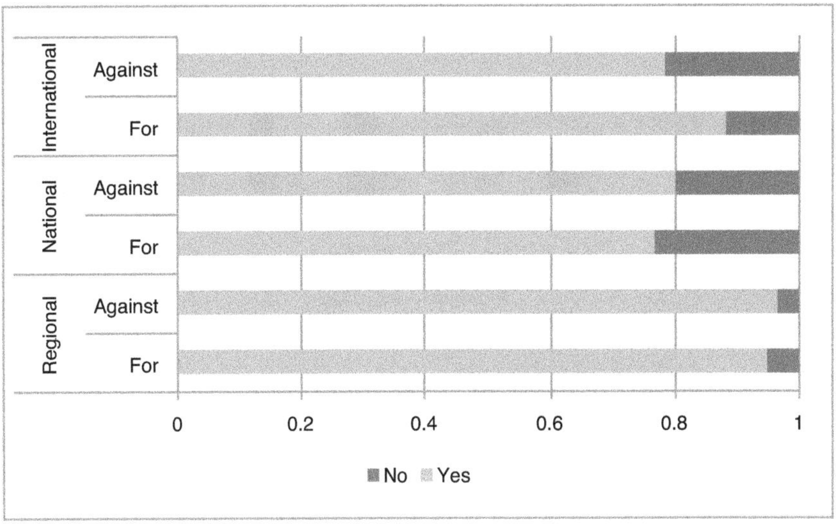


*Figure 3.20* Preferences of the media according to the attitudes towards independence
Source: SAPIM, own calculation.

*Table 3.4* Results of $\chi^2$ test

| | *Regional* | *National* | *International* |
|---|---|---|---|
| Pearson $\chi^2$ | 1.70 | 9.70 | 10.83 |
| p-value | 0.63 | 0.02 | 0.01 |
| Cramér's V | 0.06 | 0.15 | 0.16 |

Source: Own calculation.

half get news less from the press (36%) and radio (35%). The most popular Spanish nationwide television channel, *Antena 3*, ranked fifth among the Catalans. However, most of the Catalans watch the news on the regional channel, *TV 3*. Among the most popular news-based channels, 61% is Catalan, and only 32% is nationwide.[6]

This picture is even supporter by Google Trends data (Figure 3.33). In 2004–2019, about 58% of Google searches in Catalonia were for regional TV3, while only 28% for nationwide Antene 3.

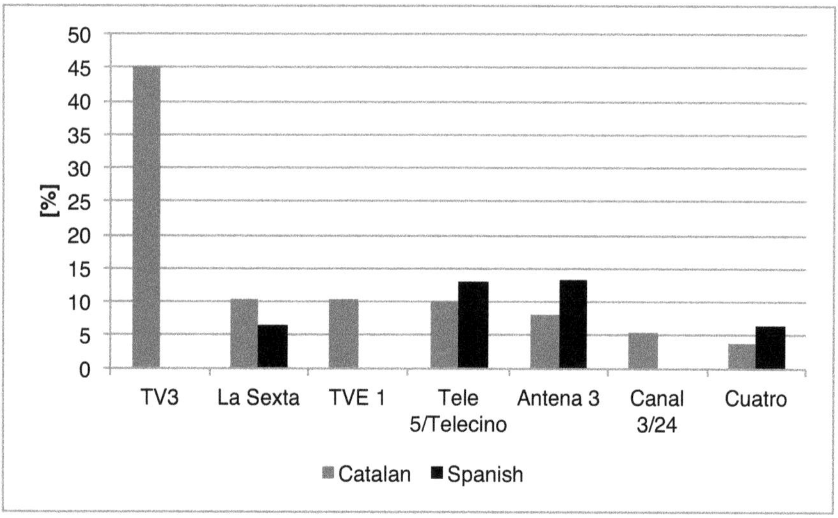


*Figure 3.21* Popularity of TV channels in Spain and Catalonia
Source: CEO (2018) and Barlovento Comunicación (2017).

| | TV3 | La Sexta | TVE 1 | Tele 5 | Antena 3 |
|---|---|---|---|---|---|
| Andalusia | 3 | 24 | 1 | 3 | 69 |
| Balearic Islands | 21 | 21 | 1 | 3 | 54 |
| Valencian Community | 9 | 25 | 1 | 3 | 62 |
| Catalonia | 58 | 12 | | 2 | 28 |
| Navarre | 4 | 27 | 1 | 4 | 64 |
| Basque Community | 3 | 31 | 1 | 6 | 59 |
| Galicia | 3 | 30 | 1 | 4 | 62 |

*Figure 3.22* Google search for the main TV channels in Spain
Source: Google Trends. Author.

Similarly, among the daily newspapers, the most popular is published in Catalonia. From the eight most-read newspapers (according to respondents), six are purely regional (CEO 2018). The most popular national newspaper, *El País*, is read by 8.6% of the Catalan respondents. The newspaper, *La Vangardia* (with headquarters in Barcelona), is published in two language mutations – Catalan (read by 18% of Catalan respondents) and Castilian (14% of the respondents). Unfortunately, the available data do not allow us to compare the popularity of the regional newspapers in the non-secessionist regions.

Finally, two-thirds of the Catalan respondents receive political news from the Catalan radios. The two most listened radios (RAC 1 and Catalunya Rádio) are together followed by 63% of respondents (CEO 2018).

Two most popular newspapers in Belgium are *Het Laatste Nieuws* in Dutch and *La Derniere Heure in French.* While *Het Laatste Nieuws* (dark gray, Figure 3.34) is searched mainly in Flanders (96%) and Brussels (62%), *La Derniere Heure* is being searched in Wallonia (86% of all searcher, light gray, Figure 3.34).

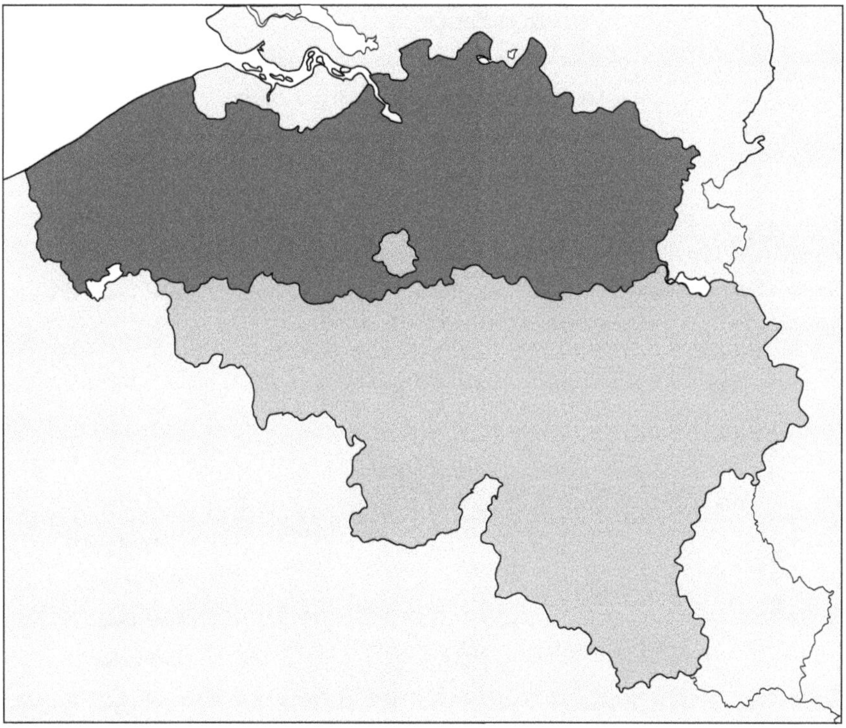

*Figure 3.23* Map of search for the main newspaper in national languages (Belgium)

Source: Google Trends. Author.

Respondents who read the regional press significantly more than the national press call for secession more often than others (73% in comparison to 67%). However, this difference is not statistically significant. Moreover, those, who read exclusively regional and not national press identify themselves significantly more with their region than with their country (Figure 3.24).

Similarly, those who regularly use international media are significantly more in favour of secession (Figure 3.25). This is highly indicated, especially by the South Tyrolean respondents (Figure 3.26) because they identify themselves more with Austria, call for the restoration of historical borders, and, therefore, tend to follow foreign (probably Austrian) media significantly more often than others.[7]

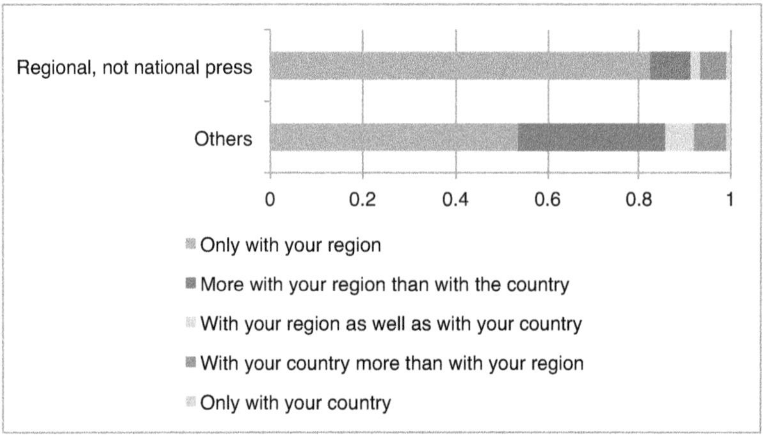


*Figure 3.24* Identification with the region according to the preferences of the media

Source: Own calculation.

*Pearson* $\chi^2 = 27.6$, *p-value* $= 0.00001$, *Cramér's* $V = 0.246$.

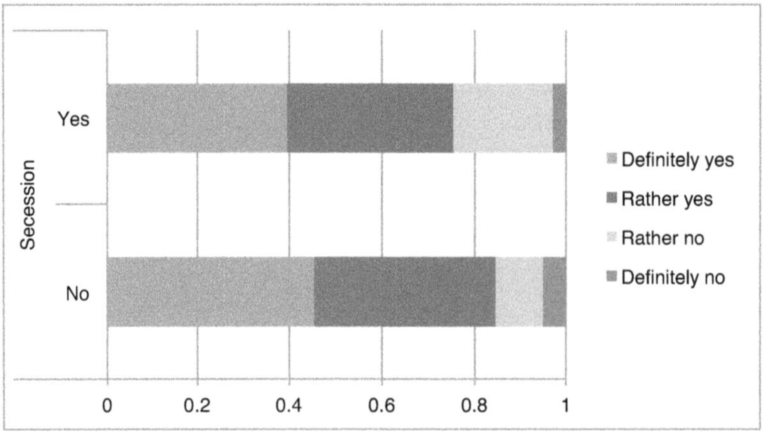


*Figure 3.25* Support of secession among the readers of the international media

Source: Own calculation.

*Pearson* $\chi^2 = 12.1$, *p-value* $= 0.00713$, *Cramér's* $V = 0.162$.

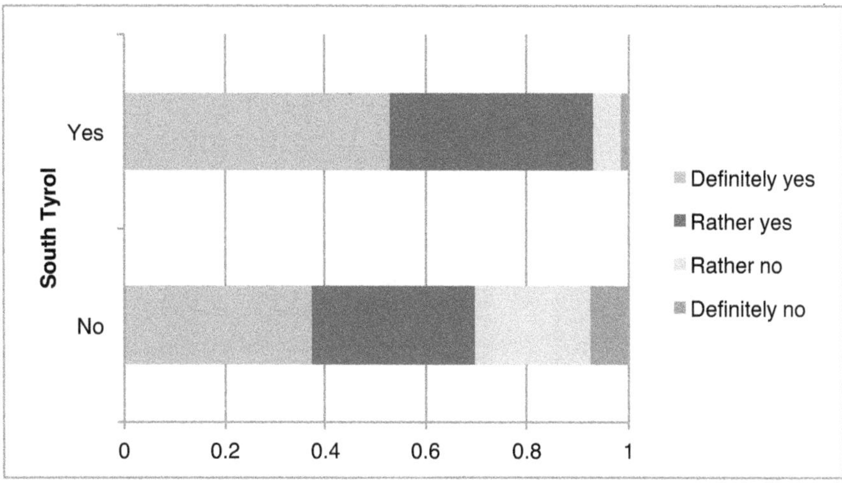


*Figure 3.26* Popularity of the international media among the South Tyroleans

Source: SAPIM, own calculation.

*Pearson* $\chi^2 = 47.6$, *p-value* = 0.00000, *Cramér's V* = 0.309.

## *Religion*

If the religion was the romantic secessionist factor, we would expect heterogeneity in religion within in the country. To compare the religionist structure we firstly used data on religiosity in EU countries and regions are available from the *Atlas of European Values* (EVS 2016).

The survey results provide us with detailed information on seven countries, which enable us to compare the religiosity among members of the secessionist parties with the average religiosity of relevant whole countries. In five countries (Italy, Austria, German, Belgium, and the Czech Republic) the religiosity among survey respondents is higher than in the entire country, while in France and especially in Spain, the religiosity among the respondents is lower (see Figure 3.27).

A considerably lower level of religiosity in Catalonia has its roots in the Spanish Second Republic (1931–1936) when the Catalan autonomous government was formed by the liberals (Dowling 2006:84). According to the survey, on a *hypothetical referendum on Catalan independence*, Catalans, who declared themselves as Mass-attending Catholics, would vote for independence significantly less often than the average population (41.2% in comparison to 51.1%, Requejo and Nagel 2014:206).

Structure of denomination differs significantly, especially in Spain (see Figure 3.39): while Spain as a whole is predominately declared as the Catholic country (64% of Catholics), among our respondents, there is just one-third of Catholics. In other countries, the differences in the main denomination are less pronounced: 7 percentage points (p. p.) in Belgium and the Czech Republic, 6 p. p. in Italy and 3 p. p. in Austria and Denmark.[8]

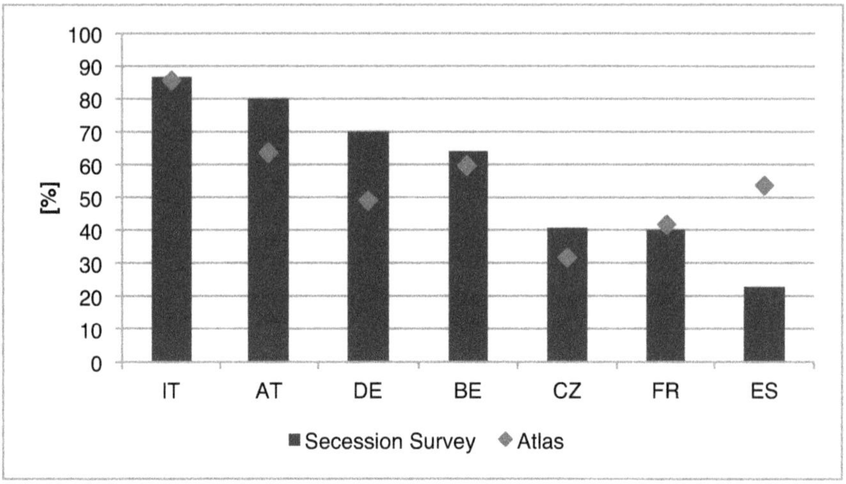


*Figure 3.27* Religiosity among respondents in the secessionist regions in comparison to the religiosity in the country

Source: ESV, SAPIM, own calculation.

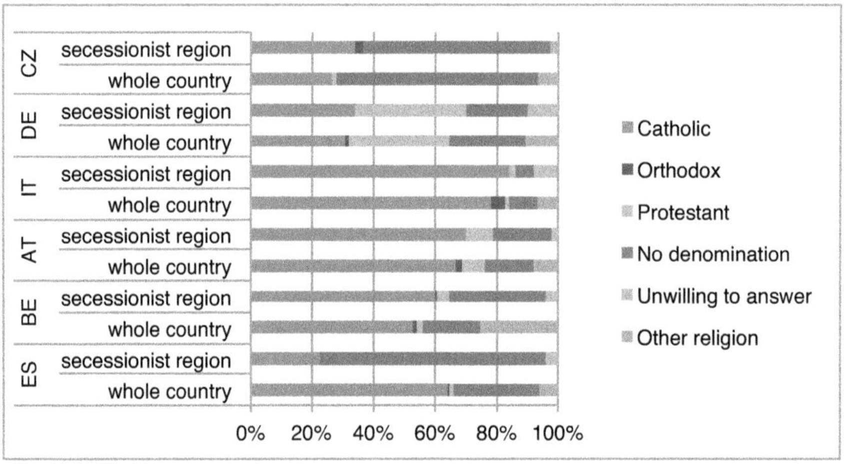


*Figure 3.28* Structure of denomination in the secessionist regions and the whole country

Source: Eurostat. SAPIM, own calculation.

In the following text, we will explore how the religiosity affects the secessionist attitudes. Believers tend to be more pro-secessionist than unbelievers (72% in comparison to 67%).[9] Believers' claims indicated that they would significantly more often support the membership of their country in the EU (48%), while unbelievers would vote against the EU membership (Figure 3.29).

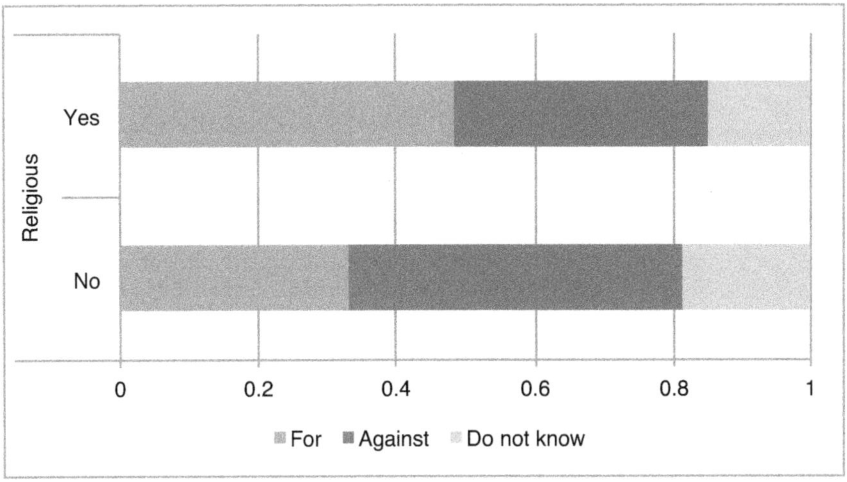


*Figure 3.29* If there was a referendum on your country's membership of the EU, how would you vote?

Source: SAPIM, own calculation.

*Pearson* $\chi^2 = 9.91$, *p-value* = 0.00702, *Cramér's V* = 0.133.

Believers identify themselves significantly more with their region while those who declare no denomination identify more often only with their country (Figure 3.30).

There is no significant difference in trust in most of the institutions (European Commission, European Government, National Government, and Local Countries). However, unbelievers tend to trust in regional authorities significantly more often than believers (51% do definitely trust or trust in comparison to only 40% of believers, Figure 3.31).

It might be expected that believers try to trust, even, in institutions more than unbelievers. Nevertheless, the results of the ANOVA do not support this hypothesis (Table 3.5). Unbelievers score of total trust in the political institutions is slightly higher in comparison to believers. However, this difference is negligible and not statistically significant.

Similarly, the expectation of the change of living standards of the newly independent country and the rest of the former country obviously do not depend on faith. However, there is a significant difference between the opinions of believers and unbelievers in the case of their families. Believers seem to be more optimistic: 82% of them believe that the living condition of their families would increase, which is by nine p. p. more than unbelievers (Figure 3.32).

Opinions on sharing power with the central government and the regional government differ among believer and unbelievers in the field of education, healthcare,

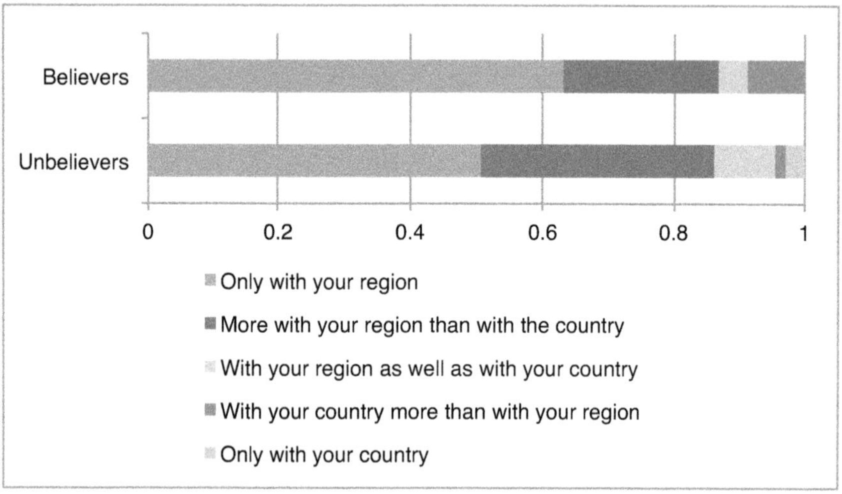


*Figure 3.30* Identification with the region among the believers and unbelievers
Source: SAPIM, own calculation.
*Pearson* $\chi^2 = 32.49$, *p-value* = 0.00000, *Cramér's V* = 0.241.

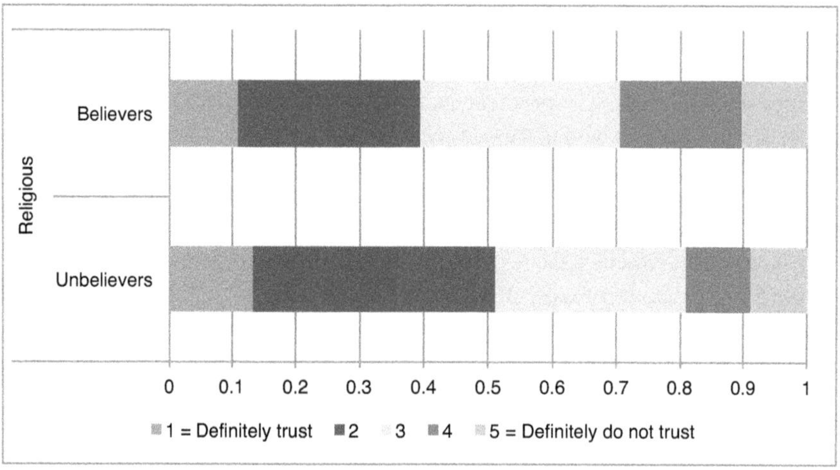


*Figure 3.31* Trust in the institutions among the believers and unbelievers
Source: SAPIM, own calculation.
*Pearson* $\chi^2 = 8.47$, *p-value* = 0.076, *Cramér's V* = 0.123.

*Table 3.5* Results of ANOVA

| | *Breakdown table of descriptive statistics* | | |
|---|---|---|---|
| | *Mean* | *N* | *Std. Dev.* |
| **Unbelievers** | 16.54 | 131 | 3.58 |
| **Believers** | 16.18 | 408 | 4.06 |
| **Total** | 16.27 | 539 | 3.95 |
| | *F-statistic* | *p-value* | |
| **Levene Test of Homogeneity of Variances** | 3.66 | 0.056 | |
| **Analysis of Variance** | 0.83 | 0.364 | |

Source: Own calculation.

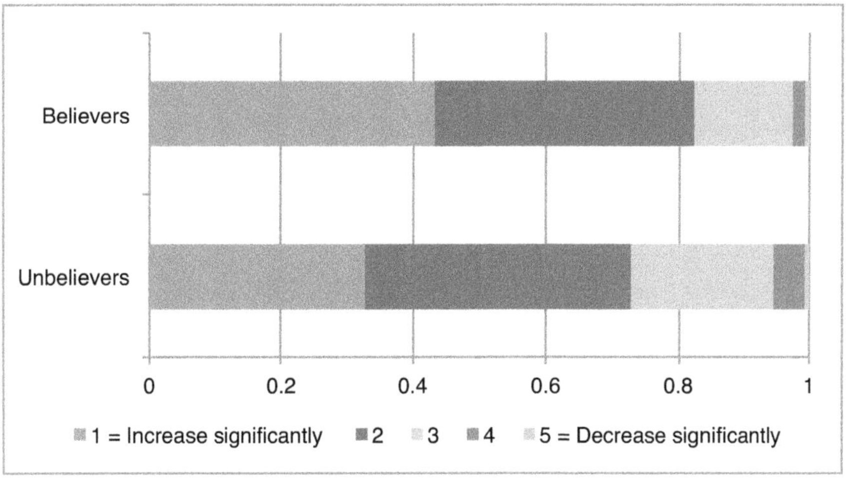


*Figure 3.32* Expectation of the living condition increase in their families among the believers and unbelievers

Source: SAPIM, own calculation.

*Pearson* $\chi^2 = 8.67$, *p-value* = 0.069, *Cramér's V* = 0.127.

social policy, and taxation. However, their attitudes toward power-sharing in safety, European policy, and foreign affairs are similar (Figure 3.33). It is obvious that, for most the regional citizens, the international policy, as well as the safety of the country (policies traditionally considered to be a government matter), are seen as distant to reach, while management of the internal affairs is assessed in line with the principle of subsidiarity. Nevertheless, believers seem to always prefer the transition of power into the hands of the regional government. The greatest difference (of 12 p. p.) was in the assessment of health care.

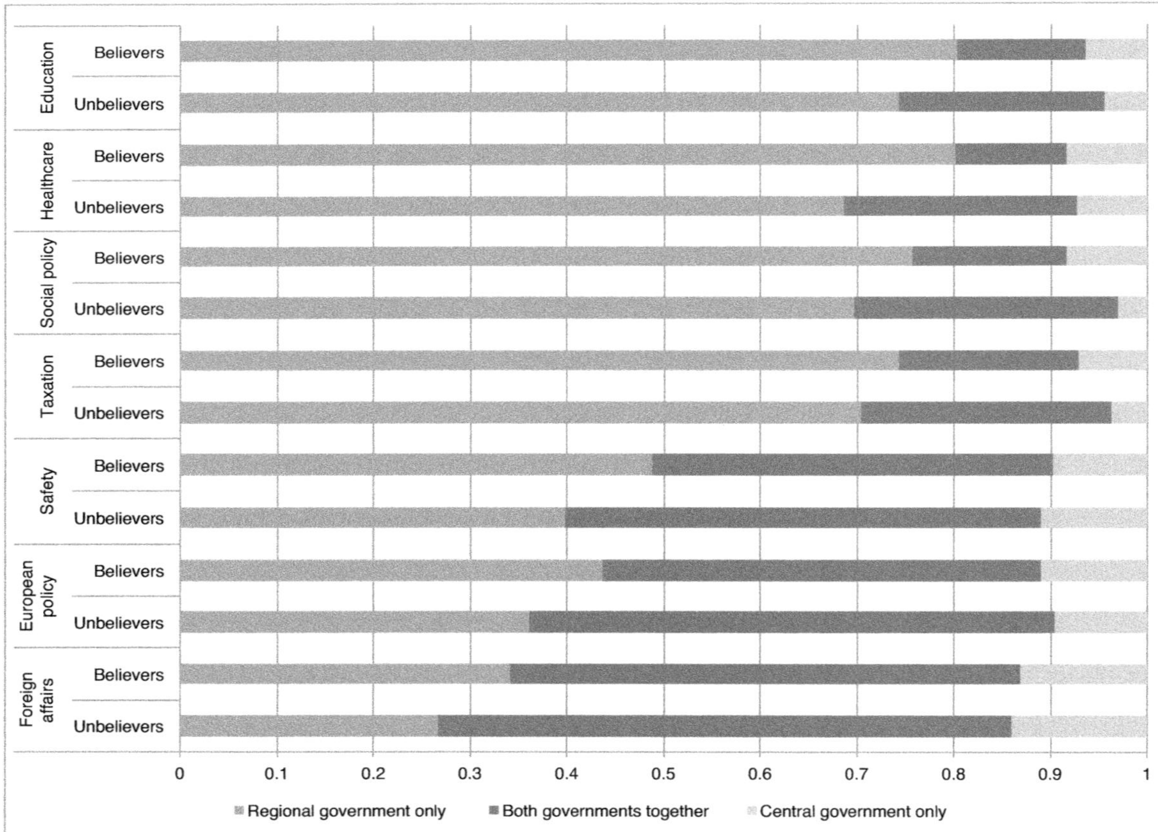


*Figure 3.33* Sharing the powers between the central and the regional government according to the believers and unbelievers

Source: SAPIM, own calculation.

*Table 3.6* Results of $\chi^2$ test

| | *Pearson* $\chi^2$ | *Cramér's V* | *p-value* |
|---|---|---|---|
| Education | 5.31 | 0.09 | 0.07** |
| Healthcare | 13.3 | 0.15 | 0.001*** |
| Social policy | 11.75 | 0.15 | 0.003*** |
| Taxation | 4.79 | 0.09 | 0.09** |
| Safety | 3.49 | 0.08 | 0.17 |
| European policy | 3.48 | 0.08 | 0.18 |
| Foreign Affairs | 2.56 | 0.07 | 0.28 |

Source: Own calculation.

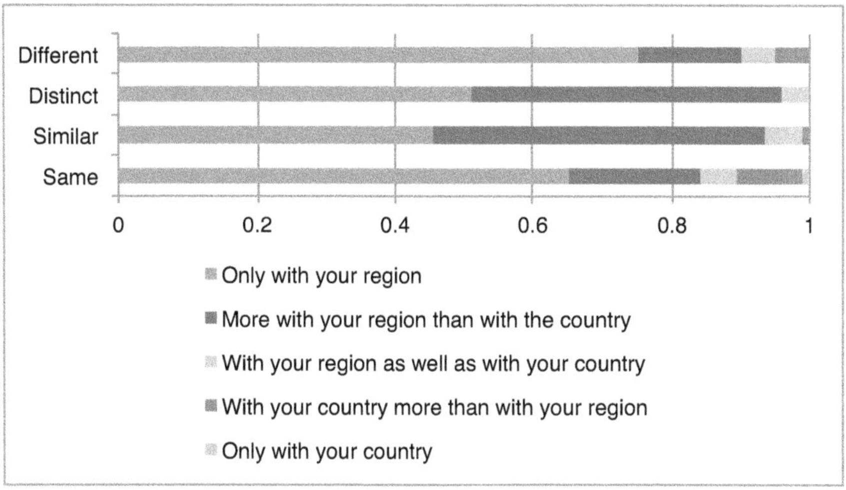


*Figure 3.34* Identification with the region according to the religion categories

Source: SAPIM, own calculation.

*Pearson* $\chi^2 = 50.62$, *p-value* = 0.000, *Cramér's V* = 0.179.

The relationship between one's denomination and identification with a region or country is consistent with our expectation. The respondents whose denomination differed most from the rest of the country identified themselves only with their region more often than those whose denomination is very similar or the same (Figure 3.34).

Heterogeneity of attitudes to religion as well as denomination seem to be a significant factor of the differences between secessionist regions and the rest of country; this is also according to the data published by the *European Values Study (EVS 2008)*. Scotland, Flanders, Northeastern Italy (as region covering South Tyrol), and Catalonia, Valencian Community, and the Balearic Islands express

*Table 3.7* Belief in God

| | *Belief in God* | *Religious services: attend at least once a week* |
|---|---|---|
| Scotland | 66 | 25 |
| United Kingdom | 65 | 17 |
| | *+1* | *+8* |
| Flanders | 59 | 19 |
| Belgium | 61 | 15 |
| | *−2* | *+4* |
| Catalonia<br>Valencian Community<br>Balearic Islands | 71 | 21 |
| Spain | 76 | 21 |
| | *−5* | *0* |
| Northeastern Italy (incl. South Tyrol) | 87 | 35 |
| Italy | 81 | 35 |
| | *+6* | *0* |

Source: EVS (2008), author.

different ratios of belief in God (Table 3.7). While the Scottish and respondents from Northeast Italy believe in God more than their country as a whole, Flemish and respondents from Catalonia, Valencian Community, and the Balearic Islands express lower degrees of religiosity than Belgium and Spain in total. The Scottish and Flemish respondents also confirm their belief by more frequent attendance of religious services.

### *3.2.2 Formal institutions*

Any decentralisation, including the secession, takes place within the legislative frame. The main decision-makers, who can formulate the legislature, are the political parties participating on the legislative process in the national assemblies. Their uprise, as well as their fall, depends on the power of the people voting in the election. In this section, we study the political preferences of the voters in the secessionist regions as it is the main input to the function of aggregation of the political preferences.

*Political preferences*

Heterogeneity in the romantic factors materialises in the political preferences of the inhabitants. In this part, we study their trust of the different levels of government as well as their election behaviour on the regional and national level. Finally,

*Table 3.8* Theoretical hypotheses

| | |
|---|---|
| H1 | *Trust in the national representatives is higher in the non-secessionist regions in comparison to the secessionist regions.* |
| H2 | *Trust in the regional representatives is higher in the secessionist regions.* |
| H3 | *General election's results in the secessionist regions differ from the total results.* |
| H4 | *Citizens in the secessionist regions are mote apathetic in terms of the general election turnout.* |

Source: Eurostat (2015), authors.

the case of Spanish secessionist regions is analysed in detail using data from European Value Studies as well as our original SAPIM data.

Table 3.8 summarises eight main theoretical hypotheses, which will be analysed in the following section.

Hypotheses *H1* and *H2* are backed by Hechter's secessionist theory of economic exploitation. According to this approach, the exploited secessionist regions are underrepresented in the national parliaments. If the national representatives do not reflect the preferences of the secessionist region, regional voters might trust the regional representatives more (Huysseune 2002).

Hypothesis *H3* suggests that the preferences of voters from secessionist regions differs significantly from the preferences of the other voters. This might result from the fact that the winner of the general election did not succeed in the secessionist region.

Analogically, we would expect that voters from secessionist regions are less enthusiastic about the general election (in the case that the national representatives do not reflect their preferences). Thus, the turnout is lower in comparison to other regions as well as to the regional election (*H4*).

Voters from secessionist regions trust in the regional representatives more than in the national representatives (*H1* and *H2*); the difference (12.9 p. p.) is nearly 4.5 times higher than in the case of the non-secessionist regions (2.3 p. p.). This difference is statistically significant. There is also a statistically significant and very high correlation between the variables *Quality of life* and *Trust in regional representatives* ($\rho = 0.71$), as well as the variables *Situation of economy* and *Trust in regional representatives* ($\rho = 0.75$). It means that if the citizens are more satisfied with their quality of life and the situation of the economy, they tend to trust significantly more in their regional representatives (however, the same is not true for the national representatives or EU Commission).

In accordance with our assumption, votes for the winner of a general election, as well as voter turnout, are lower in secessionist regions in comparison to the non-secessionist regions (*H3*, *H4*). However, none of these differences is statistically significant. Similarly, there is no significant difference between voter turnout in general elections and turnout in regional elections in secessionist regions.

*Table 3.9* Main results

| *Current situation in [%]* | *Region* | |
|---|---|---|
| | *Non-secessionist* | *Secessionist* |
| **Trust in [%]** | | |
| National representatives | 20.8 | 16.7 |
| Regional representatives | 23.1 | 29.6 |
| **General election [%]** | | |
| Votes for winner | 29.1 | 20.7 |
| Turnout | 70.6 | 63.5 |

Source: Own calculation.

### *Heterogeneity of voters' preferences: case of the Spanish Kingdom*

The 2016 General Election revealed a wide preference gap between Catalan (*Cataluna*) and the rest of Spain. However, the cluster map also depicts that even the Basque Country (*Pais Vasco*), Valencia, Galicia, Navarra, and the Canary Islands are quite heterogeneous in terms of political preferences.

The analysis of European Value Studies data (GESIS 2018) confirms a significant heterogeneity in political preferences with Spain. Secessionist regions in Spain (Galicia, Basque Country, Aragón, Catalonia, Valencian community, and Balearic Islands) are significantly more left-wing in comparison to the rest of Spain. Respondents from secessionist regions put themselves, on the scale from 1 (left) to 10 (right), on average, on the central-left (4.5) while non-secessionists place themselves on the central-right (5.1). This gap is even wider between Catalonia (4.2) and the rest of Spain (5).

Even in Spain, there is significantly lower confidence in the central government in secessionist regions in comparison to non-secessionist regions (Figure 3.36); 28% of citizens in non-secessionists regions tend to trust the government while 84% from secessionist regions do not have confidence in it.

Spanish secessionist regions also express slightly lower confidence in the EU. Nevertheless, even though the results are statistically significant, the value of Cramér's V is pretty low. The difference EU-believers in secessionist and non-secessionist regions in Spain is 4 p. p. (Figure 3.37).

Contrary to expectations, we could not prove the difference in identifying respondents from secessionist and non-secessionist Spanish regions with their region: 48% of both groups said, unanimously, that they feel "very close" to their region, and 1% of both groups claimed to be "not close" to it. The significant difference, though, could be observed in the identification with Spain. Respondents coming from the secessionist regions feel "very close" to Spain in 38% of the cases, which is 5.25 p.p. less in comparison to the respondents from non-secessionist regions. This relationship is, however, significantly deeper when focussing on Catalonia. Only 71% of Catalans feel "close or very close" to their country, which is 16 p. p. less in comparison to the rest of Spain.

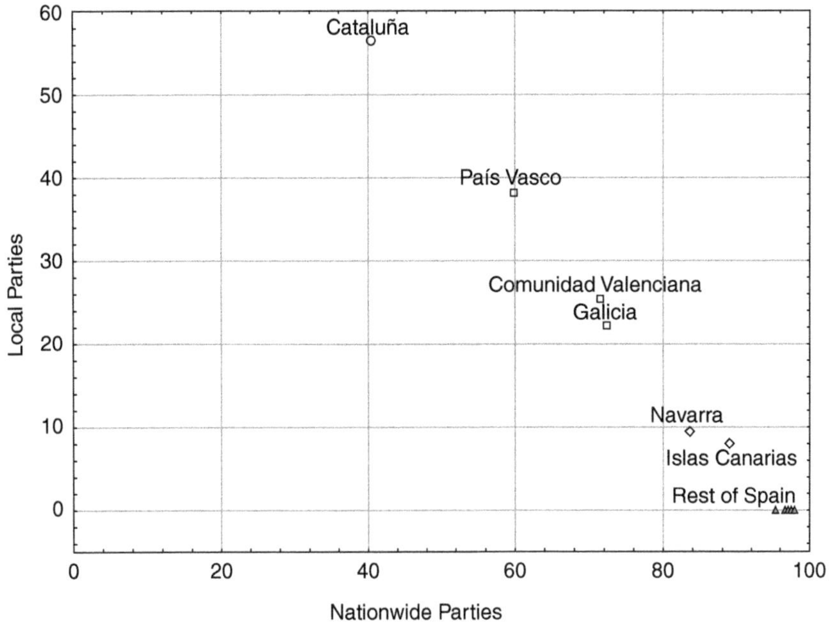


*Figure 3.35* Cluster analysis showing heterogeneity in political preferences within the Spanish Kingdom

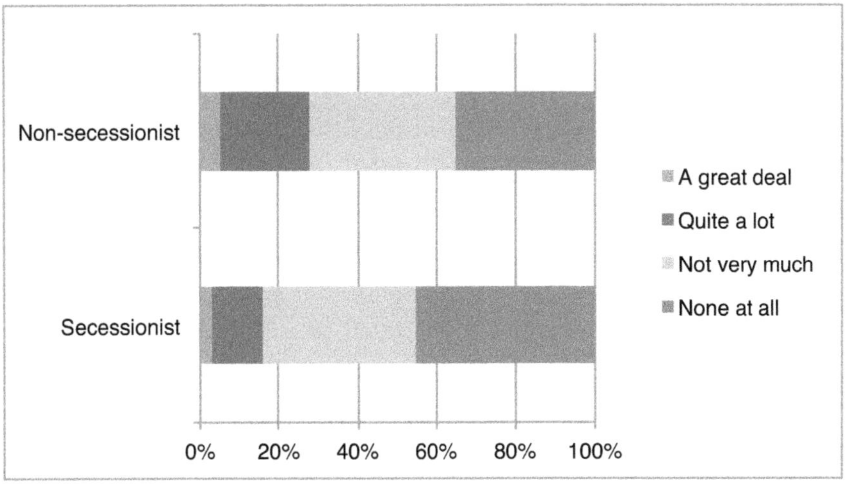


*Figure 3.36* Confidence in the central government in Spain

Source: SAPIM, own calculation.

*Pearson* $\chi^2 = 23.26$, *p-value* = 0.00004, *Cramér's V* = 0.139.

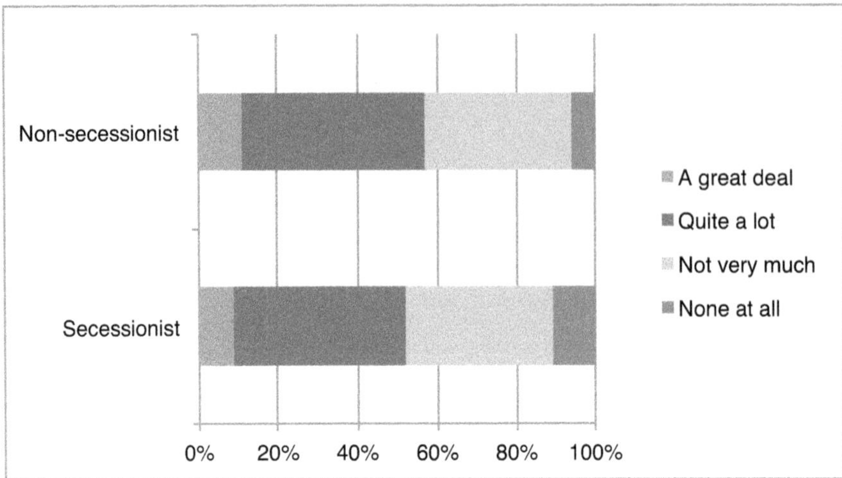


*Figure 3.37* EU-believers in Spain

Source: SAPIM, own calculation.

*Pearson* $\chi^2 = 9.15$, *p-value* $= 0.027$, *Cramér's* $V = 0.089$.

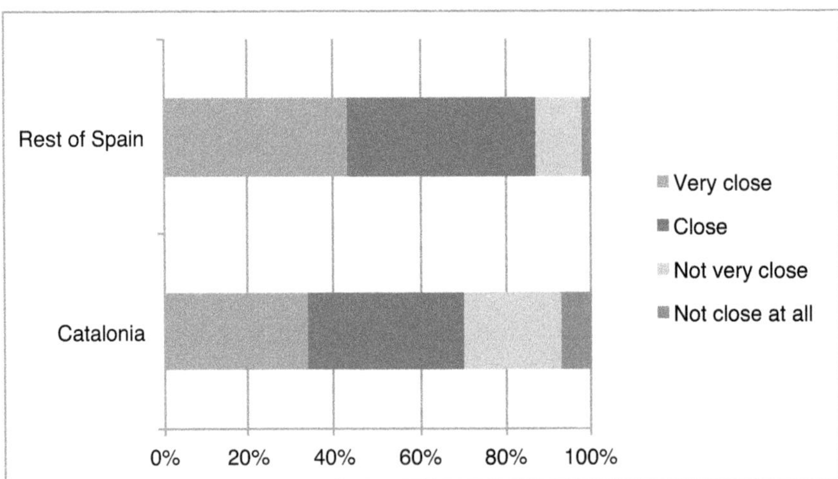


*Figure 3.38* Identification with the Spain

Source: SAPIM, own calculation.

*Pearson* $\chi^2 = 34.77$, *p-value* $= 0.0000$, *Cramér's* $V = 0.169$.

## 3.3 Economic factors

In this section, the macroeconomic as well as microeconomic factors are discussed regarding the secessionist attitudes. First, we verify if secessionism is connected to higher economic performance. The role of the scarce resources (especially, in case of the Scottish oil) is then investigated. The third part studies the impact of interregional fiscal transfers, and the fourth subchapter analyses the effect of European economic integration. The last two parts follow with the microeconomic factors – risk attitudes and discount rate – and reflects their relationship to the secessionist moods.

### *3.3.1 Macroeconomic factors*

Arguments of the secessionists as well as anti-secessionists are often based on the estimated change in the living condition. The standard of living can be approximated by the economic level. The first part of this section is therefore devoted to the Gross Domestic Product (GDP) per capita in the secessionist regions and the rest of the countries. Canonical studies focus on the greed and grievance argument, which will be studied using the case of the scarce resources. Similar, however more pecuniary, is the discussion on the fiscal decentralisation and the fiscal position. Finally, the role of the economic integration on the political decentralisation will be studied.

*GDP level*

The most crucial factors which are discussed in terms of the secession belongs to the size of the nation as well as the size and the level of the economy. For instance, Catalonia's former president Artur Mas claimed that Catalonia is the "Denmark of Southern Europe" because it is "almost Germanic in economic character" (Khan 2017). The canonical studies of Alesina and Wacziarg (1998:305) highlight that there is a trade-off between the economies of scales and costs of heterogeneity. Tables 30 and 31 show that the new countries emerged after the secession would be viable in the European context. It means that their population size, economic strength, and economic level are not extremely lower in comparison to the existing European countries. For instance, in terms of the population, Catalonia would be on a similar level as Bulgaria and Scotland would not differ from Slovakia. The break-up would seriously harm only Belgium which would, after the secession of Flanders, lose 57% of its population. Spain would lose about half of the population in the case of the simultaneous secession of Catalonia, Galicia, and the Basque Country.

As for the economic level of the regions, the potentially secessionist regions such as Catalonia and Basque are significantly richer than the rest of Spain. If they left the Kingdom, the Spanish GDP per capita would significantly decrease.

Differences between Basque GDP per capita and that of the rest of Spain (without Basque) is significantly higher in comparison to the same difference for Catalonia, though the difference between the total Spanish GDP per capita and the

Catalonian GDP is higher in comparison to the Basque indicator. This difference is caused by the fact that the population of Basque is significantly smaller (only 2.1 million inhabitants) in comparison to the Catalan population (7.5 million inhabitants). Higher GDP is, therefore, in the total Spanish GDP represented with the lower weight.

In terms of the GDP, the most serious harm would once again be experienced in Belgium (58.3% decrease) and Spain (30.2% decrease in case of simultaneous secession of all Spanish secessionist regions). However, the new post-secessionist countries would still be viable with Flanders being at a similar level as Denmark or the Basque Country on the same level as Slovakia.

This phenomenon is in line with Hechter's theory of *Internal Colonialism*. Internal Colonialism describes situations or regions that are "simultaneously economically disadvantaged and culturally distinctive from the core of the host state" (Hechter 2017:xiv). Economic exploitation is based on the assumption that the interregional solidarity is relatively weak and does not function effectively.

Discussions on economic secession often reveal the belief that secessionist regions are being exploited at the country level (Alexandrakis and Jones 2006). However, in our dataset, only six regions (Flanders, Åland, South Tyrol, Aosta Valley, Catalonia, and the Basque Country) would have a higher GDP p.c. than the rest of the country after the secession. All other regions would have lower economic levels. The highest difference is observed in the case of South Tyrol (€39,940 in comparison to €26,591 for the rest of Italy), and, conversely, in Wales (€24,572 in comparison to the €34,783 of the rest of the United Kingdom).

Huysseune (2002) shows that the secessionist movement, *Lega Nord* (in northern Italy), speaks about the North of Italy as the "colony" of the Italian South. It is also supported by Calvet (n.d.) who quotes the catchword of Catalonian secessionist parties "Spain robs us!" If the region is more developed and its citizens are more satisfied with their quality of life, they would prefer to be independent and not pay for the poorer rest of the country.

*Table 3.10* The impact of the secession on the population and GDP of the original countries

| *Country* | *Before secession* | | | *GDP [bil. €]* | | | | |
|---|---|---|---|---|---|---|---|---|
| | *Rank* | *Population (mil.)* | *Rank* | *Population* | *Change (%)* | *Before secession* | *After secession* | *Change (%)* |
| France | 2 | 66.4 | 2 | 66.1 | −0.5 | 2.059 | 2.051 | −0.4 |
| United Kingdom | 3 | 64.8 | 4 | 57.7 | −11 | 2.254 | 2.006 | −11.0 |
| Italy | 4 | 60.8 | 3 | 62.4 | −3 | 1.613 | 1.555 | −3.6 |
| Spain | 5 | 46.4 | 6 | 23.1 | −50 | 1.041 | 0.727 | −30.2 |
| Belgium | 9 | 11.3 | 22 | 4.8 | −57 | 0.401 | 0.167 | −58.3 |
| Finland | 18 | 5.5 | 19 | 5.1 | −7 | 0.205 | 0.204 | −0.7 |

Source: Own calculation.

*Table 3.11* Comparison of the hypothetical new secessionist countries with existing EU members

| *New country* | *Population* | *Rank* | *Comparable country* | *Population* | *GDP 2014 (bil. €)* | *Comparable country* | *GDP 2014 (bil. €)* |
|---|---|---|---|---|---|---|---|
| Catalonia | 7.4 | 15 | Bulgaria | 7.2 | 197 | Ireland | 193.2 |
| Flanders | 6.4 | 17 | Denmark | 5.7 | 233.4 | Denmark | 260.6 |
| Scotland | 5.3 | 21 | Slovakia | 5.4 | 172.7 | Portugal | 173.4 |
| Wales | 3.1 | 25 | Lithuania | 2.9 | 75.9 | Slovakia | 75.6 |
| Galicia | 2.7 | 27 | | | 53.9 | Luxembourg | 48.9 |
| Basque Country | 2.1 | 28 | Slovenia | 2.1 | 63.4 | Slovakia | 75.6 |
| Sardinia | 1.7 | 31 | Estonia | 1.3 | 33.3 | Serbia | 33.3 |
| South Tyrol | 0.5 | 35 | Malta | 0.4 | 20.6 | Estonia | 19.8 |
| Corsica | 0.3 | 37 | | | 8.8 | Malta | 8.1 |
| Aosta Valley | 0.1 | 38 | Liechtenstein | 0.04 | 4.7 | Kosovo | 5.6 |
| Åland | 0.03 | 40 | | | 1.4 | Montenegro | 3.5 |

Source: Eurostat (2016), authors.

*Table 3.12* Quality of life and situation of the economy

| *Current situation in [%]* | *Region* | |
|---|---|---|
| | *Non-secessionist* | *Secessionist* |
| Quality of life | 78.7 | 83.5 |
| Situation of the economy | 50.5 | 58.7 |

Source: own calculation.

As for the variables *Quality of life* and *Situation of the economy*, citizens from secessionist regions seem to be more satisfied than their fellow citizens from the rest of the country. Nearly five p. p. more respondents from secessionist regions compared to the rest of the country evaluate their quality of life as good. The difference in satisfaction with the situation of the economy is even deeper (8.2 p. p.). This is emphasised by the fact that the GDP p.c. in secessionist regions is €1,776 higher than in non-secessionist regions (€30,903 vs €29,127). Nevertheless, the difference in Eurobarometer satisfaction is not supported by the t-test, which might be caused by some extreme values in the very small data sample.

#### ECONOMIC PERFORMANCE ACCORDING TO ATTITUDES TO THE SECESSION

Respondents who declare themselves as pro-secessionist are significantly more optimistic about the economic situation in their region: 84% of pro-secessionists find the regional condition as good or very good while the same is true for 64% of anti-secessionists (Figure 3.39).

However, 19% of secessionists find the economic condition of their country as a whole to be good or very good in comparison to 39% of non-secessionists (Figure 3.40). On the contrary, 46% of secession supporters evaluate is as bad or very bad.

However, the opinion towards the EU is nearly the same among secessionists (31% of them are satisfied with the EU economic level) and non-secessionists (36% evaluate the economic conditions in EU as good or very good, Figure 3.41). These results serve as the control of the optimism bias. If the pro-secessionist tends to be much more optimistic or pessimistic than anti-secessionist, it could be revealed in the evaluation of the EU economic situation, which could be seen as relatively value-neutral.

The economic level is considered to be an important factor which can affect decision-making in an independence referendum; however, it is more pronounced for those who require secession than for those who support only some degree of

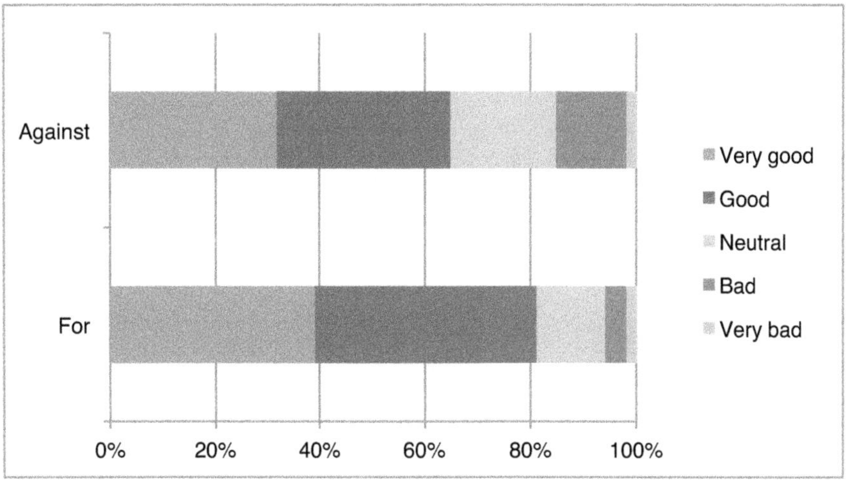


*Figure 3.39* Economic situation in the regions

Source: SAPIM, own calculation.

*Pearson* $\chi^2 = 23.94$, *p-value* $= 0.00008$, *Cramér's* $V = 0.207$.

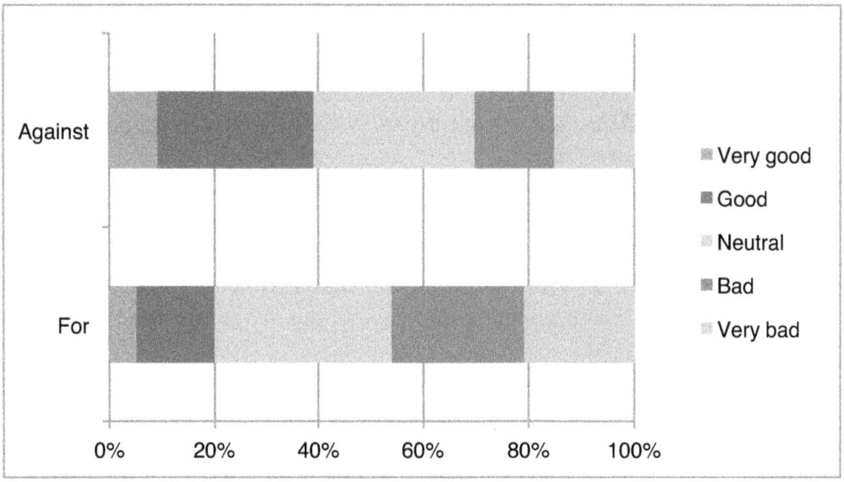


*Figure 3.40* Economic conditions in the country according to the secessionis moods

Source: SAPIM, own calculation.

*Pearson* $\chi^2 = 25.15$, *p-value* $= 0.00005$, *Cramér's* $V = 0.212$.

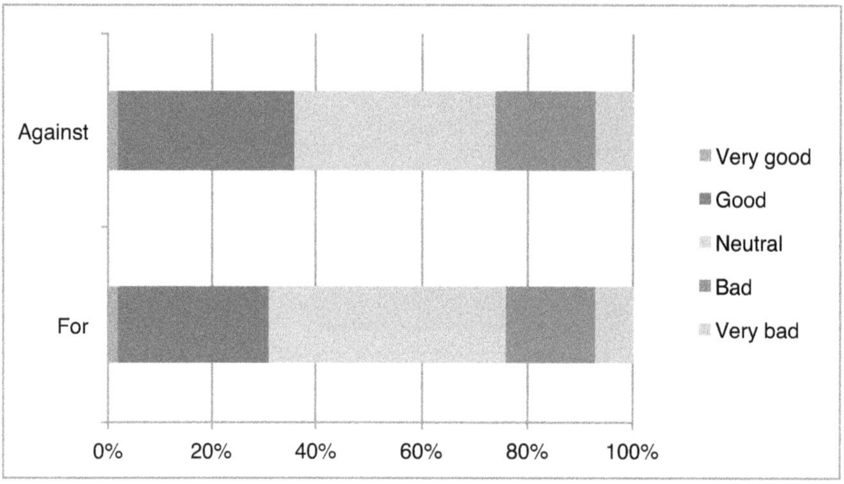


*Figure 3.41* Opinions towards the EU

Source: SAPIM, own calculation.

*Pearson* $\chi^2 = 3.223$, *p-value* = 0.076, *Cramér's V* = 0.52.

decentralisation. Based on our survey results, if the living standards in the secessionist region were high, 52% of pro-secessionist respondents claim that they would support secession; this is contrary to 34% of those who support a softer decentralisation (Figure 3.42).

A high living standard also seems to be a more important factor for respondents who otherwise expect an improvement in living conditions in the case of a secession (49% of them claim that they would support the emergence of a new state in the case of high living standards, which is 10 p. p. more in comparison to those who expect a decrease in the economic conditions; see Figure 3.43).

Last but not least, those who would support secession in case of a serious economic crisis tend to rate the economic conditions of their region as significantly better in comparison to those for whom the economic crisis would not be a crucial pro-secessionist argument (Figure 3.44). However, we cannot observe any relationship between an economic crisis as a secessionist factor and the evaluation of the economic situation in the whole country and the EU. Similarly, there is no relationship between the standard of living expectation in the newly independent country, the rest of the former country, and the family.

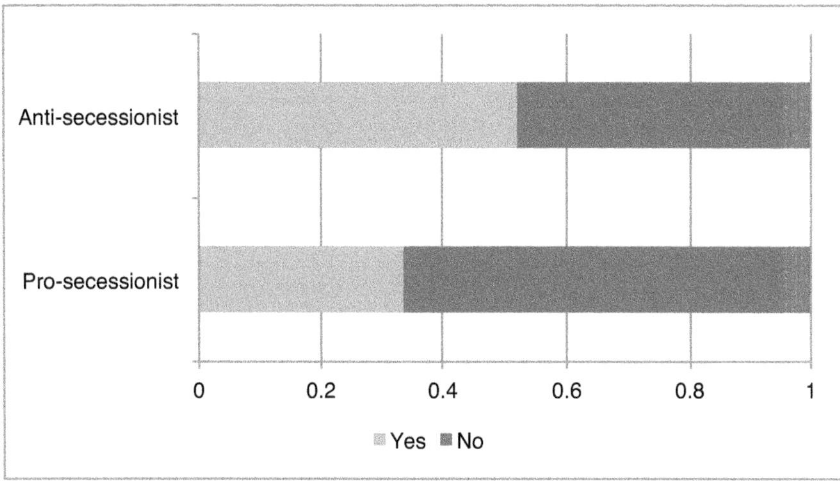


*Figure 3.42* Living standards in the secessionist regions and the rest of the country
Source: SAPIM, own calculation.
*Pearson* $\chi^2 = 15.93$, *p-value* = 0.00007, *Cramér's V* = 0.17.

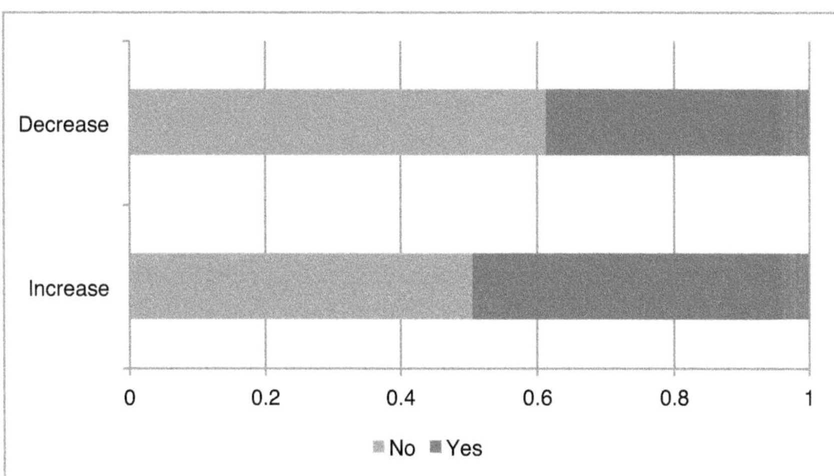


*Figure 3.43* High living standards and the emergence of a new state
Source: SAPIM, own calculation.
*Pearson* $\chi^2 = 10.66$, *p-value* = 0.0306, *Cramér's V* = 0.14.

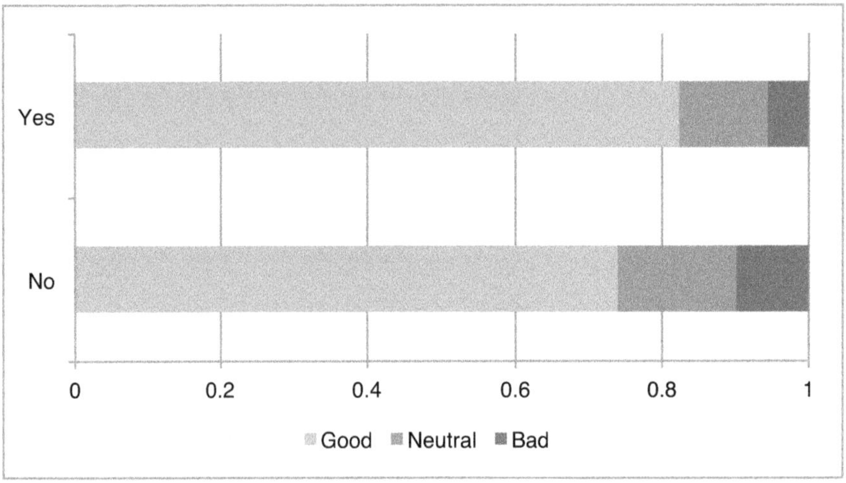


*Figure 3.44* Economic crisis as a pro-secession argument in relation to the evaluation of the economic situation in the region

Source: SAPIM, own calculation.

*Pearson* $\chi^2 = 8.77$, *p-value* = 0.0669, *Cramér's V* = 0.125.

## *Scarce resources*

> Natural resource wealth provides a source of finance for the rebel organisation and encourages the local population to support political demands for secession.
>
> Collier et al. (2003:22)

This section discusses the relationship between the distribution of scarce resources and independence support. The secessionist movements in European countries are not often fostered by scarce resources as directly as other world regions. In the current EU, Scotland is the only secessionist region connected to scarce resources distribution. First, we discuss the relationship between oil prices and the electoral support for the Scottish National Party. In the second section, the greed and grievance phenomenon is tested on the survey data.

### OIL IN THE WHEELS OF SCOTTISH SECESSION

Between 1964 and 2016, there were 39 elections in Scotland: 14 general elections (House of Commons in London), 4 European Parliament elections, and 21 local elections (Local councils and Scottish Parliament).[10] For the whole period, results for the Scottish National Party (SNP) are available (Audickas and Cracknell 2018). Oil prices were published by the Organisation of Petroleum Exporting Countries (OPEC 2019) on a daily, weekly, monthly, and yearly base. Furthermore, data on Brent Crude were used for the 1987–2016 period (EIA 2019).[11] Finally, the variable, *Election*, reflects the type of election. This variable takes on a value of 1 in the case of a general election, 2 in the case of the election to the European Parliament, 3 for a local election, 4 for a regional election, and 5 for the election to the Scottish parliament. This scale assumes that the election with the lower ordinary number will be affected less by Scottish nationalism and more by the British common political topics and vice versa.

There is a statistically significant correlation between the price of oil and the electoral support of the Scottish National Party (Pearson correlation coefficient $\rho = 0.50$ in the case of prices as published by the OPEC and $\rho = 0.49$ in the case of Brent oil prices).

The OLS model was estimated to verify the relationship between the Scottish National Party election gain and the oil prices using the control variable, *Election*, which reflects the type of elections:

$$SNP = \beta_0 + \beta_1 \times Brent_{Monthly} + \beta_2 \times Election + \varepsilon$$

It was proved that SNP is more successful in elections closer to the Scottish region, and its gain is closely connected with the crude oil price development (see Table 35).

For instance, if crude oil prices increase to 100 USD per barrel, then the SNP could receive 16.15 p. p. more votes in the election to the Scottish Parliament in comparison to the general election if the prices fall to 50 USD per barrel.[12]

The same model was estimated using the explanatory variable *time* (to control it for the trend effect), lack variables *Brent_Monthly (i)*, $i \in \{-1,-2,-3,-4\}$, and election results of other political parties. Nevertheless, none of these models had as high an explanatory power as the basic model.

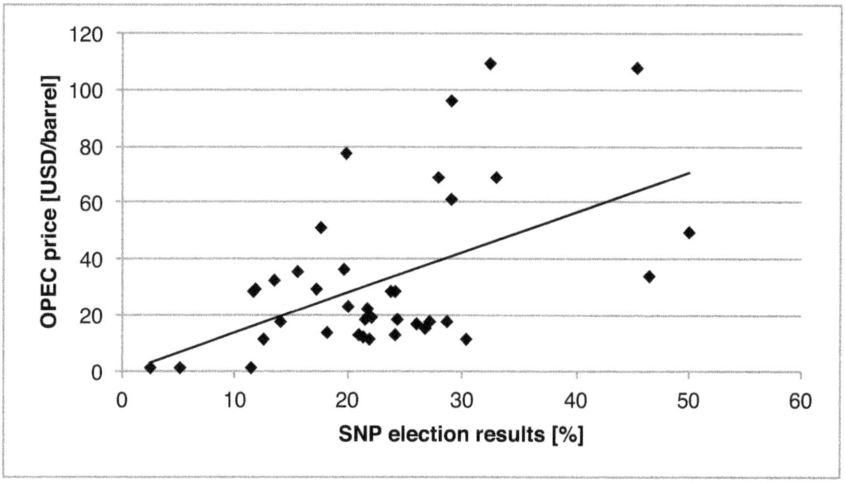


*Figure 3.45* SNP election results in relation to the OPEC price (1964–2016)

Source: OPEC (2019), Audickas and Cracknell (2018). Own calculation.

*Table 3.13* Results of OLS model

| | *Coefficient* | *Std. Error* | *p-value* | |
|---|---|---|---|---|
| **Dependent variable: SNP** | | | | |
| constant | 15.2 | 3.56 | 0.0003 | *** |
| Brent_Monthly | 0.13 | 0.04 | 0.0090 | *** |
| Election | 2.4 | 0.99 | 0.0260 | ** |
| $R^2$ | 0.40 | | | |

Source: own calculation.

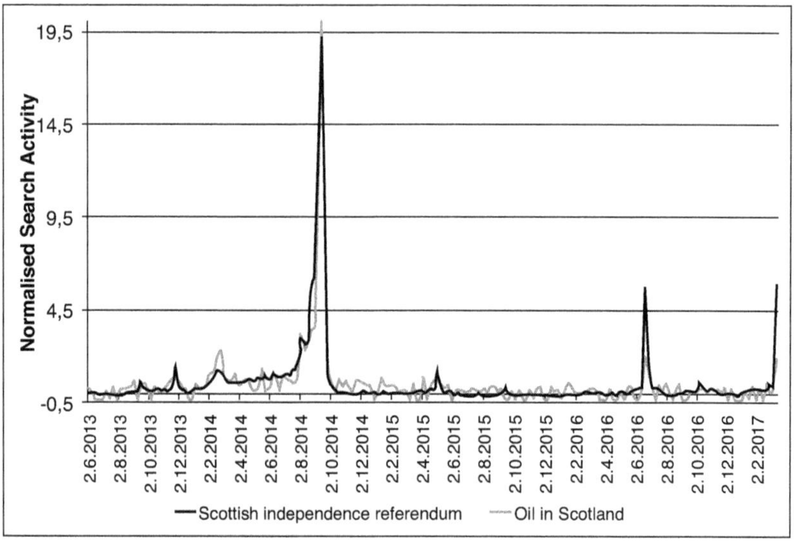


*Figure 3.46* Web Search activity in the United Kingdom for terms *Scottish independence referendum* and *oil in Scotland* (June 2013–March 2017), weekly time series

Source: Google Correlation. Own calculation.

Furthermore, there was no difference between the results of the Scottish Independence referendum in the districts connected to the oil industry and the districts without oil (in both types of Scottish districts, the average ratio of voices for the independence was 43.6%). Among four districts where the majority voted for independence, there were two districts without oil and two with oil. However, the lowest vote for Scottish independence was in the Orkney Islands (32.6% voted for independence), where the Oil industry has a 14.7% stake of the GDP.

Google Correlation data confirms the close relationship between the search for the "Scottish independence referendum" and "oil in Scotland". Within the time span from January 2013 to December 2017, the correlation between the Scottish independence and Scottish oil in search reached $\rho = 0.997$ peaking in the week from 14 September 2014 when the independence referendum took place (see Figure 3.46). The

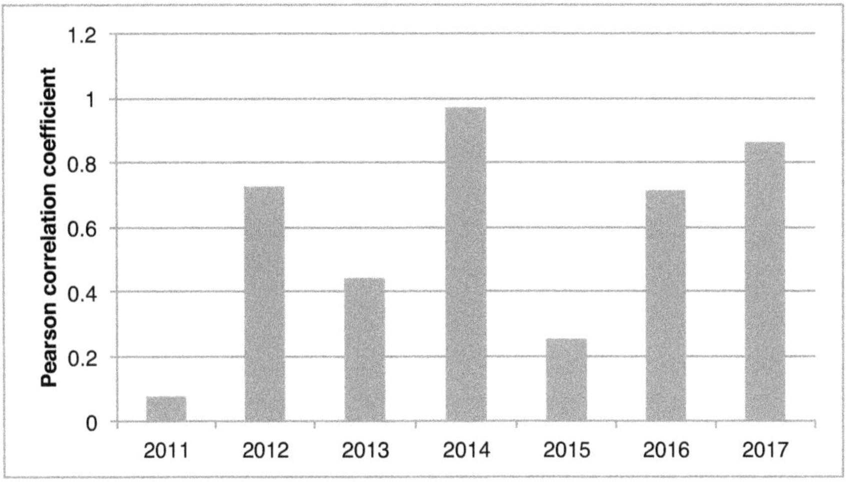


*Figure 3.47* Correlation by year between web search activity in the United Kingdom for terms *Scottish independence referendum* and *oil in Scotland* (June 2013–March 2017), weekly time series

Source: Google Correlation. Own calculation.

second peak in the week after 2 June 2016 precedes the *United Kingdom European Union membership referendum* and the last after 12 March 2017 is connected to the official demand for the second referendum on independence issued by the Scottish prime minister Nicola Sturgeon.

The strongest correlation between search for the Scottish independence referendum and the Scottish oil occurred in the year of referendum (2014) and after the Brexit referendum (2016–2017), on the other hand, before the referendums, the correlation was significantly weaker (Figure 3.47).

GREED AND GRIEVANCE IN SECESSIONIST REGIONS

Pro-secessionists agree with the statement that the "Central government has disproportionally high profits from the regional resources" (Q8c) significantly more often than members of pro-independence parties who do not call for secession (see Figure 3.48).

If respondents expect an increase in the living standard in an independent region after the secession, they significantly more often feel exploited of their scarce regional resources (85% of respondents in comparison to 61% of respondents who expect a potential decrease in the living standard after potential independence).

Furthermore, those who feel the scarce resources exploitation from the central government are also dissatisfied with the fiscal flows between the central

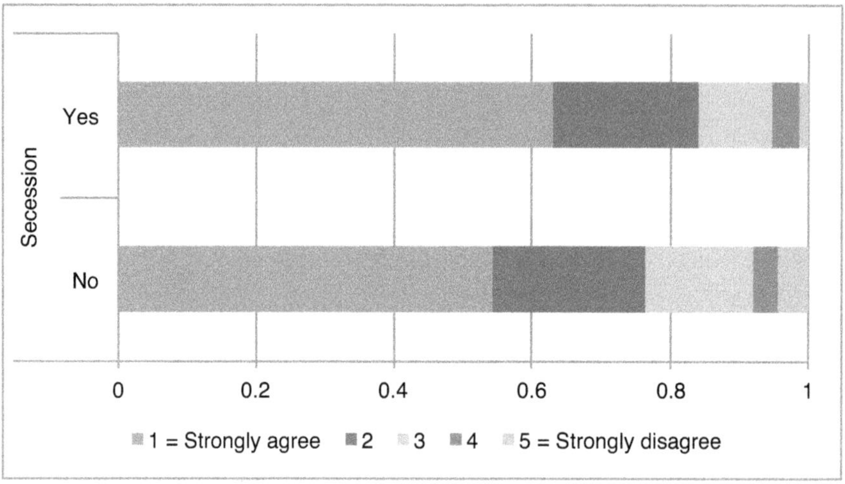


*Figure 3.48* Agreement with the statement that "Central government has disproportionally high profits from the regional resources" among the pro-secessionists and rest of the respondents

Source: SAPIM. Own calculation.

*Pearson* $\chi^2 = 8.47$, *p-value* = 0.075, *Cramér's V* = 0.124.

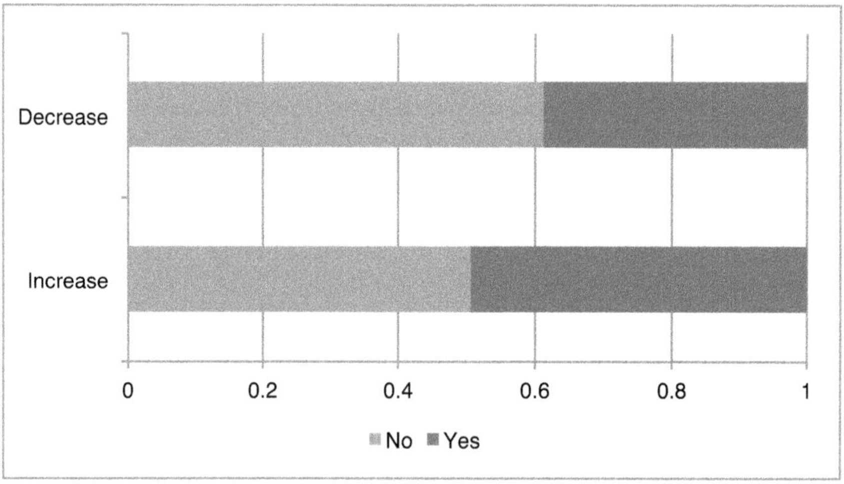


*Figure 3.49* Relationship between expected change of the living standard after independence and feeling of being exploited

Source: SAPIM. Own calculation.

*Pearson* $\chi^2 = 112.48$, *p-value* = 0.0000, *Cramér's V* = 0.23.

government and the region. That is, 94% of them believe that regional tax contributions to the central budget are higher than the amounts we receive back (in comparison to 70% of those who do not feel any exploitation, Figure 3.50).

An even wider gap is opened between respondents who feel the scarce resource exploitation and those who do not; this is with respect to their opinion on public expenditure management. Most of the respondents who blame the central government of greed (in the matter of the regional scarce resources) also claim that they could decide on public expenditures better on the national level than the central government (95% in comparison to 67% of those who disagree with the "greed and grievance" thesis; see Figure 3.51). Those respondents would also be willing to pay a higher "secessionist tax" (on average €465 in PPS in comparison to merely €163 in PPS by those who do not feel any exploitation). Nevertheless, because of the very high variability in the dataset,[13] this difference was not proven as statistically significant.

Those who suspect the central government despite the disproportionally high profits from regional resources expect an improvement in the living standards of the new country (90%; Figure 3.52) as well as their families (84%; Figure 3.53) in the case of a successful secession. These proportions are significantly higher in comparison to the expectation of those who do not consider "governmental greed" as a serious problem.

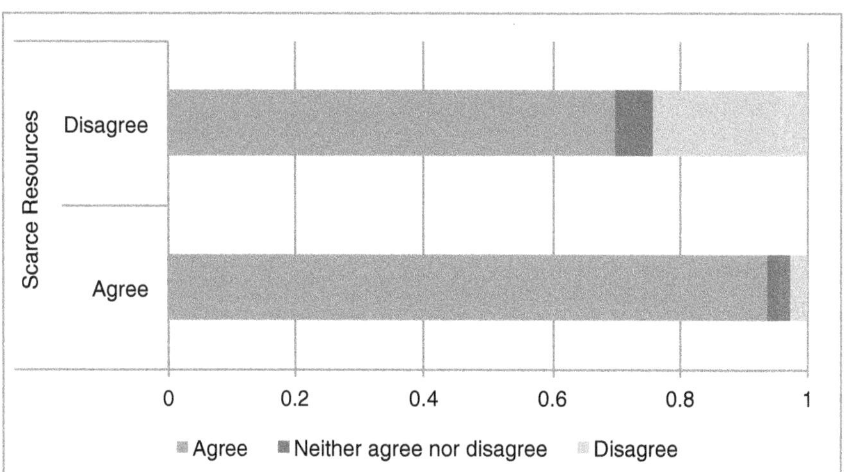


*Figure 3.50* Do you agree that your tax contributions to the central budget are higher than amounts you receive back? (According to the feeling of the exploitation)

Source: SAPIM, own calculation.

*Pearson* $\chi^2 = 197.57$, *p-value* = 0.0000, *Cramér's V* = 0.299.

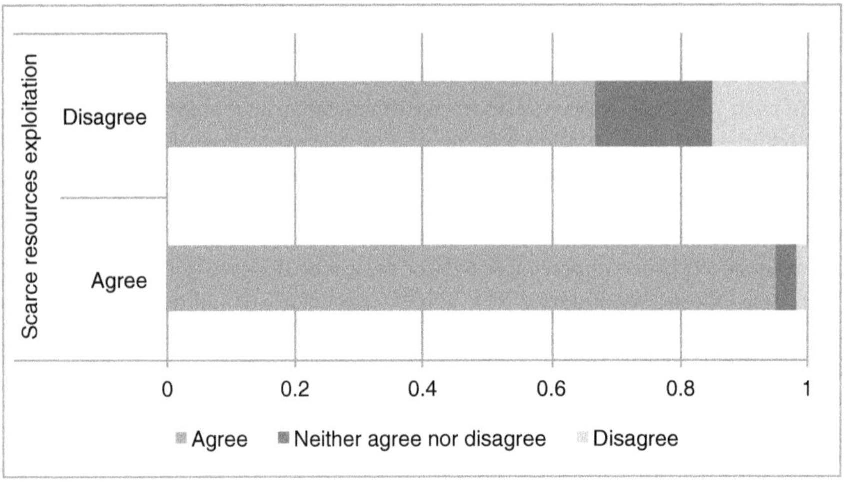


*Figure 3.51* Could your region decide on public expenditures better at the national level than the central government decides? According to the feeling of exploitation

Source: SAPIM. Own calculation.

*Pearson* $\chi^2 = 143.43$, *p-value* = 0.0000, *Cramér's V* = 0.256.

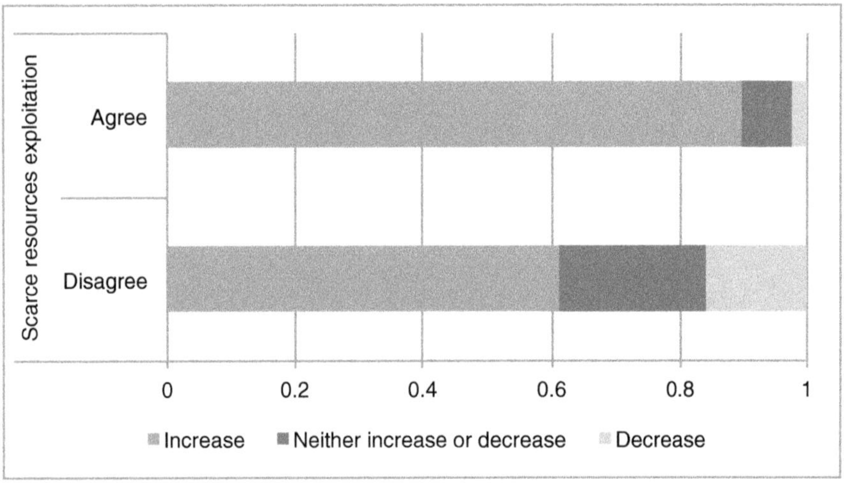


*Figure 3.52* Expectation of the change in the living standards of the new country among those who suspect the central government from the disproportionally high profit from the regional resources. (According to the feeling of exploitation)

Source: SAPIM. Own calculation.

*Pearson* $\chi^2 = 34.8$, *p-value* = 0.0000, *Cramér's V* = 0.272.

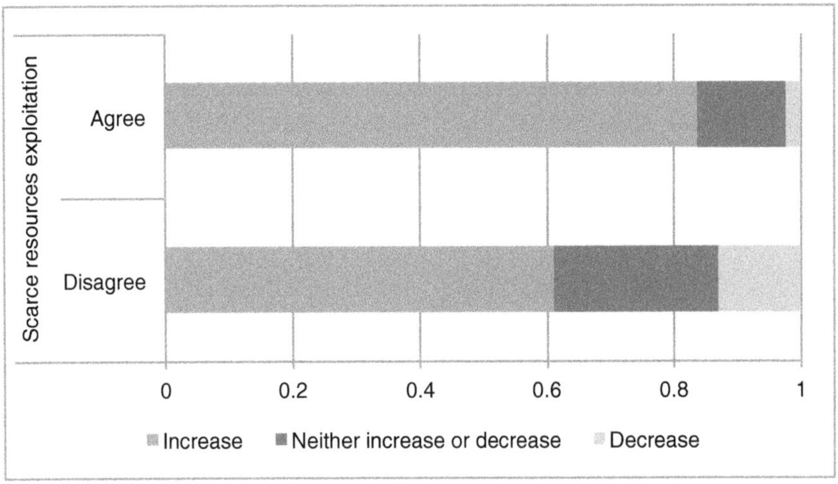


*Figure 3.53* Expectation of the change in the living standards of the family among those who suspect the central government from the disproportionally high profit from the regional resources. (According to the feeling of exploitation)

Source: SAPIM. Own calculation.

*Pearson* $\chi^2 = 19.02$, *p-value* = 0.0008, *Cramér's V* = 0.202.

## *Interregional fiscal transfers*

Respondents who support the secession of their region significantly more often calls for exclusive responsibility of their regional governments in the case of tax policy (81% of secessionists in comparison to 56% of non-secessionists; see Figure 3.54).

Significantly higher support for the tax policy decentralisation can be observed among respondents who do not trust the central government (80% of them in comparison to 57% of those who trust it; see Figure 3.55).

Similarly, those who identify themselves with their region more than with their country support fiscal decentralisation significantly (84% in comparison to 56% in the case of respondents who identify themselves with the country as a whole; Figure 3.56).

Higher support for fiscal decentralisation can be observed among people who are dissatisfied with the economic situation in their country. That is, 85% of those who find it bad or even very bad would entrust the tax policy only to the regional governments (in comparison with 51% of those who find the economic situation in their country as good or very good; Figure 3.57). There is no such strong relationship between fiscal decentralisation and the evaluation of the economic situation on the regional or European level.

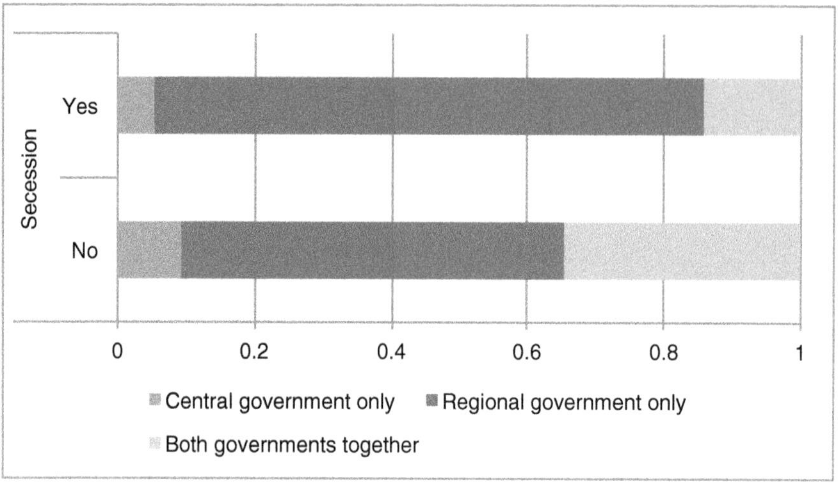


*Figure 3.54* If your region were to remain part of the current state, how should the be the taxation power shared between the central government and the regional government? (According to the attitudes to the secession)

Source: SAPIM. Own calculation.

*Pearson* $\chi^2 = 35.49$, *p-value* = 0.0000, *Cramér's V* = 0.254.

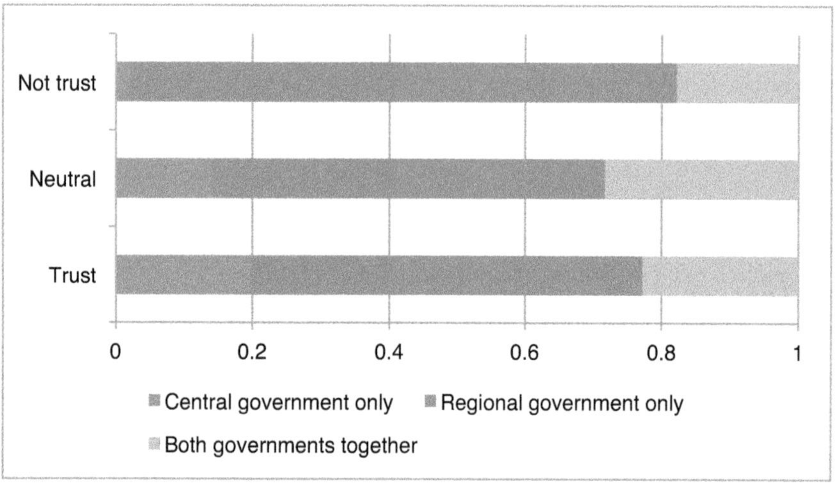


*Figure 3.55* If your region were to remain part of the current state, how should the be the taxation power shared between the central government and the regional government? (According to the trust to the central government)

Source: SAPIM. Own calculation.

*Pearson* $\chi^2 = 61.27$, *p-value* = 0.0000, *Cramér's V* = 0.238.

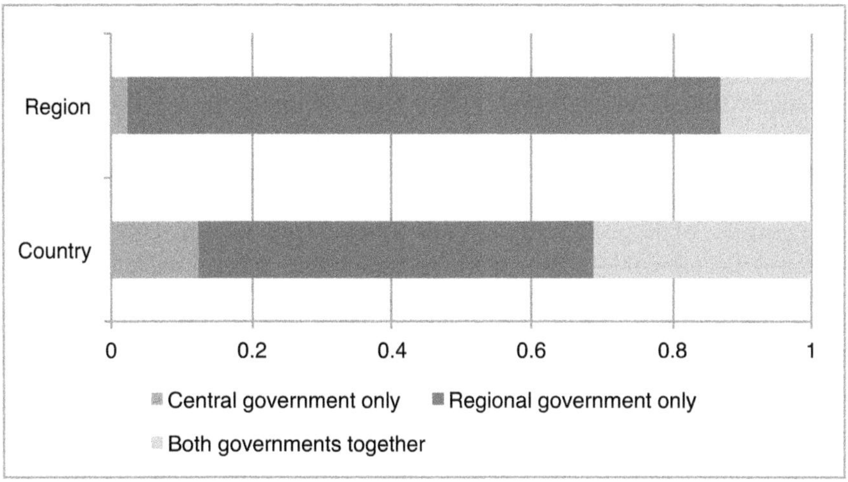


*Figure 3.56* Support for the fiscal decentralisation according to the identification with the region and the country

Source: SAPIM. Own calculation.

*Pearson* $\chi^2 = 55.34$, *p-value* $= 0.0000$, *Cramér's* $V = 0.318$.

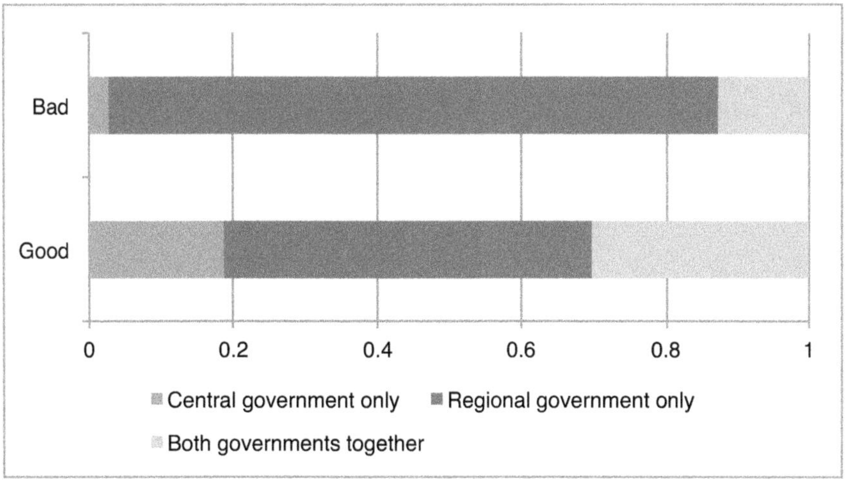


*Figure 3.57* Support for the fiscal decentralisation according to the evaluation of the economic situation in the country

Source: SAPIM. Own calculation.

*Pearson* $\chi^2 = 75.15$, *p-value* $= 0.0000$, *Cramér's* $V = 0.263$.

Shifting the tax policy to the hands of the regional government is proposed, especially by citizens who believe in the significant increase in economic level after the secession (77% of them in comparison to 33% of those who expect an economic decrease in the region; Figure 3.58). Similarly, the greater tax power of the regional government is supported by 77% of those who expect an increase in their family economic level and 80% of those who expect a decrease in the economic level of the rest of the country. In other words, the more respondents are persuaded of the good condition of their region (as compared to the rest of the country), the more they will support decentralisation in fiscal matters, which is completely in line with the theoretical assumptions.

Respondents who support secession are significantly more often convinced that their region contributes to the central budget and higher amount on taxes than it receives back (Figure 3.61). Similarly, 75% of pro-secessionists suppose that their region could decide on public expenditures better than the central government decides (in comparison to 62% of anti-secessionists).

Dissatisfied with the fiscal position of their region are especially those respondents who do not trust their national government (Figure 3.62). That is, 92% of them agree with the statement that their tax contributions to the central budget are higher than the amounts they receive back. Surprisingly, there cannot be observed an inverse relation. Satisfaction with the regional fiscal position is independent of the respondent's trust in the regional government.

In line with our expectation, people who find the economic situation in their country unsatisfactory tend to be dissatisfied with their regional fiscal position

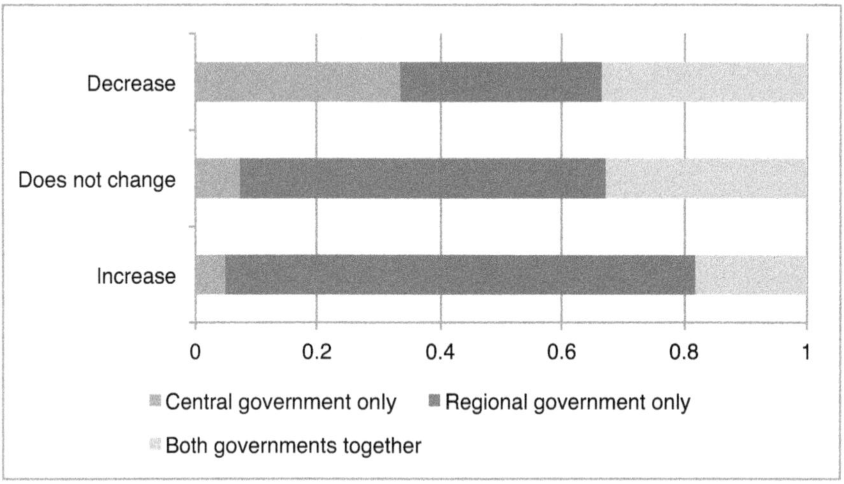


*Figure 3.58* Support for the fiscal decentralisation according to the expectation of the economic development after the independence in the newly independent country

Source: SAPIM, own calculation.

*Pearson* $\chi^2 = 63.25$, *p-value* = 0.0000, *Cramér's V* = 0.244.

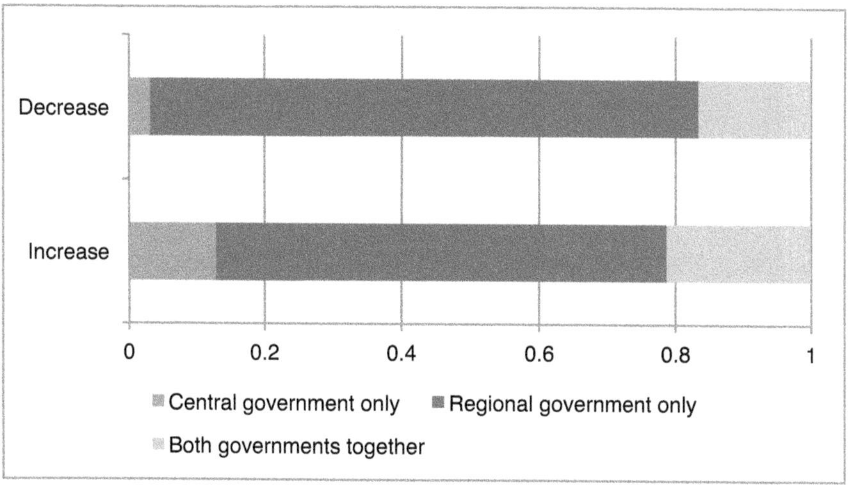


*Figure 3.59* Support for the fiscal decentralisation according to the expectation of the economic development after the independence in the former country

Source: SAPIM. Own calculation.

*Pearson* $\chi^2 = 23.51$, *p-value* $= 0.00276$, *Cramér's* $V = 0.15$.

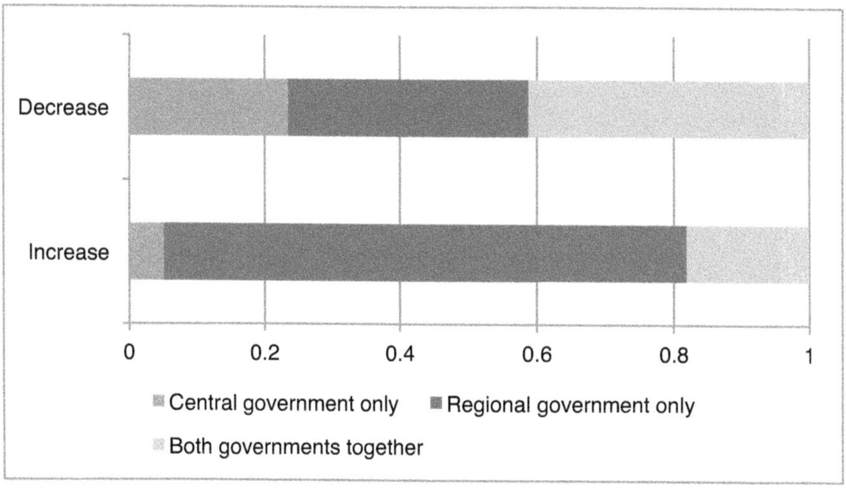


*Figure 3.60* Support for the fiscal decentralisation according to the expectation of the economic development after the independence in the family

Source: SAPIM. Own calculation.

*Pearson* $\chi^2 = 51.57$, *p-value* $= 0.0000$, *Cramér's* $V = 0.22$.

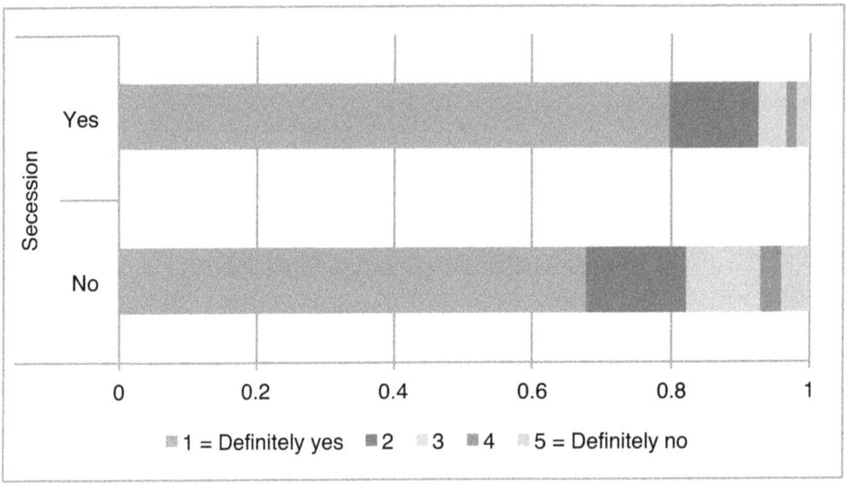


*Figure 3.61* Is the regional tax contributions to the central budget higher than amounts received back? (According to the attitudes to the secession)

Source: SAPIM. Own calculation.

*Pearson* $\chi^2 = 15.34$, *p-value* = 0.00404, *Cramér's V* = 0.166.

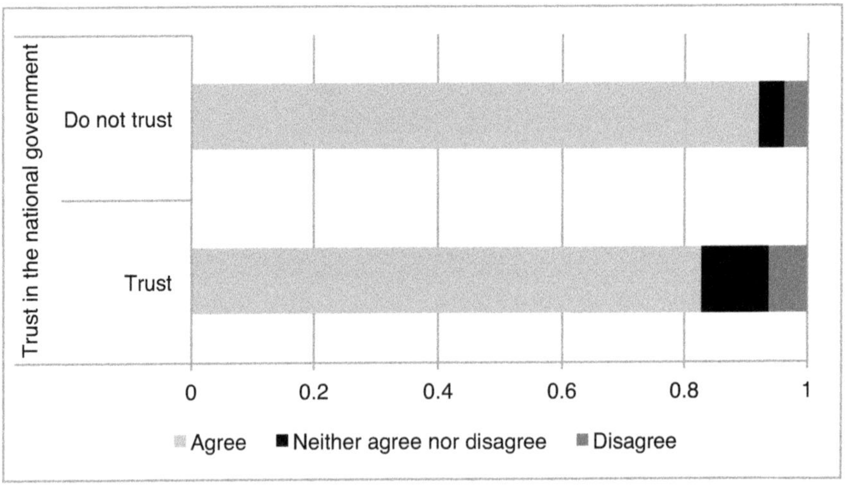


*Figure 3.62* Satisfaction with the fiscal position according to the trust in the national government

Source: SAPIM. Own calculation.

*Pearson* $\chi^2 = 46.589$, *p-value* = 0.00008, *Cramér's V* = 0.146.

(91% find the economic situation to be bad in comparison to 82% who find it to be good; see Figure 3.63).

A considerable difference in perception of grievance is closely connected to the expectation of an increase in the regional living standards in the case of independence. While 61% of those who expect a decrease in the case of independence feel some grievance in terms of the fiscal position, the same is true for 92% of those who expect an improvement in living standards after the secession.

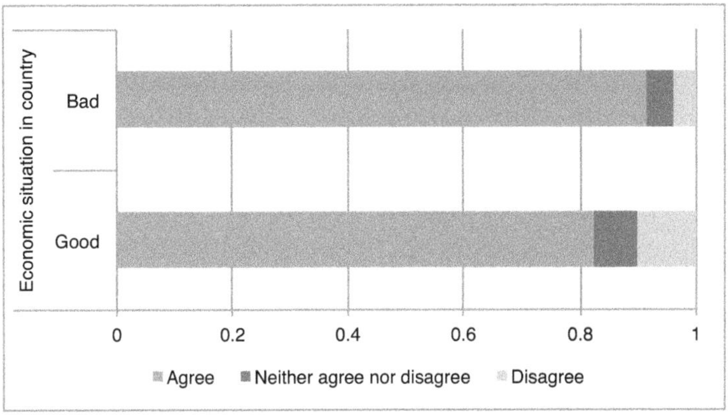


*Figure 3.63* Satisfaction with the fiscal position according to the assessment of the economic situation in the country.

Source: SAPIM. Own calculation.

*Pearson* $\chi^2 = 36.608$, *p-value* = 0.00238, *Cramér's* $V = 0.129$.

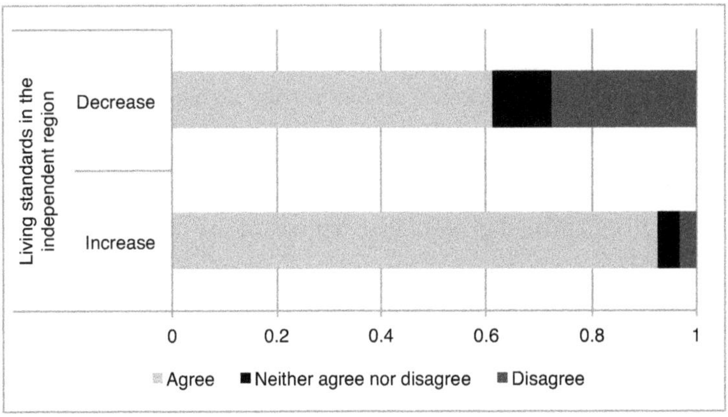


*Figure 3.64* Satisfaction with the fiscal position according to the expectation of the living standard change in case of the independence

Source: SAPIM. Own calculation.

*Pearson* $\chi^2 = 108.33$, *p-value* = 0.0000, *Cramér's* $V = 0.225$.

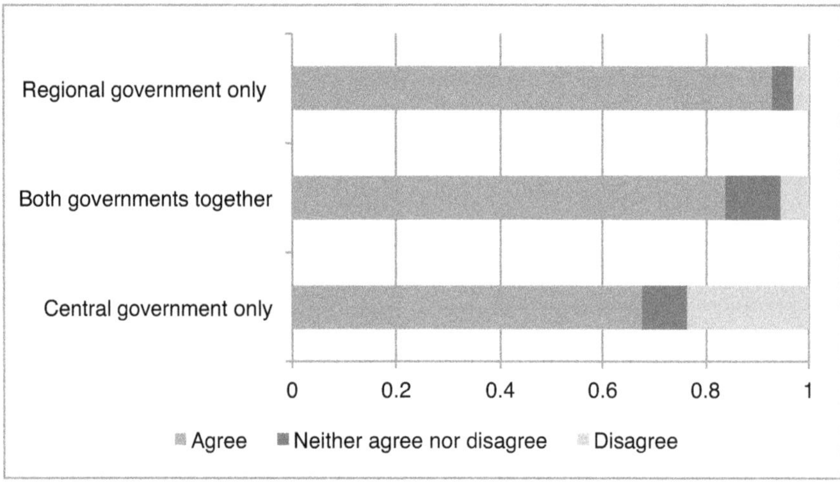


*Figure 3.65* Satisfaction with the fiscal position according to the preferences of sharing power over the tax policy

Source: SAPIM. Own calculation.

*Pearson* $\chi^2 = 40.07$, *p-value* = 0.0000, *Cramér's V* = 0.192.

Finally, those who would entrust the tax policy to the regional government agree with the statement on the unfair fiscal position more often than those who would leave it in the hands of the central government (93% in comparison to 68%; Figure 3.65).

### *Economic integration*

If the European integration was desirable for the economy and well-being of the secessionist regions, we might expect that citizens should tend to trust in the EU more (and that they trust in the EU representatives more national representatives). Furthermore, it is reasonable to expect that such secessionist regions benefit from EU membership more than the rest of the countries even in terms of the EU funds.

Although the average trust in the EU is higher in the secessionist region in comparison to the non-secessionist region, this difference of 1.7 p.p. is not statistically significant. For both the secessionist and non-secessionist regions, the trust in political representatives is derived from the principle of subsidiarity: citizens tend to trust their regional representatives most, their national representatives less, and, least of all, the EU representatives.

However, secessionist parties might be pro-European; their voters do not share such Europeanism. According to the results presented in this section, secessionist parties highlight the theoretical importance of the EU in the economy of their

*Table 3.14* Trust in European institutions according to the secessionist attitudes

| | *Region* | |
|---|---|---|
| | *Non-secessionist* | *Secessionist* |
| Trust in (%) | | |
| European Union | 49.8 | 51.5 |
| European Commission | 10.8 | 10.5 |
| EU funds p.c. (€) | 178.0 | 226.5 |

Source: own calculation.

regions. They also back the romantic Europeanism based on the post-sovereign idea of the Europe of regions instead of the Europe of states.

However, citizens living in the secessionist regions do not trust in the EU and its representatives more than other citizens. Actually, the trust in the European Commission in such regions is nearly three times lower than their trust in the regional representatives.

Two different attitudes cause the difference in the sentiments towards the EU between the secessionist parties and their voters. According to the parties, a small nation cannot be isolated from the rest of Europe; it needs to benefit from the European economic integration as is suggested for example by Alesina and Spolaore (1997) and Alesina et al. (1997). On the contrary, the citizens are not willing to accept the trade-off between the independence on the original national state and the dependence on the supranational EU. These different attitudes should be made clear before every independence referendum anytime and anywhere in the EU.

### *3.3.2 Microeconomic factors*

Last part of this chapter is devoted to the decision making of the individual economic subjects. Firstly, we will test if the secessionists are risk averse, risk neutral of risk lovers. In the second subchapter their discount rate as the mirror of their patience is studied, including its impacts on the decision-making in terms of secession.

#### *Risk attitude*

Risk attitude is approximated by the respondent's willingness to take part in the lottery with the probability of winning being 10%. The willingness to take part in such a lottery is nearly the same among secessionists (66%) as well as those who do not want the secession (69%).[14] Pro-secessionists are also less willing, on average, to buy the ticket than the non-secessionists (€24.6 in Purchasing Power Parity (PPP) in comparison to €28.7 in PPP). However, this difference is again insignificant as proved by the ANOVA. On average, respondents are therefore pronouncedly risk averse.

Most of the respondents are risk-averse (57% in nominal expression), 8% of them are risk-neutrals who would pay exactly €100 to buy a lottery ticket, and only

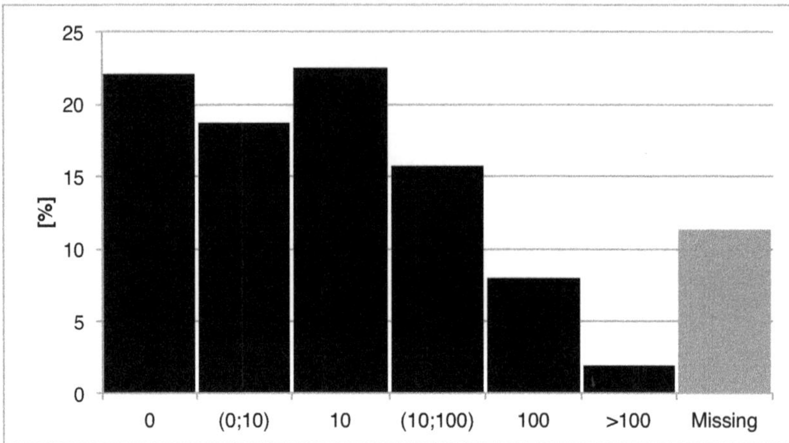


*Figure 3.66* The probability of winning a lottery jackpot of €1,000 is 10%. How much in euros would you be willing to pay for a lottery ticket? (Relative frequency)

Source: SAPIM. Own calculation.

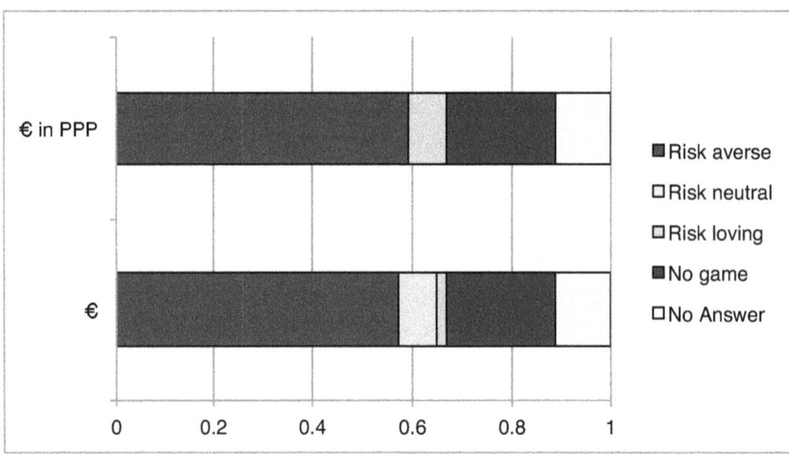


*Figure 3.67* Comparison of respondents' structure of risk attitudes in relation to the currency unit

Source: SAPIM. Own calculation.

2% are risk loving. Using the Purchasing Power Parity, the risk-neutrality disappears in favour of the risk-lovers as well as risk-averse (Figure 3.67). Regarding the aim of the descriptive analysis, the replies in nominal euros were used as their reflection (even the neutral respondents). Amounts expressed in Purchasing Power Parity were used for the quantitative analysis.

Results based on the replies in current euro differ significantly from results after converting the amounts according to the Purchasing Power Parity.

White-collar workers tend to be significantly more risk-averse in comparison to blue-collar workers (Figure 3.68), which is in line with our assumption.

There is no significant dependence between risk attitude and willingness to vote for secession, nor is there one on the willingness to vote for the country's exit from the EU (Figure 3.69). However, those who are in favour of institutions of the EU

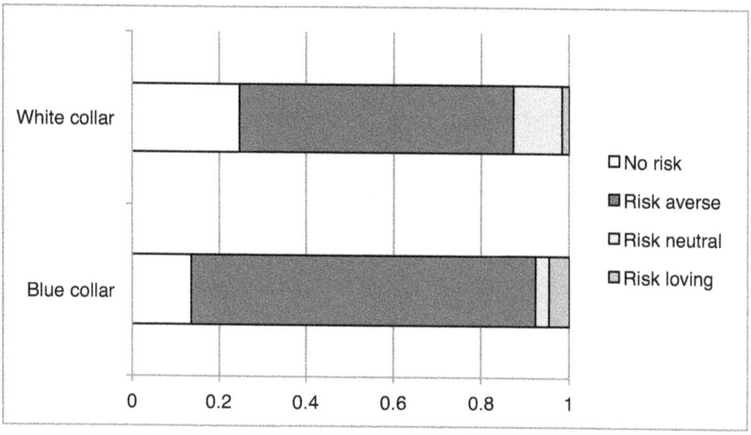


*Figure 3.68* Risk attitudes between white- and blue-collar workers

Source: SAPIM. Own calculation.

*Pearson* $\chi^2 = 10.74$, *p-value* = 0.013, *Cramér's V* = 0.162.

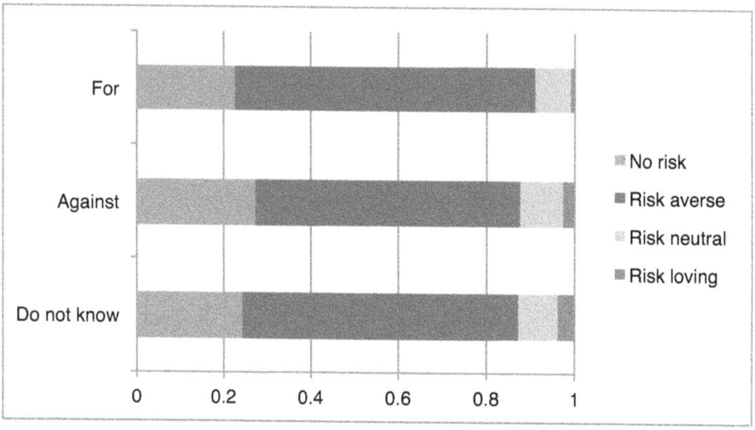


*Figure 3.69* Risk attitudes according to the attitudes towards secession

Source: SAPIM. Own calculation.

*Pearson* $\chi^2 = 4.55$, *p-value* = 0.60, *Cramér's V* = 0.067.

tend to be more often risk-lovers or are, at least, risk-neutral than those who are neutral toward EU institutions or those who do not trust them.

Those who trust in the European Commission are also willing to pay significantly more than others (€75 in comparison to €19–28; Figure 3.70). The same is true for true believers in the European Parliament (€78.4 in comparison to €19–28, Figure 3.71). The greatest difference might be observed between those who asses

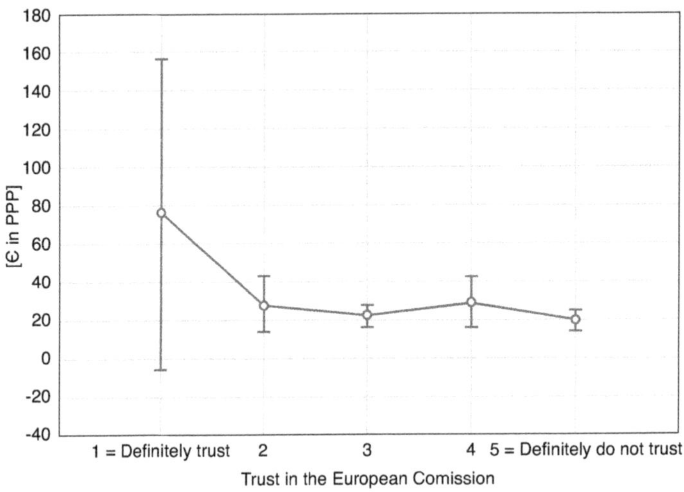


*Figure 3.70* Risk attitudes and the trust in the European Commission

Source: SAPIM. Own calculation.

*Scheffe test p-value: category 1 towards other categories < 0.05.*

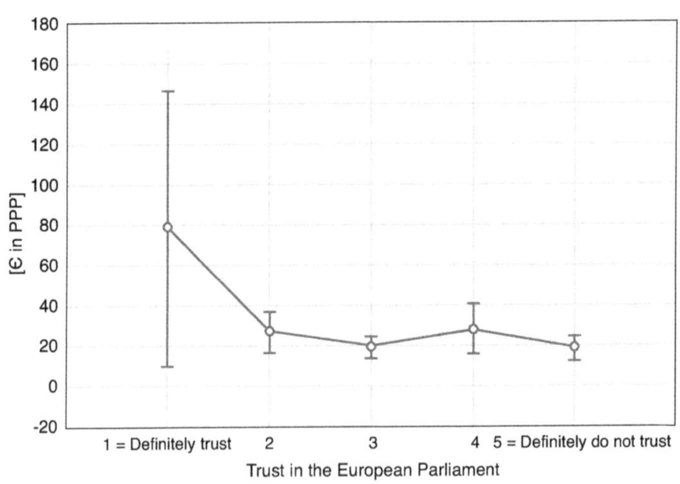


*Figure 3.71* Risk attitudes and the trust in the European Parliament

Source: SAPIM. Own calculation.

*Scheffe test p-value: category 1 towards other categories < 0.01.*

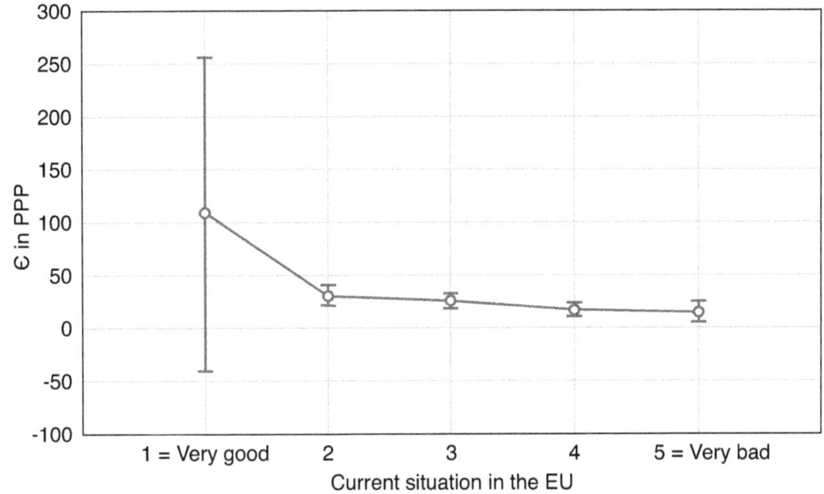


*Figure 3.72* Risk attitudes and assessment of the current economic situation in the EU

Source: SAPIM. Own calculation.

*Scheffe test p-value: category 1 towards other categories < 0.01.*

the current economic situation in the EU as very good (€106.9 in comparison with €14–30; Figure 3.72). There are, therefore, risk-lovers, as their willingness to pay is sufficiently greater than €100.

Based on our data, the risk attitude does not depend significantly on sex (although men seem to be a little bit more risk-taking than women), working class (blue-collars are slightly, but not significantly more risk-loving than white collars), or religion (believers and unbelievers express the same attitudes towards risk). Those results are summarised in Table 3.15.

Differences between individual countries seem to be pronounced on average. However, the null hypothesis of the same mean cannot be rejected by the ANOVA because of the high standard deviations (Figure 3.73). The significant difference between willingness to pay for the lottery ticket in the Czech Republic (€67 in PPP) and the rest of the countries (€23.7 in PPP on average) is statistically significant with Scheffe's test where p-value = 0.0005. However, the condition of Levene's Test significance is not met. The significance of the differences was also not proved by the non-parametric $\chi^2$ test.

Contrary to our hypothesis, secessionist preferences are not connected to the risk-attitudes of the respondents. However, such a result might be explained by the selection bias. The survey was conducted among members of pro-independence parties and movements. It is, therefore, possible that the respondents tend to express a similar risk attitude which would be different from the attitudes of non-party members.

*Table 3.15* Risk attitudes according to sex, working class and religion (results)

| | | *Amount (€ in PPP)* | *p-value* |
|---|---|---|---|
| Sex | Female | 23.8 | 0.82 |
| | Male | 26.1 | |
| Working class | Blue-collar | 30.5 | 0.36 |
| | White-collar | 27.5 | |
| Religion | Non-believer | 28.3 | 0.97 |
| | Believer | 28.5 | |

Source: SAPIM. Own calculation.

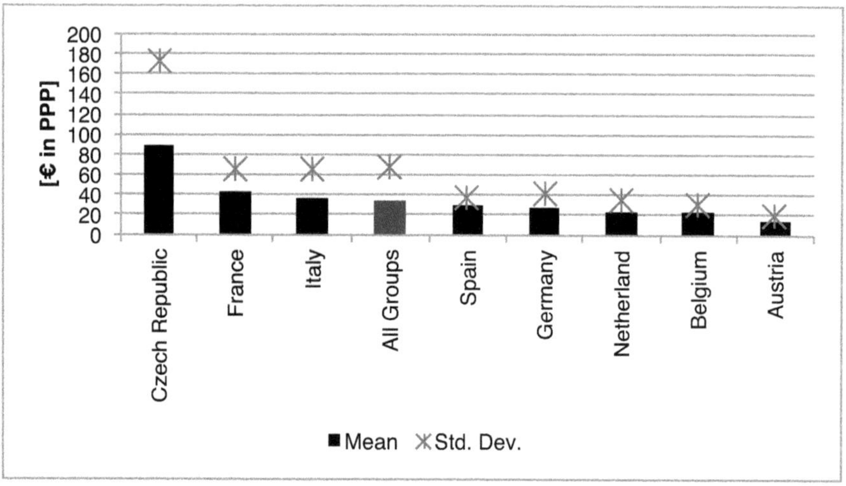


*Figure 3.73* Willingness to pay in the EU countries
Source: SAPIM. Own calculation.

Those estimates might have been checked using the Google Trends data. It is reasonable to expect that the risk-lovers play lottery more often than the risk-averse people. Furthermore, those, who play lottery, would be expected to control the results on-line. Using the right key word, the difference in the interest in the lotteries among the regions can be easily recognised.

Since 2004 there has been the EuroMillions lottery played in the Western Europe. Currently citizens in nine countries can play. The key word "EuroMillions" is not language-sensitive, it can be used for search in all the regions.

As Figure 3.74 clearly depicts that the interest in the lottery EuroMillions is not significantly higher in the secessionist regions in comparison to the non-secessionist regions. For example, Flemish Google searchers look for the key

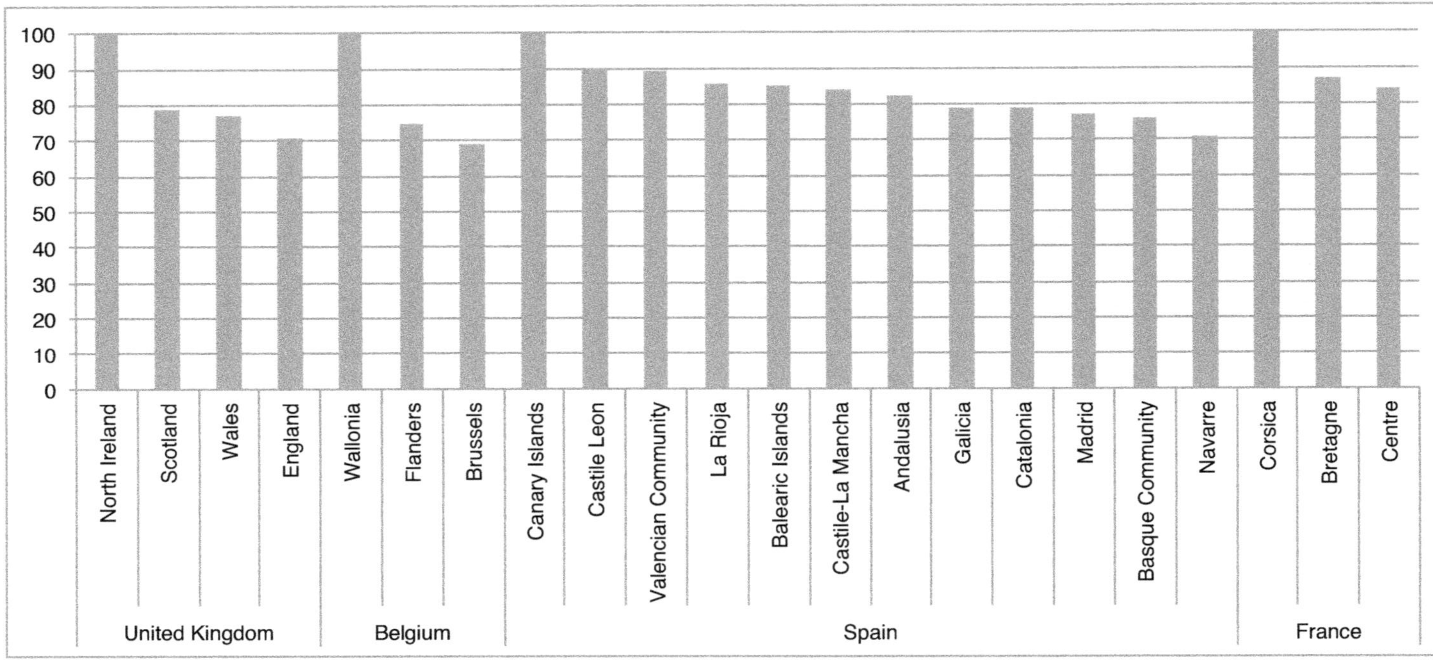


*Figure 3.74* Interest in the lottery EuroMillions in the selected regions (2004–2019)

Source: Google Trends. Own calculation.

word "EuroMillions" significantly less often the inhabitants of Wallonia, who seem to be less risk-averse. Similarly, the risk aversion as approximated by the search for the key word "EuroMillions" is nearly the same in secessionist Galicia, Catalonia, and Basque Community as in the non-secessionist and centrist Madrid. Scotland and Wales seems to be slightly more risk averse than people in England; however. They are significantly less in comparison to the Northern Ireland. The only secessionist region which shows signs of being risk-loving is the Corsica in France.

Similar results are available when looking for the *Eurojackpot* as the similar transnational lottery: according to the Google Trends data, the greatest interest (probably connected to the highest degree of risk-loving) occurs in Andalusia (99) and Extremadura (94) as regions without stronger pro-secessionist tensions; on the other hand, the search in Basque (35) and Galicia (46) is comparable with Madrid (32) and Catalalonia (54) seems to be again even less risk-averse than Castile-La Mancha (71).

Nevertheless, it should be taken in account that there might be some popular regional lotteries which are searched by the citizens more often than the international one which distorts the survey data.

Nevertheless, according to the results of our survey, the secessionist cannot be seen as the risk-lovers who "can make one heap of all their winnings and risk it on one turn of pitch-and-toss".[15] This leads to the careful conclusion that their decisions on the future of their region might be supported by a deeper understanding of the secessionist problem.

### *Discount rate*

Slightly more than four fifths of respondents answered question *Q5*:

> You could be given €100 today or €100 plus bonus a year later. How high would the bonus have to be for you to be willing to choose the latter option?

Regarding the aim of the statistical modelling, it is remarkable that about 93% of respondents replied with a round number (a number ending with zero or five). Figure 3.75 summarises the most frequent answers (categories with more than ten responses, including category €1). The most frequent answer is €100, which means that the bonus should equal the present value of sum (17% of respondents), following by one tenth of present value (€10; 12% of respondents).

Such rounded responses are typical, especially for the data on income or wealth, consumption, and expectation. However, this is not so typical in the field of financial topics (such as mortgages; Gideon et al. 2017). Further, counting with such rounded numbers might be misleading if the replies are taken *at face value, even though many may, in fact, be rounded* (Manski and Molinari 2010:219). Such rounding is not only a specific psychological feature but also it might affect the functionality of econometric models. Rounding tendencies are translated into the

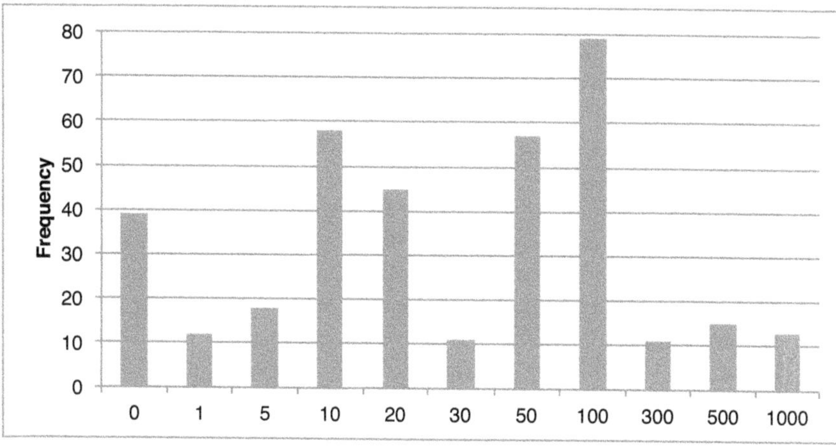


*Figure 3.75* The most frequent amounts
Source: SAPIM. Own calculation.

*Table 3.16* Categories of discount rate

| *Category* | | *r (%)* | *N* |
|---|---|---|---|
| 1 | low | ⟨0;5⟩ | 75 |
| 2 | modest | (5;50⟩ | 191 |
| 3 | high | (50;100⟩ | 85 |
| 4 | very high | >100 | 113 |

Source: Author.

lower variability of the dataset, which weakens the usage of OLS models. Furthermore, some respondents replied with extremely high numbers (such as 10,000 or even one billion euros; those answers were excluded as obvious outliers). Thus, to avoid data distortion to satisfy the research aim, we used an ordinal database on four categories as listed in Table 3.16.

In line with the theory, we test the theoretical hypothesis that respondents with a *lower* discount rate support secession significantly more than respondents with a higher discount rate. The average discount rate of pro-secessionists is lower (137.3% to 193.5%); nevertheless, this difference is not statistically significant.[16]

There is no explicit assumption on the difference between male and female discount rates in the literature. Soytas and Kose (2014) mention the meta-analysis of 33 studies, which leads to the conclusion that female discount rates are lower in comparison to that of males (which means they are more patient). This presumption was not confirmed in our data. The female discount rate is lower within the group of lowest and highest discount rates. Nevertheless, this difference is not statistically significant. Only within the category of a *medium discount rate* is there a significantly higher female rate in comparison to the male rate (Table 3.17).

The general tendency of women to express higher discount rates is confirmed by $\chi^2$ test (Figure 87).

This difference is statistically significant for the pro-secessionists. Women who do support secession express significantly higher discount rates than men (38.4% in comparison to 24.8%; p-value = 0.001). With this exception, gender differences are not significant. This might be explained by similar attitudes to the present-future relations among members of the autonomist parties and movements.

Respondents with a higher level of education (university graduates) express lower discount rates, which is consistent with the assumption that "education can

*Table 3.17* Discount rate according to the sex of respondents

| | | *Female* | *Male* | *p-value* |
|---|---|---|---|---|
| 1 | low | 1.25 | 1.59 | 0.66 |
| 2 | medium | 38.04 | 25.41 | 0.00 |
| 3 | high | 98.57 | 98.57 | 0.99 |
| 4 | very high | 431.7 | 530.2 | 0.56 |

Source: Author.

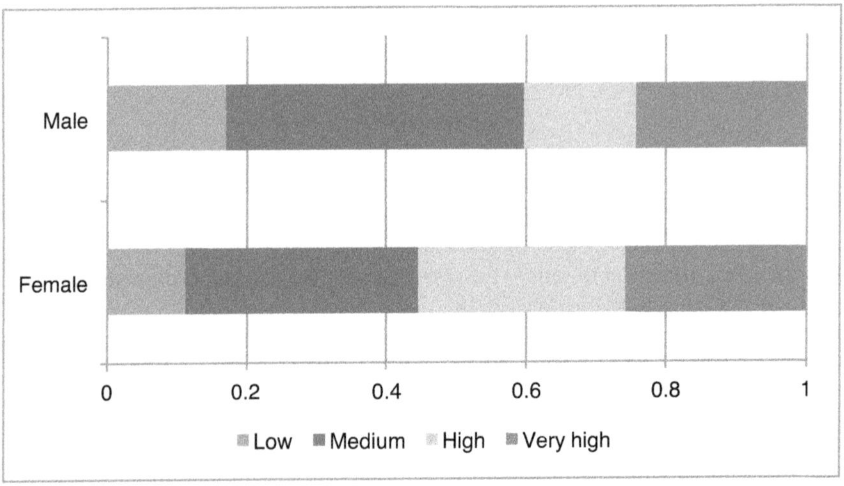


*Figure 3.76* Discount rates according to sex

Source: SAPIM. Own calculation.

*Pearson* $\chi^2 = 8.57$, *p-value* = 0.035, *Cramér's* $V = 0.136$

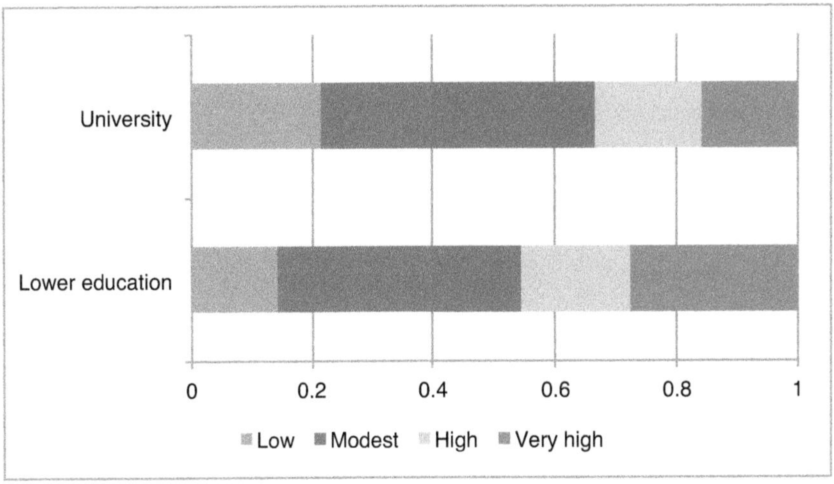


*Figure 3.77* Discount rate according to education level
Source: SAPIM. Own calculation.
*Pearson* $\chi^2 = 8.67$, *p-value* = 0.034, *Cramér's V* = 0.137

be understood as an investment in patience" (Becker and Mulligan in Bauer and Chyitlová 2009). The average discount rate of respondents with a university degree represents just one-third of the average discount rate or respondents with a lower educational level (the difference between the discount rate of 65% in comparison to 190% is statistically significant).

Despite the assumption of a lower discount rate among the religious people (Cartera et al. 2012), there was no relationship between discounting the future and religiosity. Similarly, those who expect a potentially better living condition for their family or new country after the secession do not express lower discount rates than their counterparts.

On 13 September 2013, one year before the Scottish independence referendum, 1,002 respondents were asked two questions:

1 Would you support or oppose Scotland becoming independent if you were convinced you would be £500 a year better off as a result?
2 Would you support or oppose Scottish independence if you were convinced it would leave you personally no better and no worse off financially?

(ICM 2013)

The pecuniary incentives turned out to significantly influence the respondents' attitudes towards the secession. If there were no change in the personal economic level, 44% of respondents would vote against the independence, while 47% of

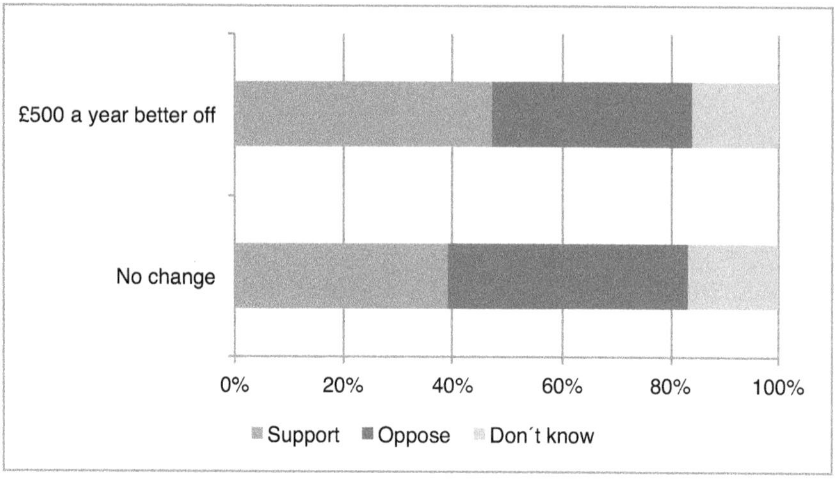


*Figure 3.78* Scottish attitudes towards the secession and the pecuniary incentives
Source: ICM (2013). Own elaboration.

respondents would vote for the independence if there would be an increase in income (Figure 3.78).[17]

## 3.4 Cobb-Douglas function

These results from the previous chapters suggest that respondents can optimise their utility functions to reflect their income. In this part, we, therefore, try to estimate the utility function of the secessionist party members.

Firstly, the set of variables useful for the factor analysis is constructed (see Table 3.18).

Correlation matrix for these nine variables was estimated (see Figure 3.79). Variables *Q7e* and *Q7f* turned not to be correlated with other variables, so they were excluded from the further analysis. Significant correlation exists between variables *Religion* and *Mother tongue* on the one side and between *Q2.1* and *Q3.1* on the other side, other correlations are weaker.

Eigenvalues suggest using just four variables (*Religion*, *Mother tongue*, *Q2.1* and *Q3.1*). Figure 3.80 of factor loadings confirms closeness of both economic respectively romantic factors.

The new variables – factors *R* and *E* – were then calculated as

$$R = 0{,}664 \times Religion_{kat} + 0{,}563 \times Mother_{tongue} - 0{,}194 \times Q3.1 + 0{,}052 \times Q2.1$$

$$E = -0{,}176 \times Religion_{kat} + 0{,}04 \times Mother_{tongue} + 0{,}746 \times Q3.1 + 0{,}549 \times Q2.1$$

*Table 3.18* Romantic and economic factors

| *Factor* | | | |
|---|---|---|---|
| *Romantic* | | *Economic* | |
| Religion | Compliance of the respondent with the prevailing religion in the country | Q2.1 | Economic situation in region |
| | | Q3.1 | Economic situation in newly independent country |
| Mother tongue | Compliance of the respondent with the prevailing language in the country | Q7e | Support of secession in case of high living standard |
| | | Q7f | Support of secession in case of serious economic crisis |
| Qs4_1 | Identification with the region | Q8a | Tax sovereignty |
| | | Q8b | Expenditures sovereignty |

Source: Author.

| | *Religion* | *Mother tongue* | *Qs4_1* | *Q3.1* | *Q2.1* | *Q7e* | *Q7f* | *Q8a* | *Q8b* |
|---|---|---|---|---|---|---|---|---|---|
| Religion | 1.00 | | | | | | | | |
| Mother tongue | **0.31** | 1.00 | | | | | | | |
| Qs4_1 | **−0.12** | **−0.41** | 1.00 | | | | | | |
| Q3.1 | 0.08 | **0.13** | −0.14 | 1.00 | | | | | |
| Q2.1 | **0.17** | **0.22** | −0.10 | **0.12** | 1.00 | | | | |
| *Q7e* | *0.00* | *0.04* | *0.04* | *−0.17* | *−0.10* | *1.00* | | | |
| *Q7f* | *0.04* | *−0.05* | *0.04* | *0.01* | *−0.11* | *−0.02* | *1.00* | | |
| Q8a | 0.09 | 0.02 | −0.01 | 0.30 | −0.03 | −0.10 | −0.03 | 1.00 | 0.40 |
| Q8b | 0.09 | 0.00 | −0.05 | 0.30 | 0.03 | 0.00 | −0.07 | 0.40 | 1.00 |

*Figure 3.79* Correlation matrix

Source: Author.

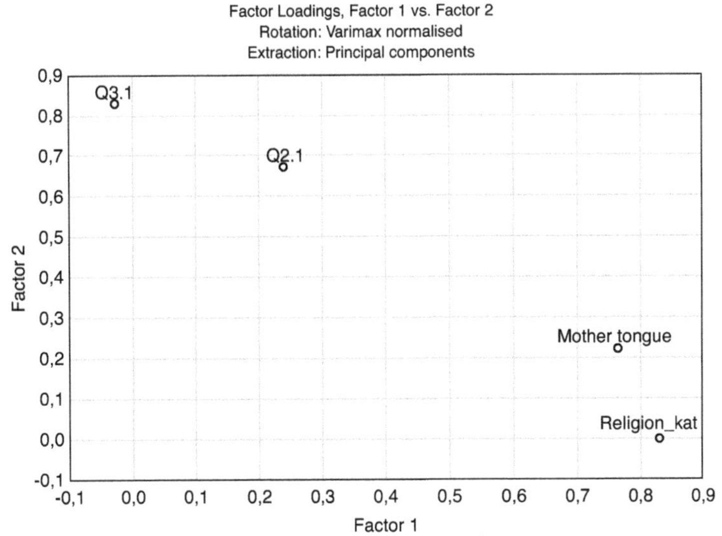


*Figure 3.80* Factor loadings

Source: Author.

As the lowest value within both factor is element $x_i = -1.67$, the constant $k = 1.67$ was added to all variables of the OLS model to estimate the Cobb-Douglas function. The estimates of the unrestricted and restricted model are introduced in Table 3.19.

After re-transformation of the level constant, the Cobb-Douglas function for the secessionist regions is of the form

$$u = 56,8 \times R^{\frac{2}{3}} E^{\frac{1}{3}}$$

In other words, while romantic factors are considered to be more important than the economic factors, the weight of the economic factors is in no case neglictable.

*Table 3.19* Estimates of the unrestricted and restricted model

| | $\log u$ | *coeff.* | *st. dev.* | *p-value* | |
|---|---|---|---|---|---|
| *model 1* | $\log \widehat{\beta_0}$ | 4.46 | 0.09 | <0.0001 | *** |
| | $\log \hat{R}$ | −0.07 | 0.12 | 0.58 | |
| | $\log \hat{E}$ | −0.29 | 0.11 | 0.008 | *** |
| | $R^2$ | | | | 0.88 |
| *restriction* $\beta_1 + \beta_2 = 1$ | | *coeff.* | *st. dev.* | *p-value* | |
| *model 2* | $\log \widehat{\beta_0}$ | 4.04 | 0.08 | 2.75e-171 | *** |
| | $\log \hat{R}$ | 0.67 | 0.09 | 5.81e-014 | *** |
| | $\log \hat{E}$ | 0.33 | 0.09 | 0.0001 | *** |

Source: Author.

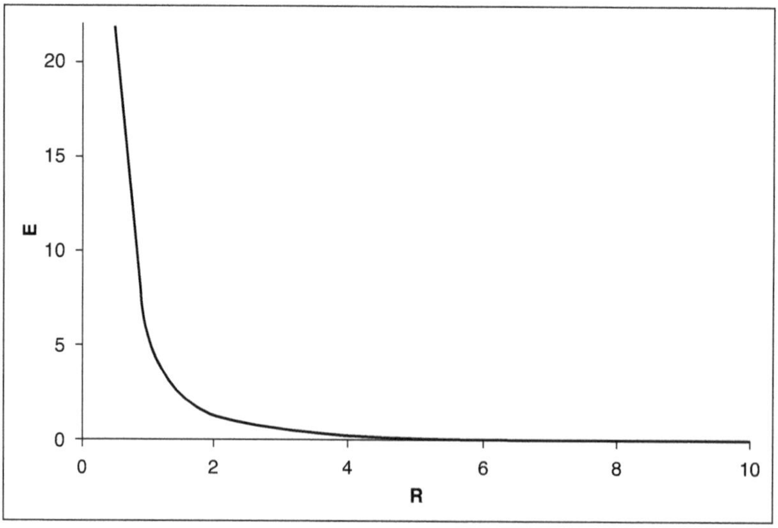


*Figure 3.81* Cobb-Douglas function for the secessionist regions

Source: Author.

## Summary

Secessionist regions report higher levels of human capital, and they put more emphasis on the human capital building than other (non-secessionist) regions. Secessionists follow more often the international media and less often the national media than those who do not support full a secession. The regional media, especially, has very high support.

Religiosity, as well as denomination, differs substantially among secessionist regions and the rest of their country. Moreover, believers identify themselves more often with their region, while people without denomination identify more often with their country. The heterogeneity in the romantic factors measured by the Herfindahl-Hirschman index of language, religion, and ethnicity is considerably higher in secessionist regions. According to the HHI values, the most fragile European countries (in terms of the romantic factors) is Spain and Belgium. However, homogeneous nations are Malta, Portugal, and Greece. The smaller countries are relatively more homogeneous. Cultural homogeneity is, furthermore, connected to better economic results. Thus, by using this approach, the other potentially secessionist region of Navarra in Spain may be identified, though it is not so often discussed.

In the case of a secession, all the potentially new independent countries would be viable on their own in terms of population, territory, GDP, as well as the GDP per capita. Secession would be most painful to Belgium, which would lose more than half of its GDP. Flanders would be at the state of the same economic as well as population size as Denmark. Secessionist tensions and higher economic level are connected to the call for fiscal decentralisation.

Citizens from the secessionist regions are significantly more satisfied with the quality of life as well as the economic situation, and they are more optimistic in terms of the economic perspectives. The economic level of Catalonia, Basque, and Flanders of South Tyrol is pronouncedly higher in comparison to the rest of the countries. The economic level is also an important factor when they decide on the secession votes: the higher the economic level, the greater the support of independence in the referendum would be. The Scottish example shows that the oil prices are closely connected to the secessionist moods; indeed, most of the pro-secessionist respondents feel that the central government has disproportionally high profits from their regional resources.

Most of the respondents are risk averse. A lower aversion can be recognised among the blue-collar workers. Nevertheless, pro-secessionists express higher discount rates when gender is taken into account. Similarly, a lower education level is connected to a higher discount rate, which is fully in line with the general expectation.

## Notes

1 Answer "definitely yes" or "rather yes".
2 These statistics cover only those respondents who answered questions Qi9a (97%), Qi9b (92%), and Qi9c (89%). When the non-answers include the share of the national and the international media, the followers are the same (73%).

3 This was the case, for instance, in the case of the Czech region, "Moravia". The members of the regional secessionist party "Moravane" want to replace the existing regions by the former historical lands of Bohemia, Moravia, and Silesia.
4 Respondents could have chosen more than just one criterium.
5 KU Leuven is ranked as the first best Belgian university, Universiteit Gent, 3rd, and Universiteit Antwerpen, 4th. Similarly, Scottish University of St. Andrew is ranked third among British universities, Universitat de Barcelona is ranked first and, Universitat Pompeau Fabra, second, among Spanish universities.
6 The rest consists of other marginal channels. Moreover, 4.1% of respondents do not follow any news-channel regularly.
7 See Chapter 4, section 4.2.
8 It would be appropriate to compare the secessionist region with the rest of the country *without* that region; however, such data were not available.
9 Nevertheless, this difference is not statistically significant:

$$\chi^2 = 1.16, p - value = 0.282, Cramér's\ V = 0.045.$$

10 The first Scottish Parliament election was run in 1999. In the previous periods, there was the Scottish regional elections based on the *Local Government (Scotland) Act 1973.*
11 U. S. Energy Information Administration.
12 $SNP = 15.2 + 0.13 \times Brent\_Monthly + 2.4 \times Election + \varepsilon$

Then for [Brent_Monthly, Election] = [100; 5] and [50;1] there is (15.2 + 100 × 0.13 + 5 × 2.4) – (15.2 + 50 × 0.13 + 1 × 2.4) = 16.1.
13 Standard deviations of 291 and 6,252 respectively.
14 The difference between both ratios is not significant (p-value of the test is 0.46).
15 Rudyard $\chi^2$ Kipling – *If.*
16 The basic requirements of Analysis of Variance (ANOVA test and Levene test) are not met. Moreover, the hypothesis is not supported by the test:

$$Pearson\ \chi^2 = 2.14, p - value = 0.54, Cramér's\ V = 0.067.$$

17 If the response of "Don't know" was removed; in the case of no change, 47% of respondents would vote for secession; and in the case of income increase by £500, secession would be supported by 56% of respondents (Ibidem).

# 4 Secessionist profile of Flanders and South Tyrol

Studies on secession deal predominantly with only two European regions which run the independence referendum: Scotland and Catalonia. The structure of respondents in our survey allows us to study two regions which are not a focus of media interest: Flanders in Belgium and South Tyrol in Italy. Secessionist tensions in those regions are of a dramatically different quality. While Flanders belongs to typical secessionist regions playing with the idea of full independence, South Tyroleans consider irredentism, which leads to unification with Austria based on historical development. In this section, the "secessionist profile" of both regions is introduced.

## Economic performance of Flanders and South Tyrol

The economic level in Flanders is 5% higher than that in Belgium without Flanders. A deeper difference might be observed between South Tyrol and Italy without South Tyrol since the economic level of South Tyrol is higher by 54.5% in comparison to the rest of Italy (see Figure 4.1).

Considering these differences, it is not unexpected that Flemish members of secessionist parties and movements are very optimistic – 91% of them evaluate the economic condition of their region as good or very good, while the economic conditions in their country is seen as good or very good only by 16% of respondents and, on the level of the EU, 20% of respondents (Figure 4.2).

Most of the respondents are, therefore, very optimistic about the future living standards of the potentially independent and sovereign Flanders (93% of respondents expect a potential increase in the economic level), and three-quarters expect a potential increase in the economic level of their family. However, 50% of respondents expect a decrease in the living standards of the rest of the former country (Figure 4.3).

Regarding the wide gap between the region and the rest of the country in Belgium-Flanders and Italy-South Tyrol, we could expect an even more pronounced difference between economic evaluation of their region in comparison

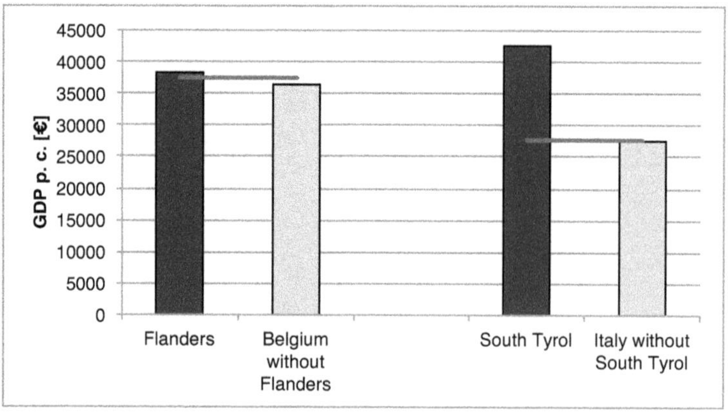


*Figure 4.1* Comparison of the economic level in the Flanders/South Tyrol and rest of Belgium/Italy

Source: Eurostat. Own calculation.

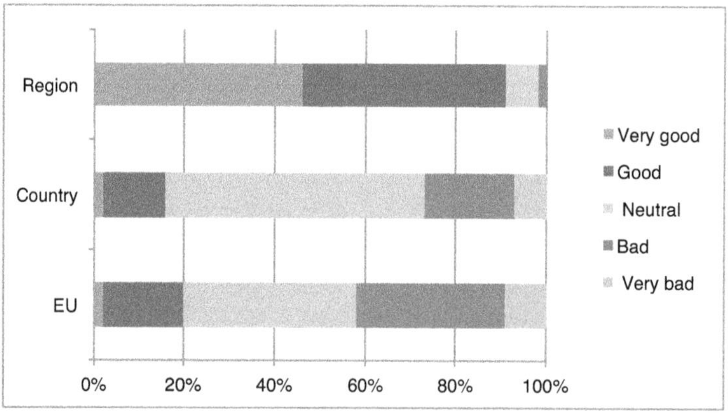


*Figure 4.2* How do you assess the current economic situation in Flanders, Belgium, and EU?

Source: SAPIM. Own calculation.

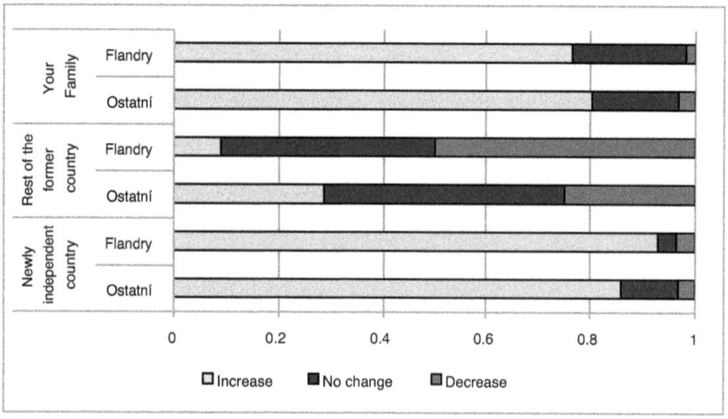


*Figure 4.3* In the case of your region's independence, how would the living standards of your family, newly independent Flanders, and rest of the former Belgium be changed?

Source: SAPIM. Own calculation.

to the country. That is, 88% of respondents from South Tyrol assess the economic level of their region as good or very good, while 16% are equally optimistic of their country, and 37% on the EU (Figure 4.4).

The improvement in the living condition of independent South Tyrol is expected by 88% of the respondents. Meanwhile, 83% of respondents expect an increase in the living standards of their family, but only one quarter expect an increase in the rest of the former country (Figure 4.5).

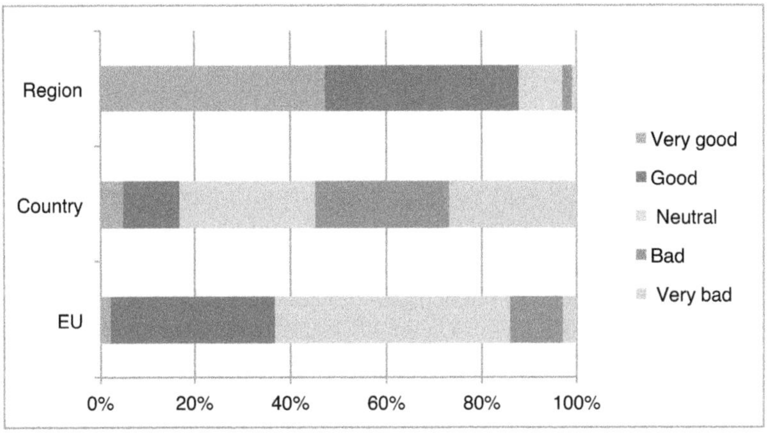


*Figure 4.4* How do you assess the current economic situation in South Tyrol, Italy, and EU?
Source: SAPIM. Own calculation.

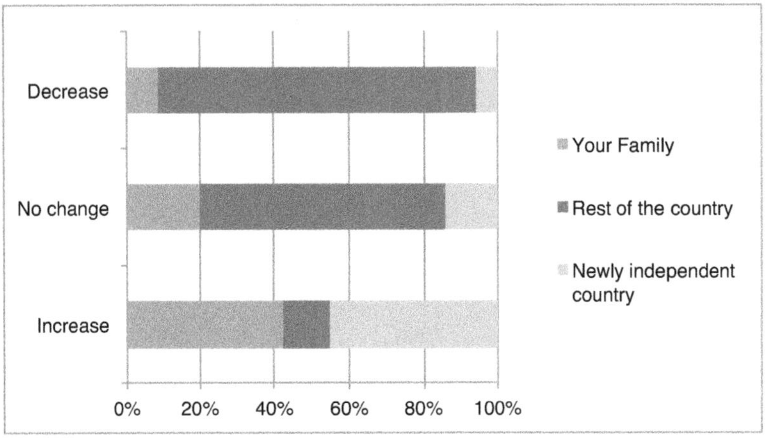


*Figure 4.5* In the case of your region's independence, how would the living standards of your family, newly independent South Tyrol, and rest of the former Italy be changed?
Source: SAPIM. Own calculation.

Considerable differences between real economic conditions and respondents' expectations might be explained by the milder difference in the economic level of Flanders and the rest of Belgium in comparison to the significant difference between South Tyrol and Italy.

## 4.1 Flanders

Belgium has its modern roots in 1789 after the Brabantine revolution. The Congress of Vienna resulted in the formation of the United Kingdom of the Netherlands (located in the territory of today's Benelux). In 1830, Belgium was re-established (Sklenářová 2011). Belgium has lacked, from its very beginning, the *national genius* (Vos 2002), which led to the emergence of the pro-secessionist Flemish movement based on romantic nationalism (Ibidem).

The Flemish region is, together with Scotland and Catalonia, considered to be one of the crucial secessionist regions in modern Europe. The main autonomist force, N-VA, is growing and reaching greater election success since it gradually replaced the then-leader of the secessionist wing, Flemish Block (Vlaams Block). Federal election success of NV-A in 2007 can be explained by its coalition with CD&V (Christen-Democratisch en Vlaams; a traditional Christian democratic political party which has been in 4 out of 6 governments during the 1995–2019 period).

Maddens mentions that Flemish autonomist parties were successful in the interwar period, falling rapidly after the Second World War as they were suspect in collaborating with German occupiers (Maddens 2017:55). In the 21st century, there might be observed the so-called *Flemish Paradox*. According to the results of the IPSO survey from 2014, the separatist parties in Flanders receive nearly 40% of votes although only 6.4% of voters claimed to be separatists (Maddens 2017:56).

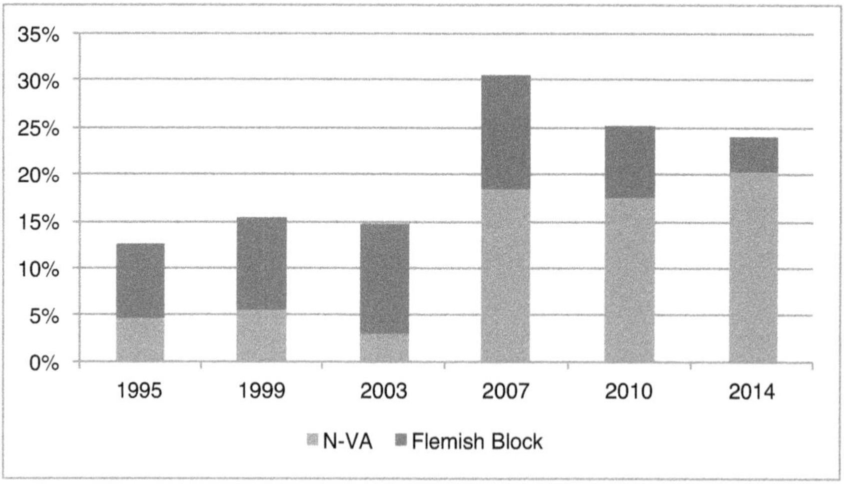


*Figure 4.6* Federal election: results of Flemish secessionist movements in 1995–2014

Source: IBZ (2019). Own calculation.

In the 2018 local election, the Flemish nationalist parties succeeded significantly: N-VA won the election in Antwerp, East Flanders, Flemish Brabant, and run second in Limburg and West Flanders. Together with the second biggest autonomist party, Vlaams Belang, they received 38% of the votes.

Respondents from Flanders are significantly more often for secession than respondents from other regions: 91% of them called for the independence of Flanders as a separate sovereign state (Figure 4.8).

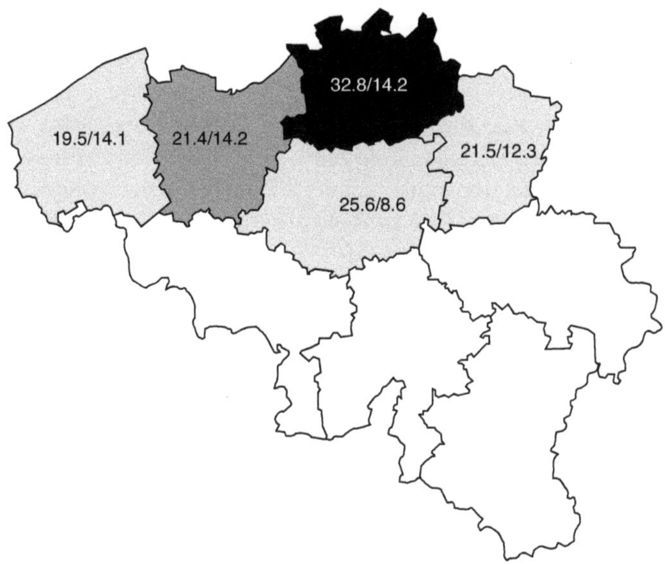


*Figure 4.7* Local election 2018 – results of the Flemish nationalist parties

Source: IBZ (2019). Own calculation

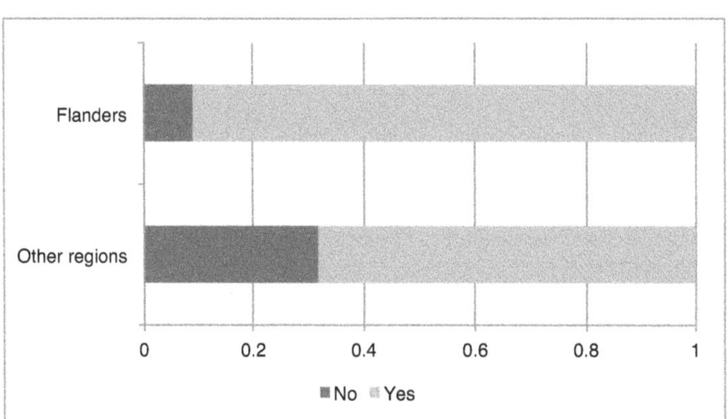


*Figure 4.8* Support for secession in Flanders in comparison to other regions

Source: SAPIM. Own calculation.

*Pearson* $\chi^2 = 12.65$, *p-value* = 0.0004, *Cramér's V* = 0.147

Flemish members of the autonomist parties are also significantly, more often than others, in favour of the emergence of the new sovereign state (91% of them; Figure 4.9). However, none of the respondents considers secessionist rhetoric as a threat to the central government in Brussels. This is consistent with Flemish's greater degree of satisfaction with the central government (see further).

Path-dependency is playing a significant role as well. While most of the secessionists (92%) in other regions call for a republic in a state system regarding the newly independent state, 100% of the respondents want Flanders to remain a monarchy. However, the Flemish are consistent with the rest of the respondents regarding the opinion on the membership of a newly independent country in the EU. That is, 72% of the Flemish, as well as 75% of the other respondents, want to remain in the EU. Nevertheless, 60% of the Flemish respondents would vote for the exit of modern Belgium from the EU in comparison with 46% of pro-secessionist respondents from other regions (Figure 4.10). According to the results of Eurobarometer, citizens of Flanders tend to trust the EU significantly more often than citizens of the rest of Belgium (70.1% in comparison of 64% of citizens in Brussels and 50% in Wallonia).

Flemish pro-independence citizens trust the regional government significantly. Nevertheless, their national government in Brussels also has a higher degree of Flemish confidence in comparison to the respondents from other regions. The explanation is straightforward: during the survey (summer 2018), the Flemish pro-independence party N-VA (Nieuw-Vlaamse Alliantie) was, for nearly four years, the largest party in the Belgium federal government. Its ministers held interior,

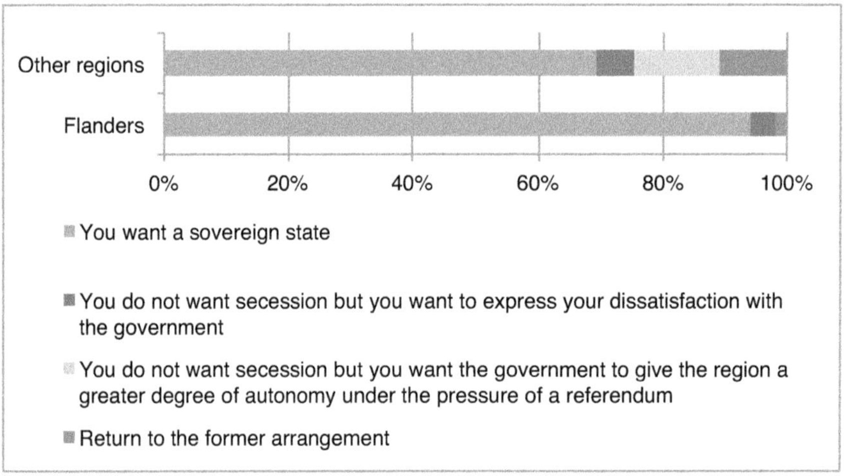


*Figure 4.9* Type of disintegration required

Source: SAPIM. Own calculation.

*Pearson* $\chi^2 = 15.86$, *p-value* $= 0.0012$, *Cramér's V* $= 0.169$.

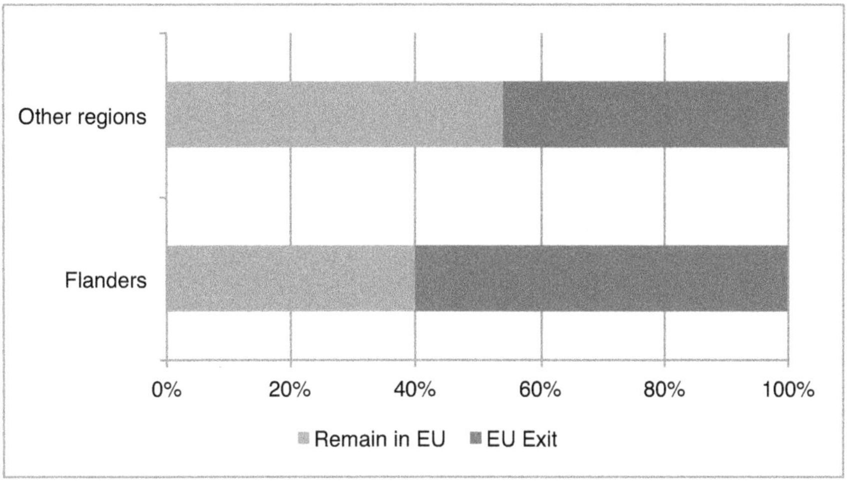


*Figure 4.10* Attitudes toward the EU exit

Source: SAPIM. Own calculation. P-value = 0.07.

immigration, and finance ministries. However, because of the disagreement on the United Nations migration pact, the N-VA left the government in December 2018 (Brunsden and Peel 2018).

According to Eurobarometer 472 data, Flemish citizens also trust the Belgian government significantly more (69%) even in comparison to other Belgians (46%). They are more optimistic regarding the future of their region than the people of Brussels (68%) or the Wallonians (47%) since 72% of the Flemish citizens are *very* or at least *rather optimistic*.

However, Flemish pro-independence party members trust significantly less in the European Parliament and Commission than their European counterparts (see Figure 4.11).

This lukewarm approach to EU institutions is further proven in the Flemish assessment of economic conditions in their region, Belgium as a whole, and in the EU. Flemish respondents consider the situation in their region as significantly better than respondents from other pro-independence regions (91% in comparison to 75% of others), which is also consistent with the Eurobarometer 472 data (Figure 4.12). Similarly, they consider the situation in the entire country as significantly worse than others (just 16% are satisfied with it in comparison to 26% of other respondents). Nevertheless, they are, also, considerably less satisfied with the economic level of the EU. While more than one-third of other respondents asses it as good or very good, in Flanders, share such optimism is only shared by one-fifth of the respondents (Figure 4.13).

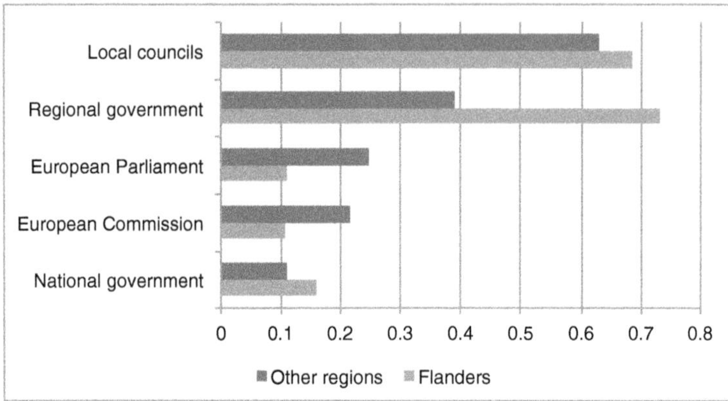


*Figure 4.11* Trust in the institutions in Flanders in comparison to other EU regions
Source: SAPIM. Own calculation.

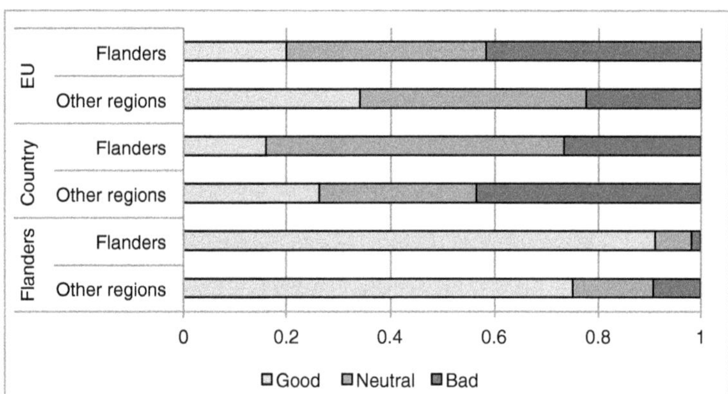


*Figure 4.12* Assessment of the economic situation in the region, country, and EU
Source: SAPIM. Own calculation.

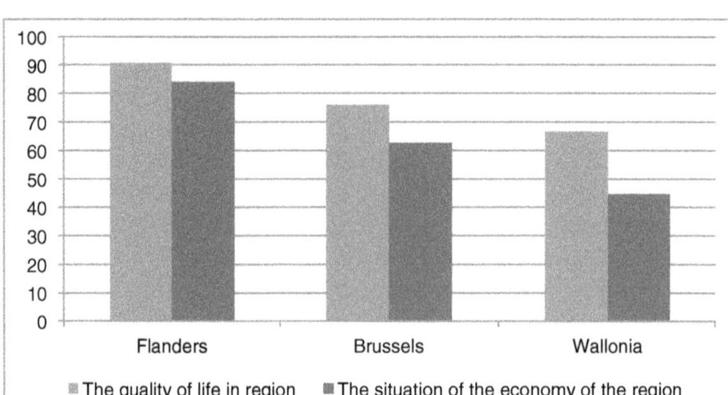


*Figure 4.13* The ratio of citizens who judge the quality of life in their region and the situation of their regional economy as very good or rather good
Source: Eurobarometer 472. Own calculation.

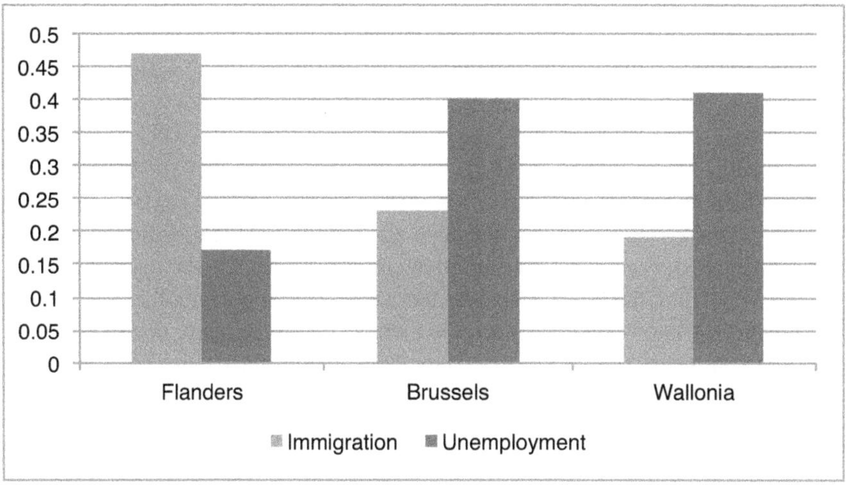


*Figure 4.14* "What do you think are the two most important issues facing our region at the moment?"

Source: Eurobarometer 472. Own calculation.

Different economic conditions are further confirmed by the answers to the question from Eurobarometer 472: "What do you think are the two most important issues facing (OUR REGION) at the moment?" While 47% of the Flemish consider immigration as the biggest problem, for 40% of other Belgians, the most serious problem is unemployment (Figure 4.14).

Such cautious attitudes toward the EU are, however, not supported by the Flemish opinion on EU membership, which they share with all other respondents. Geographical as well as historical matters influence the relationship with the EU. The Flemish are proud of the role Belgium plays in the world politic (De Wilde 2014). However, after the economic crisis in 2009, the N-VA "has gradually shifted from a pro-European to a Eurorealistic stance" (Maddens 2017:59).

Pro-secessionist party members in Flanders reached a higher education level than respondents from other regions; 57% of Flemish respondents are university graduates (in comparison to merely a quarter of others), and all of them are white-collar workers. Most of the respondents (96.4%) speak Dutch as the mother tongue, three-quarters used it at school, and 73% at work.

The linguistic frontline divides Belgium into French-speaking Walloons and Dutch-speaking Flemish, as well as bilingual Brussels and a small a German-speaking community (consisting of merely 70,000 inhabitants; Deprez and Vos 2016:18). The roots of Dutch as the first language were not straightforward in Flanders. Flemish elites adopted Dutch, especially, in the *Gouden Eeuw* (Dutch Golden Age) in the 17th and 18th century. However, after the Belgian independence, the Flemish started to speak French. The Dutch language was then kept just outside the frame of formal education, which led to its deformation into *Flemish* as the local dialect (Kemezis 1974) used at elementary schools, town halls of small municipalities, and lower courts (Vos 2002). The constitutional reform in 1970 led to a federalisation of Belgium connected to the education reform, which resulted in a creation of three autonomous educational systems: the Flemish system covering 58% of pupils and students, the French system covering other 41%, and, finally, the German system taking care of the remaining 1% (Hörner et al. 2007:105).

The Flemish read the national press more often than the regional press. This difference is also statistically significant in comparison to readers from other secessionist regions in Europe, as they are much more interested in the regional media. It is also related to the lower Flemish interest in international media.

Though Belgium is a federal state, the Flemish call for a higher degree of autonomy, even in the sharing of powers. They want, significantly more often than others, a decentralisation of social policy, health care, taxation, and education. That is,

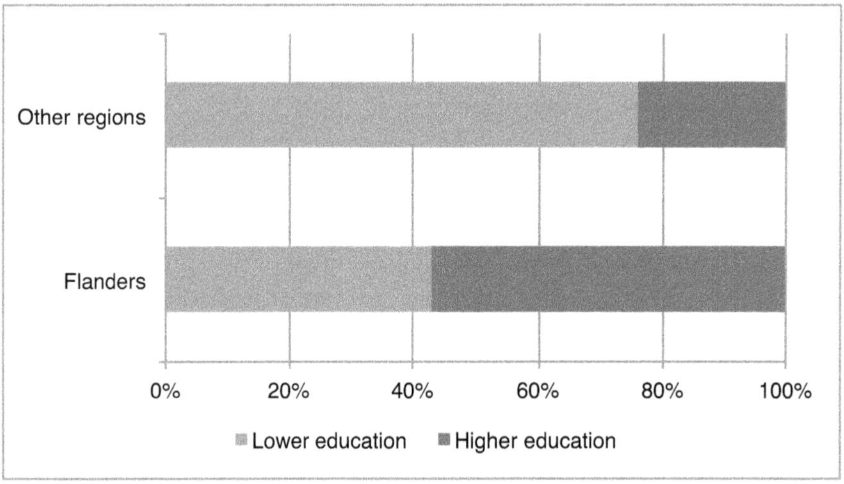


*Figure 4.15* Education structure of the secessionist parties' members in Flanders in comparison to other EU regions

Source: SAPIM. Own calculation.

*Pearson* $\chi^2 = 28.89$, *p-value* = 0.0000, *Cramér's V* = 0.221

*Table 4.1* Results of the $\chi^2$ test

| | *Pearson* $\chi^2$ | *Cramér's V* | $p - value$ |
|---|---|---|---|
| Regional media | 15.06 | 0.165 | 0.0018 |
| National media | 9.07 | 0.132 | 0.028 |
| International media | 152.86 | 0.554 | 0.000 |

Source: SAPIM. Own calculation.

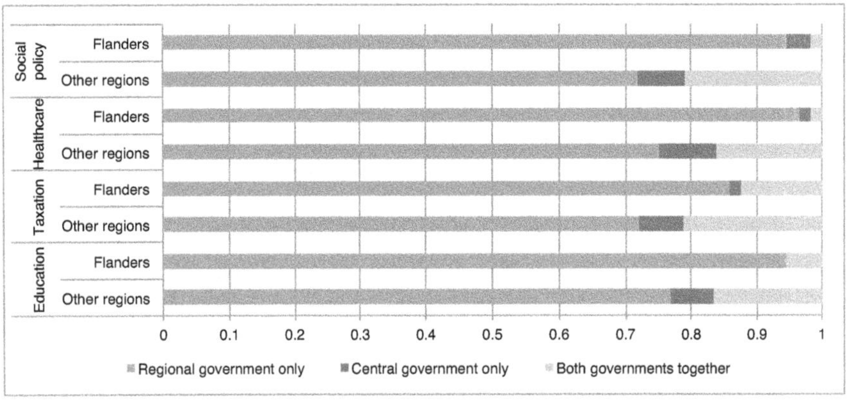


*Figure 4.16* If Flanders were to remain part of the current state, how should the following powers be shared between the central government and the regional government? Comparison with respondents from other secessionist regions

Source: SAPIM. Own calculation.

*Table 4.2* Results of $\chi^2$ test

| | *Pearson* $\chi^2$ | *Cramér's V* | *p-value* |
|---|---|---|---|
| Education | 9.74 | 0.133 | 0.0077 |
| Taxation | 5.22 | 0.098 | 0.073 |
| Healthcare | 13.10 | 0.154 | 0.00143 |
| Foreign Affairs | 3.13 | 0.0759 | 0.208 |
| Safety | 1.62 | 0.0544 | 0.444 |
| European policy | 1.67 | 0.0553 | 0.433 |
| Social policy | 14.25 | 0.1617 | 0.0008 |

Source: SAPIM. Own calculation.

these should be exclusively in the hands of the regional government (Figure 4.16). Nevertheless, their opinion of sharing the executive power does not differ from other respondents in the field of foreign affairs, safety, and European policy (Table 4.2).

## 4.2 South Tyrol

The Tyroleans live in the federal state of Tyrol in Austria (*Bundesland Tirol*), the Italian German-speaking region of South Tyrol, as well as the Italian-speaking region of Trentino (Minahan 2016). It was declared independent in 1919. Nevertheless, this independent movement was suppressed when the *Treaty of Saint-German* was signed, and the so-called Brenner Pass was established. During the 1920s, the region *Südtirol* suffered the aggressive policy of Italianisation of the Germans who were, even, forced to change their surnames (Pföstl ND:2). After the Second World War, new borders of the region were drawn; thus, it was not purely German (ibidem).

Respondents from South Tyrol strongly differ from all other respondents in their mother language. While, for nearly 86% of respondents from other regions, their mother tongue is also the official language of their country, for 98.3% of South Tyrolean respondents, their mother tongue is not Italian (Figure 4.17). It was implicitly confirmed even by the language they choose when answering the questionnaire, as 294 respondents chose German and only six chose Italian (the rest of them, three respondents, answered in English).

While most of the respondents speak German as their mother tongue, in schools, 64% of them used Italian and half of them (52.8%) German. Finally, at work, both languages (German and Italian) are used equally (Figure 4.18).

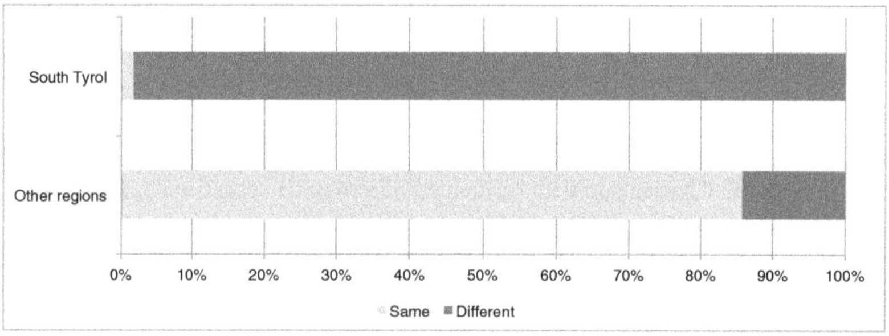


*Figure 4.17* Do the respondents have same mother language as the citizens from the rest of the country?

Source: SAPIM. Own calculation.

*Pearson* $\chi^2 = 401.03$, *p-value* = 0.0000, *Cramér's V* = 0.649

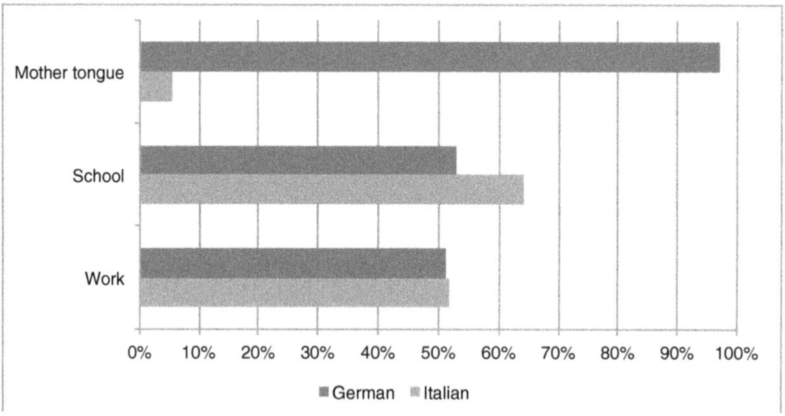


*Figure 4.18* Usage of German and Italian language in different situations among the citizens of the South Tyrolean region

Source: SAPIM. Own calculation.

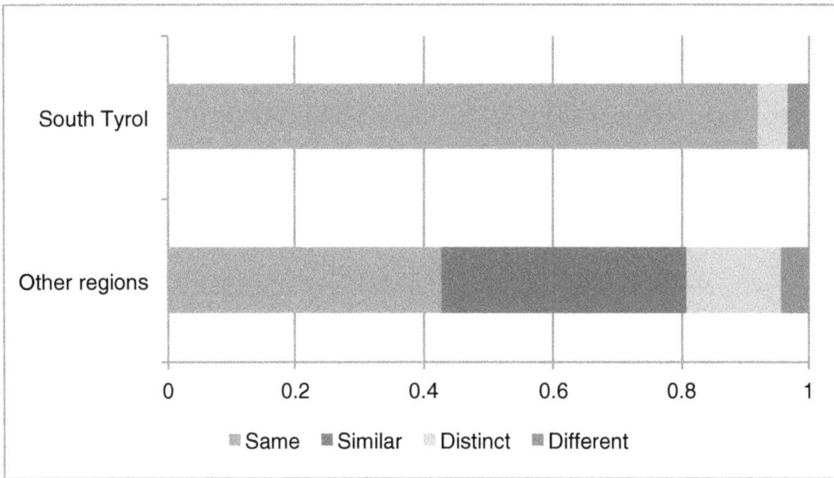


*Figure 4.19* Homogeneity on the confession among the respondents from the South Tyrol in comparison to the respondents from other EU regions

Source: SAPIM. Own calculation.

*Pearson* $\chi^2 = 166.89$, *p-value* = 0.0000, *Cramér's* $V = 0.564$

One-third of South Tyrolean respondents used both languages at work simultaneously. Similarly, 46% of respondents use both languages simultaneously at school.

Most of the South Tyrolean respondents are of a Catholic confession (85%), which results in untypically high degree of homogeneity with the rest of the country. While only 43% of respondents confess the same religion as their mother country in other regions, in South Tyrol, the denomination is the same in 92% of cases. What is more, there is a higher degree of religious similarity with Italy than with Austria, where Catholicism is confessed by approximately 66% of citizens (compare Eurobarometer 83.4).

South Tyrolean respondents follow the regional and international media significantly more (and national media significantly less) than respondents from other secessionist regions (Figure 4.20). The international media is followed by 93% of respondents in South Tyrol in comparison to about two-thirds of respondents in other regions. On the contrary, about 28% of Tyroleans do not follow the Italian media.

None of the respondents would like the newly independent state to be a monarchy. This shows that path-dependency is not absolute: South Tyrol used to be a county and, later, a crown land of Austria-Hungary. However, the newly

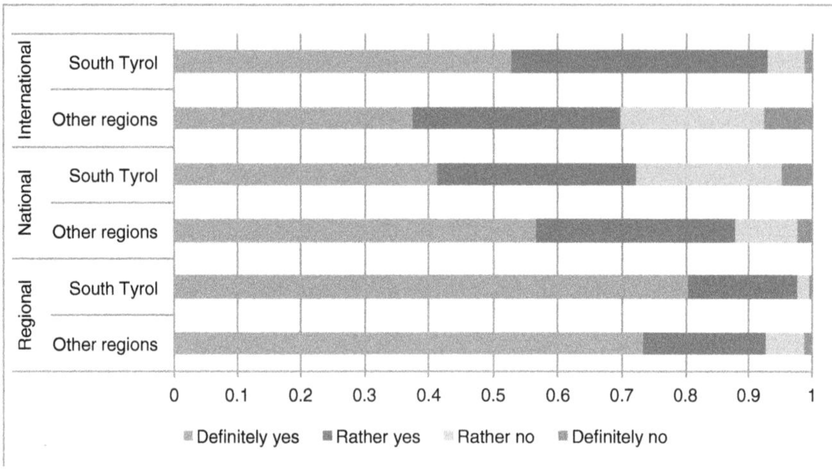


*Figure 4.20* Which media do you use?

Source: SAPIM. Own calculation.

*Table 4.3* Results of $\chi^2$ test

| | *Pearson Chi-square* | *Cramér's V* | *p-value* |
|---|---|---|---|
| Regional | 8.57 | 0.12 | 0.035 |
| National | 21.99 | 0.21 | 0.00007 |
| International | 47.58 | 0.31 | 0.0000 |

Source: SAPIM. Own calculation.

independent state is proposed to be a *Republik Süd Tirol* or *Bundesrepublik Tirol* (Minahan 2016:436).

When asked why they would vote for independence of their region, South Tyrolean respondents did not explain their preferences by their desire to have a sovereign state, expressing dissatisfaction with central government in Roma, or pressure on the government to receive a greater degree of autonomy as often as respondents of other regions. According to their answers, their main goal is the reunification (*Wiedervereinigung*) with Austria as shown in Table 4.4.

*Table 4.4* Why would the South Tyrolean vote for independence of their region?

| | |
|---|---|
| Reunification with Austria | Reunification of Tyrol and Austria. |
| | Reincorporation into Austria. |
| | Back to Austria. |
| | Back to the Austrian Fatherland/Back to the Austrian Motherland. |
| | *Anschluss* to Austrian Fatherland. |
| | Return to Austria. |
| Reunification of Tyrol | Reunification of Tyrol. |
| | The secession of South Tyrol of Italy and the reunification with North and East Tyrol in the state of Austria. |
| | So that the homeland (North, South, and East Tyrol) meets again. |
| Remedy of historical injustice | South Tyrol is not Italy; South Tyrol has always been German. The Treaties of St. Germain are against international law. |
| | Freedom for South Tyrol; we belong to Italy; we are not Italians, but we are treated like that! South Tyrol is suppressed, and if you follow the story, then you would know how horrible. |
| | It is wrong that we are in Italy. |
| | We, the South Tyroleans, have voluntarily been part of Austria since 1363. The injustice of the annexation of South Tyrol carried out in 1920 by the irredentist-led Aggressor and Alliance breaker, Italy, can (against the will of the Tyrolean people) never be tolerated. We are and will remain part of Tyrol. We will stand up for the unification of Tyrol and fight with democratic means. Our goal can only be the self-determination and separation from a state with which we have NOTHING, culturally, to do with; neither language nor customs or traditions. |
| | We belong to this state by injustice, and we do not identify with it. |
| Culture | Return from South Tyrol to the German Culture and Speech Community. |
| | My region has a different culture than my state. |

Source: SAPIM. Own calculation.

# Conclusion

Heterogeneity of preferences leads to various types of conflicts. One of the most pronounced in modern Europe is the secessionist tension leading to disintegration under the umbrella of the European integration. A view of the map of European secessionist regions reminds us of Europe on the eve of the Vienna Congress.

It is not the task of economic science to formulate a normative thesis on the justness, rightness, or even correctness of the secession, nor to discuss the right to self-determination. However, the Political Economy of Conflict can help identify the roots and consequences of secessionist tensions and estimate the role of economic (rational) as well as romantic (emotional) factors.

In the first part of this thesis, we define secession as the permanent and intentional separation of existing state territories and its citizens to found an independent sovereign state all kinds of separatism, dissolution, and irredentism.

Secession might take on both forms of conflicts: armed as well as unarmed. Armed conflicts emerge if property rights are not recognised and (or) accepted. We have shown that the most effective solution is the bargain between the secessionist region and the central government based on territorial rights.[1] Such bargaining reflects the real value that independence has for the secessionists as well as the real value the indivisibility of the state has for the centralists. However, armed conflicts harm the whole land, regardless of whether it is won by secessionists or by the central power. That is why secessionists' conflicts in previously annexed lands (such as the Baltic countries in the 20th century) are usually solved with lower costs and with international agreement. Such bargaining agreements may be illustrated by the secessionist negotiations of Slovenia, which promised in 1991 to pay $1.4 billion of Yugoslavia's debt as well as its share of the army's costs (Bohlen 1991, compare Mrak and Arhar 2004 who discuss allocation of the debt after the break-up of the Yugoslavia), or by the historical examples from the Czech lands as mentioned in the first chapter.

Unarmed secessionist conflicts are nowadays much more common. They are based on the homogeneity of preferences within the group of citizens living on the certain territory and heterogeneity of their preferences as regarded to the rest of the country. Such set of preferences resemble the country with the secessionist regions to the glass with oil and water: it is possible to create emulsion using either significant power, or the stabilizers, however, such mixture hardly ever has the static internal structure.

The aim of this thesis was to examine secession as the conflict, which has its roots in the heterogeneity of preferences.

The first objective – identification of the causes of the secessionist processes – was fulfilled in the first chapter, where the individual romantic and economic factors were. Romantic factors are connected to the romantic nationalism, they are non-pecuniary and contribute to the creation of the human group identity. Ethnicity, language and religion as the traditional romantic factors can be extended by culture as the institutional factor and the effect of education. *Ethnicity* is closely connected to the nation and nationality, state, and its citizens; it consists of the psychological, national, territorial, political, and historical elements. *Language* is an important part of the human capital; it plays role even in the international negotiations on the emergence of the new state. Finally, it is also closely connected to the education. Higher degree of human capital can both support as well as absorb the secessionist tensions, moreover, it were the teachers, who headed for the secessionist leaders. *Religion* is considered to be an important unifying element within the secessionist communities, which also draws the sharp line between the secessionist group and rest of the country. Finally, *culture* builds the national identity; it is connected to the self-recognisation of the secessionists as it covers the cultural heritage which connect the current region which its history.

The implicit barriers of romantic factors persists even after the dismantling the barriers of trade as the trans-border shift of goods and services in the custom unions shows.

Economic factors are more easily measurable in comparison to the romantic factors. For the aim of our research they could be divided to the macroeconomic (economic level, scarce resources, fiscal and monetary policy, and economic integration) and microeconomic (risk attitude as well as discount rate).

The *economic level* in terms of the gross domestic product per capita can be pro-secessionist as well as anti-secessionist factor. Among the secessionist regions there are extremely wealthy as well as very poor. Secessionist forces might appear due to the growth of economic inequality which can be result even of rapid economic development. On the contrary, the economically strong regions rich in raw materials might seek for the disintegration because of the feeling of relative deprivation.

The *scarce resources* are geographically conditioned, the greed and grievance problem is therefore closely connected to the property ownership and the recognition of the territorial claims. In the recent European Union, the only pro-secessionist scarce resource is the oil and the natural gas in the North Sea. It has been playing distinguish role in the discussion of the Scottish secession at the least since the "It's Scotland's Oil" campaign: the Scottish National Party increased its gain in the election by nearly 25 p. p. after the discovery of oil, nevertheless, such correlation does not per se imply causality.

*Fiscal policy* might mitigate as well as accelerate the secessionist tensions. Fiscal decentralism can result into the effective provision of more public goods because of the increase in preference homogeneity. On the other hand, claims for the secession might be just the instrument how to receive higher degree of fiscal autonomy (so-called vanity secession, where an interest group blackmails the government with the threat of secession to gain an economic profit e. g. in terms of gaining better taxation conditions. Fiscal decentralisation might also give more power to the local government. For instance, the tax autonomy provides the region with a potential instrument for financing future real secessions. However, the fiscal autonomy can also result in fiscal profligacy when the regions' expenditures increase because of soft budget constraints.

Political disintegration might be fuelled by the *economic integration* as the costs of the secession are higher in the case of new trade barriers, which lead to smaller inner markets. The optimal country size under the umbrella of transnational integration can be therefore smaller. The small countries might have also an advantage in the integrated world because the division of labour enable the state to focus on the very narrow niche. Actually, the smallest states (with population less than three million) have the highest concentration and diversification index.

Microeconomic factors cover the *risk attitude* and discount rate. Economic subjects are thought to be risk averse, because the secession leads to a significant change in the status quo. *Discount rates* reflect the time preferences of economic subjects which also includes one's ability to defer immediate pleasure in exchange for higher future profit. The secessionists are therefore expected to have a lower discount rate as they are more patient and can endure discomfort.

To meet the second objective (determination of the individual factor's importance for the citizens of the secessionist regions in the European Union) the hypotheses on the romantic and economic factors of secession were testes using the original data. The unique *Survey on autonomist and pro-independence movements* (SAPIM) was conducted in co-operation with the European Free Alliance (EFA) among the members of 34 secessionist parties and movements in 17 European countries. This survey, however, covers only the respondents who actively declare themselves as the pro-independence supporters. The SAPIM unfortunately does not include *the other citizens* – those who are not organised in the pro-independence movements; those who are actually against the disintegration; or those who are completely neutral towards the secessionist questions. To cover also these groups of citizens, the additional data sources (especially Eurobarometer, Atlas of European Values, Norwegian Centre for Research Data, or OECD) were used. Furthermore, the hypothesis connected to the linguistic factors and the risk attitudes were tested using Google Trends data. This dataset enabled researchers to follow the real preferences of citizens searching the key words in various (including local) languages in the specific time and place. Google Trends data hide considerable untapped potential for the further research on the preferences in the secessionist regions.

As for the methods, standard descriptive statistics were used to describe the data. Furthermore, the standard non-parametric Chi-squared test, t-test, Analysis of Variance, and linear regression were used. Heterogeneity of preferences was approximated by the Herfindahl-Hirschman Index. The special relationship between the homogeneity within the group and heterogeneity inter the groups of citizens, the cluster analysis is exceptionally useful. To estimate the significance of the romantic respectively economic factors in the decision-making on the secession, the Cobb-Douglas function was estimated using the Factor Analysis.

Our research confirms that the secession is influenced not only by romantic nationalism but also by a rational economic way of thinking. Heterogeneity in those economic factors can also be mitigated using fiscal decentralisation, higher tax autonomy, as well as better property rights recognition. It is of vital importance to admit that the romantic and economic factors are closely interconnected. For example, the religion is considered to be the romantic factor. Nevertheless, in the spirit of the Max Weber's theory, it might have considerable economic impact. Similarly, the scarce resources might be looked at as the economic factor, but the emotion connected to the alleged greed and grievance can turn it into the romantic factor.

On the end of the first chapter, eight hypotheses on the romantic and 11 on the economic factors were postulated. In this part, we summarise the main findings. We have found the linguistic frontline between certain secessionist regions and rests of their countries. The linguistic frontline divides Belgium into French-speaking Walloons and Dutch-speaking Flemish. Similarly, for 98.3% of South Tyrolean respondents, their mother tongue is not Italian, which was implicitly confirmed even by the language they choose when answering the questionnaire: most of the respondents chose German.

The media selection declares linguistic preferences in regions: supporters of the full independence of their region does not follow the national media so often as those who want just some degree of decentralisation. Furthermore, the international media is followed by 93% of respondents in South Tyrol in comparison to about two thirds of respondents in other regions, which is influenced by the role of Austrian media in the region. We have found, that according to the cluster analysis, the most fragile countries with respect to cultural heterogeneity represented by religion and language are those which have secessionist regions. The lower heterogeneity in terms of cultural as well as political preferences is connected to the higher economic level. Results from Catalonia also confirm, that secessionists feel closer to their region than to the country as whole: 16 p. p. less Catalans in comparison to the rest of Spain feel "close or very close" to their country.

Importance of the path dependency is seen especially in the attitudes towards the institutions. While most of the secessionists (92%) in other regions call for a republic in a state system regarding the newly independent state, 100% of the respondents want Flanders to remain a monarchy. Furthermore, respondents from the South Tyrol do not require separation, but the reunification (Wiedervereinigung) with Austria.

Even religion is connected to the secessionism: the respondents whose denomination differed most from the rest of the country identified themselves only with their region more often than those whose denomination is very similar or the same, Structure of denomination differs significantly, especially in Spain, with the greatest degree of heterogeneity in the Basque Country and Catalonia. Furthermore, believers tend to be more pro-secessionist than unbelievers and they identify themselves significantly more with their region while those who declare no denomination identify more often only with their country.

Secessionist tendencies are clearly connected to the heterogeneity in political opinions. For example, the analysis of European Value Studies data confirms a significant heterogeneity in political preferences with Spain. Secessionist parties in Spain frequently present themselves as left-wing. While 44% of respondents from other regions claim they identify themselves with their region, and another 44% claim they identify with their region more than with their country, 74% of South Tyrolean identify exclusively with their region and none of the respondents identify only with Italy. Voters from secessionist regions also tend to trust in the regional representatives more than in the national representatives; the difference (12.9 p. p.) is nearly 4.5 times higher than in the case of the non-secessionist regions (2.3 p. p.).

As for the economic factors, the relationship between the secessionism and economic condition of the region as well as of the rest of the country was revealed. A high living standard is more important factor for respondents, who otherwise expect an improvement in living conditions in the case of a secession. If there were no change in the personal economic level, 44% of respondents would vote against the independence, while 47% of respondents would vote for the independence if there would be an increase in income. The economic level in Flanders is 5% higher than that in Belgium without Flanders. A deeper difference might be observed between South Tyrol and Italy without South Tyrol since the economic level of South Tyrol is higher by 54.5% in comparison to the rest of Italy. Most of the respondents are very optimistic about the future living standards of the potentially independent and sovereign Flanders: 93% of respondents expect a potential increase in the economic level, and three-quarters expect a potential increase in the economic level of their family. However, 50% of respondents expect a decrease in the living standards of the rest of the former country. Flemish members of secessionist parties and movements are very optimistic: 91% of them evaluate the economic condition of their region as good or very good, while the economic conditions in their country is seen as good or very good only by 16% of respondents. On the other hand, among the respondents, there cannot be observed any relationship between an economic crisis and support for secession.

With the exception of Scotland, the scarce resources are not a key topic for the secessionists as the regions are not rich in special resources. Nevertheless, as for Scotland, there is a statistically significant correlation between the price of oil and the electoral support of the Scottish National Party in 1964–2019. If crude oil prices increase to 100 USD per barrel, then the Scottish National party could receive 16.15 percentage points more votes in the election to the Scottish Parliament in comparison to the General election if the prices fall to 50 USD per barrel. In general, if respondents expect an increase in the living standard in an independent region after the secession, they significantly more often feel exploited of their scarce regional resources (85% of respondents in comparison to 61% of respondents who expect a potential decrease in the living standard after potential independence). Pro-secessionists also agree with the statement that the "Central government has disproportionally high profits from the regional resources" significantly more often than members of pro-independence parties who do not call for secession (84% vs. 76%). Most of the respondents who blame the central government of greed (in the matter of the regional scarce resources) also claim that they could decide on public expenditures better on the national level than the central government (95% in comparison to 67% of those who disagree with the "Greed and Grievance" thesis), which is closely connected to the fact that more than 80% of respondents agree that the central government has disproportionally high profits from their resources (including oil and raw materials). Those who feel the scarce resources exploitation from the central government are also dissatisfied with the fiscal flows between the central government and the region. That is, 94% of them believe that regional tax contributions to the central budget are higher than the amounts they receive back (in comparison to 70% of those who do not feel any exploitation).

While opinions on the monetary policy were not experienced, the fiscal policy plays a dominant role in the secessionist decision-making. Respondents who support the secession of their region significantly more often call for exclusive responsibility of their regional governments in the case of tax policy (81% of secessionists in comparison to 56% of non-secessionists). Significantly higher support for the tax policy decentralisation can be observed among respondents who do not trust the central government; higher support for fiscal decentralisation can be observed especially among people who are dissatisfied with the economic situation in their country. Finally, the more respondents are persuaded of the good condition of their region (as compared to the rest of the country), the more they will support decentralisation in fiscal matters, which is completely in line with the theoretical assumptions. Moreover, nearly nine from ten respondents think that their tax contributions to the central budget are higher than amounts their region receives back. The same proportion thinks that, at the national level, they could decide on public expenditures better than the central government decides. Those respondents would also be willing to pay a higher "secessionist tax" (on average €465 in purchasing power standard (PPS) in comparison to merely €163 in PPS by those who do not feel any exploitation).

Economic integration seems to be a less pronounced factor. Although the average trust in the EU is higher in the secessionist region in comparison to the non-secessionist region, this difference of 1.7 p. p. is not statistically significant. Furthermore, citizens living in the secessionist regions do not trust in the EU representatives more than other citizens. Actually, the trust in the European Commission in such regions is nearly three times lower than their trust in the regional representatives.

Importance of the microeconomic factors was not proved at all. The willingness to take part in a lottery is nearly the same among secessionists (66%) as well as those who do not want the secession (69%). On average, respondents are pronouncedly risk averse. There is no significant dependence between risk attitude and willingness to vote for secession. Similarly, while the average discount rate of pro-secessionists is lower (137.3% to 193.5%), this difference is nevertheless not statistically significant.

Finally, the importance of the educational infrastructure was proved. A higher educational infrastructure does not influence the support of secession. Neither the pro-secessionists nor the anti-secessionists find the existence of a "sufficient amount of universities in the region" as the crucial factor which would move them to support the secession.

Subchapter 3.4 was devoted to the two objective as it presents estimates of the contribution of the romantic and economic factors to their secessionist utility function. Estimates of the Cobb-Douglas function show that while romantic factors are considered to be more important than the economic factors, the weight of the economic factors is in no case negligible: they stay for one-third of the utility from secession according to the *Survey on autonomist and pro-independence movements* respondents.

We have seen that secession as the conflict has its roots in the heterogeneity. While the heterogeneity in the romantic factors cannot be easily smoothed, the economic factors leave some space opened for the negotiation between the centre and region. It can be done especially on the field of the property rights as well as the set-up of the fiscal rules leading to the proper degree of fiscal autonomy. Nevertheless, the pure economic science can suggest only the optimal results under the existing restrictions. The solution of the secessionist conflicts as a normative, rather than a positive task, remains wholly in the hands of the policy and decision-makers.

## Note

1 Subchapter 1.5.1.

# Appendices

# Appendix A

## Questionnaire (English version)

*In the current European Union, there is an increasing interest in a higher degree of regional autonomy. In Scotland and Catalonia, a referendum on independence was held. However, the pro-independence parties and movements have also succeeded in elections in Flanders, Corsica, and Italy.*

*Therefore, we would like to ask you to fill a short questionnaire to help us understand the reasons that are important for a discussion on independence and autonomy.*

*Thank you for your kind help.*

*Hana Lipovská,*
*Faculty of Economics and Administration*
*Masaryk University*
*Czech Republic*
lipovska@mail.muni.cz

Qi1: Age
Qi2: Sex

- Male
- Female

Qi3: Place of residence (town/region and country)
Qi4: Education (highest achieved education)

- Primary
- Lower secondary
- Upper secondary
- Tertiary (bachelor's degree)
- Tertiary (master's degree or higher)

Qi5: Employment (please describe your job in a few words: for example, "teacher", "salesman", "cashier", "accountant")
Qi5a: Your current state

- A public sector employee
- A private sector employee

- Self-employed
- Unemployed
- Student
- Parental Leave
- Retirement

Qi6: Religious denomination

- Catholic
- Orthodox
- Protestant
- No denomination
- Unwilling to answer
- Other religion (specify):

Qi7: Which of the following languages

- is your mother tongue?
- did you use at school?
- have you used at work?

German
Dutch
Flemish
French
Swedish
Finnish
Italian
Spanish
Catalan
English
Gaelic
Welsh
Galician
Basque
Czech

Qi8: Do you want your children to master the local language in addition to the official language?

(Definitely yes – rather yes – yes – rather no – no – definitely no)

Qi9: Which media do you use?

(Definitely yes – rather yes – yes – rather no – no – definitely no)

- Regional
- National press
- International

Qs1: If you had to decide today on the future of your country, you would opt for:

a) Independence of your region as a separate sovereign state
b) Autonomy of your region within the existing country
c) A unitary state with the central government
d) A federation

Qs1a: You would vote for independence of your region because

a) You want a sovereign state
b) You do not want secession, but you want to express your dissatisfaction with the government
c) You do not want secession, but you want the government to give the region a greater degree of autonomy under the pressure of a referendum
d) Other reasons:

Qs1b: The new sovereign state should be

a) A monarchy
b) A republic

Qs2: If your region became a new independent state, would you like it to be an EU Member State?

(Definitely yes – rather yes – yes – rather no – no – definitely no)

Qs3: If there was a referendum on your country's membership of the EU, how would you vote?

a) For
b) Against
c) Do not know

Qs4: You politically identify

- Only with your region
- More with your region than with the country
- With your region as well as with your country
- With your country more than with your region
- Only with your country

Qs5: How much do you trust the

- Qs5.1: European Commission
- Qs5.2: European Government
- Qs5.3: National government
- Qs5.5: Regional government/authorities
- Qs5.7: Local council

(I definitely trust – . . . – I definitely do not trust)

Q1.1 What maximum monthly contribution (in Euro) would you be willing to pay as a special tax related to the costs of independence?

Q1.2 What minimum monthly benefit (in Euro) would you like to receive to continue living in the current country instead of a new independent state?

Q2 How do you assess the current economic situation in

- Q2.1 Your region?
- Q2.2 Your country?
- Q2.3 The EU?

(Very good – . . . – very bad)

Q3 In the case of your region's independence, how would the living standards of the following be changed?

- Q3.1 The newly independent country
- Q3.2 The rest of the former country
- Q3.3 Your family

(Increased significantly – . . . – decreased significantly)

Q4: The probability of winning a lottery jackpot of €1000 is 10%. How much euro would you be willing to pay for a lottery ticket?

Q5: You could be given €100 today or €100 plus bonus a year later. How high would the bonus have to be for you to be willing to choose the latter option?

Q6: If your region were to remain part of the current state, how should the following powers be shared between the central government and the regional government?

(Central government only – regional government only – both governments together)

- Q6a: Education
- Q6b: Taxation
- Q6c: Healthcare
- Q6d: Foreign Affairs
- Q6e: Safety
- Q6f: European policy
- Q6g: Social policy

Q7: Under what circumstances would you rather support secession (the emergence of a new state)?

- Q7a: Sufficient amount of universities in the region
- Q7b: Excellent infrastructure (motorways, railway)
- Q7c: Good political representation
- Q7d: The Prime minister or other central government leading politicians coming from the region
- Q7e: High living standard
- Q7f: Serious economic crisis

Q8: Do you agree with the following statements?

(Definitely yes – rather yes – yes – rather no – no – definitely no)

- Q8a: Our tax contributions to the central budget are higher than the amounts we receive back.
- Q8b: At the national level, we could decide on public expenditures better than the central government decides.
- Q8c: Central government has disproportionally high profits from our resources (including oil and raw materials)

# Appendix B

## Product concentration and diversification indices of exports and imports for European countries, sorted by population (2016)

| | *Concentration Index* | *Diversification Index* | *Population* |
|---|---|---|---|
| Gibraltar | 0.53 | 0.78 | 0.03 |
| Faeroe Islands | 0.65 | 0.76 | 0.05 |
| Andorra | 0.19 | 0.54 | 0.07 |
| Iceland | 0.44 | 0.80 | 0.35 |
| Malta | 0.33 | 0.66 | 0.47 |
| Luxembourg | 0.10 | 0.52 | 0.60 |
| Cyprus | 0.23 | 0.58 | 0.87 |
| Estonia | 0.11 | 0.44 | 1.3 |
| Latvia | 0.09 | 0.43 | 1.9 |
| Slovenia | 0.10 | 0.42 | 2.6 |
| Lithuania | 0.11 | 0.44 | 2.79 |
| Croatia | 0.06 | 0.45 | 4.2 |
| Ireland | 0.24 | 0.67 | 4.85 |
| Norway | 0.31 | 0.64 | 5.3 |
| Slovakia | 0.19 | 0.46 | 5.4 |
| Finland | 0.14 | 0.52 | 5.5 |
| Denmark | 0.09 | 0.43 | 5.8 |
| Bulgaria | 0.08 | 0.46 | 7.5 |
| Switzerland | 0.28 | 0.64 | 8.5 |
| Austria | 0.06 | 0.35 | 8.8 |
| Hungary | 0.12 | 0.39 | 9.77 |
| Sweden | 0.09 | 0.34 | 10.2 |
| Portugal | 0.07 | 0.40 | 10.3 |
| Czech Republic | 0.12 | 0.41 | 10.6 |
| Greece | 0.23 | 0.55 | 10.8 |
| Belgium | 0.09 | 0.36 | 11.5 |
| Netherlands | 0.07 | 0.32 | 17.2 |
| Romania | 0.11 | 0.42 | 19.6 |
| Poland | 0.06 | 0.37 | 38.6 |

| | *Concentration Index* | *Diversification Index* | *Population* |
|---|---|---|---|
| Spain | 0.10 | 0.33 | 46.7 |
| Italy | 0.05 | 0.34 | 60.5 |
| United Kingdom | 0.10 | 0.31 | 66.8 |
| France | 0.09 | 0.32 | 67.3 |
| Germany | 0.10 | 0.30 | 82.8 |

# Appendix C
## European Free Alliance members

| *Party/Movement* | *Country* | *NUTS 2 region* |
|---|---|---|
| Nieuw-Vlaamse Alliantie | Belgium | BE2 |
| Lista Za Rijeku | Croatia | HR031 |
| Moravané | Czech Republic | CZ06, CZ07, CZ08 |
| Ålands Framtid | Finland | FI2 |
| Insemeper a Corsica | France | FR83 |
| Mouvement Région Savoie | France | FRK27 |
| Partit Occitan | France | FRI1 |
| Partitu di a Nazione Corsa | France | FR83 |
| Union Démocratique Bretonne | France | FR52 |
| Unser Land | France | FR42 |
| Bayernpartei | Germany | DE2 |
| Lausatia Alliance | Germany | DE40B |
| Südschleswigschen Wählerverbands | Germany | DEF |
| SchlEswig Partei | Germany | DEF |
| Liga Veneta Repubblica | Italy | ITD |
| Süd-Tiroler Freiheit | Italy | ITH1 |
| Fryske Nasjonale Partij | Netherlands | NL12 |
| Ruch Autonomii Slaska | Poland | PL22 |
| Bloc Nacionalista Valencia | Spain | ES52 |
| Bloque Nacionalista Galego | Spain | ES11 |
| Eusko Alkartasuna | Spain | ES21 |
| Esquerra Republicana de Catalunya | Spain | ES51 |
| Federació PSM Entesa Nacionalista | Spain | ES53 |
| Unitat Catalana | Spain | ES51 |
| Mebyon Kernow | United Kingdom | UKK3 |
| Plaid Cymru | United Kingdom | UKL |
| Scottish National Party | United Kingdom | UKM |
| Yorkshire Party | United Kingdom | UKE |

| *Party/Movement* | *Country* | *NUTS 2 region* |
| --- | --- | --- |
| Enotna Lista | Austria | Slovenian minority |
| Omo Ilinden Pirin | Bulgaria | Macedonian minority |
| Rainbow | Greece | Macedonian minority |
| Slovenska Skupnost | Italy | Slovenian minority |
| Erdelyi Magyar Neppart | Romania | Hungarian minority |
| Magyar Keresztńydemokrata Szövetség | Slovakia | Hungarian minority |

# Appendix D
## Overview of main data sources

| *Variable* | *Data source* | *Year* |
|---|---|---|
| Mother tongue | Eurobarometer 386 | 2012 |
| | World Atlas | 2017 |
| Religion | Eurobarometer 83.4 | 2015 |
| | Atlas of European Values (EVS 2016) | 2008 |
| General election in Spain | Ministerio del Interior | 2016 |
| Religion in Spain | Centro de Investigacionec Sociológicas | 2015 |
| European Election Database | Norwegian Centre for Research Data | 2009 |
| Regional dataset | European Commission | 2016 |
| Political and economic situation | Flash Eurobarometer 427 | 2015 |
| | Flash Eurobarometer 472 | 2018 |
| Purchasing Power Parity | OECD | 2000–2017 |
| | GESIS | |
| PISA | OECD | 2012 |
| Education expenditures | Fundación BBVA-Ivie | 2013 |
| | HM Treasury/Office for National Statistics | 2015 |
| | ImpresaLavoro | 2013 |
| | Ruano and Profirou (2016) | 2015 |

Source: Author.

# References


Abbot, Philip. *The Many Faces of Patriotism*. Rowman & Littlefield, 2007. ISBN 978-07-4255-071-1.

*Act* No *128/2000* Coll. of the Czech Republic, on *Municipalities (The Municipial Order)*.

Adler-Nissen, Rebecca. The Faroe Islands: Independence Dreams, Globalist Separatism and the Europeanization of Postcolonial Home Rule. *Cooperation and Conflict*, 2014, 49(1), pp. 55–79.

Aaken, van Anne. 2012. *Behavioral International Law and Economics Harvard International Law Journal*, pp. 421–481. U. of St. Gallen Law & Economics Working Paper No. 2013–21.

Aksel Sundström, Daniel Stockemer. What determines women's political representation at the local level? A fine-grained analysis of the European regions. *International Journal of Comparative Sociology*, 2015, pp. 1–21. DOI: 10.1177/0020715215595691.

Alesina, Alberto. The Size of Countries: Does It Matter? *Journal of the European Economic Association*, 2003, 1(2–3), pp. 301–316.

Alesina, Alberto, Spolaore, Enrico. In the Number and Size of Nations. *The Quarterly Journal of Economics*, 1997, 112(4), pp. 1027–1056.

Alesina, Alberto, Spolaore, Enrico, Wacziarg, Romain. Economic Integration and Political Disintegration. *American Economic Review*, 2000, 90(5), pp. 1276–1296.

Alesina, Alberto, Wacziarg, Romain. Openness, Country Size and Government. *Journal of Public Economics*, 1998, 69, pp. 305–321.

Alexandrakis, Constantine, Jones, Robert T. Secession and Exit: An Analysis of Two Competing Hypotheses. In *The Elgar Companion to Public Economics*, ed. Ott, A.F. and Cebula, R.J. Edward Elgar Publishing no 3537, 2006, chapter 22.

Alland, A. Catalunya. *One Nation, Two States: An Ethnographic Study of Nonviolent Resistance to Assimilation*. Springer, 2006.

Allen, Larry. *Global Financial System 1750–2000*. Reaktion Books. 2004. ISBN 978-18-6189-570-7.

Almeidam, Rita, K., Carneiro, Pedro. *The Return to the Firm Investment in Human Capital*. IZA Discussion Paper No. 1937, 2006.

Althusius, Johannes. *Politica*. [1614] An Abridged Translation of Politics Methodically Set Forth and Illustrated with Sacred and Profane Examples, ed. and Trans. Carney, Frederick S. Foreword by Elazar, Daniel J. (Indianapolis: 1995 Liberty Fund). Available online: https://oll.libertyfund.org/titles/692

Ambrosio, Thomas. *Irredentism: Ethnic Conflict and International Politics*. Greenwood Publishing Group, 2001. ISBN 978-02-7597-2608-8.

Anderton, Charles, H. Conflict Economics in Christian Perspective. *Faith & Economics*, 2001, 37, pp. 1–9.

Andreas, Peter. *Political Economies of Conflict: Old Wine in New Bottles?* WPF Seminar New Wars, New Peace, 2012. Available online: https://sites.tufts.edu/reinventingpeace/2012/02/06/political-economies-of-conflict-old-wine-in-new-bottles/

Andreotti, Fabio. *Why Freedom Is Favored by Secession and Subsidiarity*. Foundation for Economic Education, 2017. Available online: https://fee.org/articles/why-freedom-is-favored-by-secession-and-subsidiarity/

Arnold, Matthew, Leriche, Matthew. *South Sudan: From Revolution to Independence*. Oxford: Oxford University Press, 2013. ISBN 978-01-902-5754-5.

Arribas, Iván, Pérez, Francisco, Tortosa-Ausina, Emili. *Measuring International Economic Integration: Theory and Evidence of Globalization*. MPRA Paper 16010, University Library of Munich, 2006.

Audickas, Lukas, Cracknell, Richard. *UK Election Statistics: 1918–2018: 100 Years of Elections*. London: House of Commons Library, 2018, Briefing Paper No. CBP7529.

Backhaus, Jürgen G., Doering, Detmar. *The Political Economy of Secession: A* Source *Book*. Neue Zürcher Publishing, 2004.

Baev, Pavel K. External Interventions in Secessionist Conflicts in Europe. *European Security*, 1999, 8(2), Summer, pp. 22–51.

Balcells, Albert *Catalan Nationalism: Past and Present*. Springer, 1996.

Baldwin, Richard, Wyplosz, Charles. *Ekonomie evropské integrace [The Economics of European Integration]*. Praha: Grada Publishing, 2013. ISBN 978-80-247-4568-8.

Baranyai, Nóra. Regionalism in Upper Silesia: The Concept of Autonomous Regions in Poland. In *Ten Public Policy Studies Pécs*, Pálné, Kovács I. and Kákai, L. University of Pécs Department of Political Studies, 2013, pp. 9–28. ISBN 978-615-5001-85-7.

Barlovento Comunicación. *Análisis Mensual del Comportamiento de la Audiencia Televisiva*, 2017. Available online: https://www.barloventocomunicacion.es/publicaciones/

Bauer, Michal, Chyitlová, Julie. *The Impact of Education on the Subjective Discount Rate in Ugandan Villages*. IZA Discussion Paper No. 4057, 2009.

Becker, Garry. Why So Many Mices Are Roaring? *Businessweek*, 6th November 1994.

Bell, David Avrom. *The First Total War: Napoleon's Europe and the Birth of Warfare as We Know It*. Houghton Mifflin Harcourt, 2007. 420 s. ISBN 978-06-1834-965-4.

Berdún, Sílvia Juventeny. Much 'More Than a Club': Football Club Barcelona's Contribution to the Rise of a National Consciousness in Catalonia (2003–2014). *Soccer & Society*, 2019, 20(1), pp. 103–122. DOI: 10.1080/14660970.2016.1267624

Bernoulli, Daniel. Exposition of a New Theory on the Measurement of Risk. *Econometrica*, 1954, 22(1). [Specimen Thoeriae Novae de Mensura Sortis, Commentarii Academiae Scientiarum Imperialis Petropolitanae, 1738].

Besanko, David, Braeutigam, Ronald. *Microeconomics*. John Wiley & Sons, 2010. ISBN 978-047-0563-58-8.

Bieri, Matthias. Separatism in EU. *CSS Analysis in Security Policy*, 2014, 160, pp. 1–4.

Binner, Jane, Chaudhry, Sajid, Mullineux, Andrew, Swofford, James, L. Scotland as an Optimal Currency Area. *Scottish Journal of Political Economy*, 2018, 65(4), pp. 315–327. DOI: 10.1111/sjpe.12181

Blanch, *Pelai Pagès* i. *War and Revolution in Catalonia, 1936–1939*. Brill, 2013.

Boettke, Peter J. *Socialism and the Market: The Natural Economy*. Taylor & Francis, 2000. ISBN 978-041-5195-87-4.

Bohlen, Celestine. Slovenia Is Moving to Independence. *The New York Times*, 6th June 1991.

Bolton, Patrick, Roland, Gérard. *The Break Up of Nations: A Political-Economy Analysis*. Mimeo ECARE, 1995.

Bolton, Patrick, Roland, Gérard, Spolaore, Enrico. Economic Theories of the Break-Up and Integration of Nations. *European Economic Review*, 1996, 40, pp. 697–705.

Bookman, Milica Zarkovicz. *The Economics of Secession*. London: Macmillan Press, 1993.

Boykin, Scott. The Ethics of Secession. In *Secession, State and Liberty*, Gordon, David. Transaction Publishers, 1998.

Boyle, Katharine, Englebert, Pierre. The Primacy of Politics in Separatist Dynamics. *African Perspective*, 2008, 2, pp. 31–63.

Braddon, Derek L., Hartley, Keith. *Handbook on the Economics of Conflict*. Edward Elgar Publishing, 2011. ISBN 978-08-5793-093-4.

Bradford, James, C. *International Encyklopedia of Military History*. Abingdon, UK: Routledge, 2004. ISBN 978-11-3595-034-7.

Brauer, Jurgen, Caruso, Raul. *Economists and Peacebuilding*. In *Handbook on Peacebuilding*, ed. Macgintry, Roger. London: Routledge, 2013, pp. 147–158. ISBN 978-11-3892-270-9.

Breton, Albert. Economic Approaches to Language and Bilingualism. In *New Canadian Perspectives*. Ottawa: Canadian Heritage, 1998.

Breuilly, John. *Nationalism and the State*. 2nd edition. Chicago: University of Chicago Press, 1994. ISBN 978-02-2607-414-6.

Brilmayer, Lea. Secession and Self-Determination: A Territorial Interpretation. *Yale Journal of International Law*, 1991, 16.

Brown, Andrew, G. *Reluctant Partners: A History of Multilateral Trade Cooperation, 1850–2000*. Studies in International Economics. University of Michigan Press, 2003. ISBN 978-04-7211-305-7.

Brubaker, Rogers. In the Name of Nation: Reflections on Nationalism and Patriotism. *Citizenship Studies*, 2004, 8(2), pp. 115–127.

Brunsden, Jim, Peel, Michael. Flemish Nationalists Quit Belgian Government. *Financial Times*, 9th December 2018. Available online: www.ft.com/content/b864e2ee-fb49-11e8-aebf-99e208d3e521

Buchanan, Alan. Toward a Theory of Secession. *Ethics*, 1991a, 101(2), pp. 322–342.

Buchanan, Alan. *Secession: The Morality of Political Divorce from Fort Sumter to Lithuania and Quebec*. Westview Press, 1991b. ISBN 978-08-1331-133-3.

Buchanan, Alan. *The Quebec Secession Issue: Democracy, Minority Rights, and the Rule of Law*. Ottawa: Privy Council Office, 1999.

Buchanan, James M., Faith, Roger L. Secession and the Limits of Taxation: Toward a Theory of Internal Exit. *The American Economic Review*, 1987, 7(5), pp. 1023–1031.

Budíková, Marie, Králová, Maria, Maroš, Bohumil. *Průvodce základními statistickými metodami*. Grada, 2010. ISBN 978-80-247-3243-5.

Cabada, Ladislav. *Koalice a koaliční vztahy České republiky v evropském kontextu [Coalitions and the Czech Republic Coalition Relations in the European Context]*. Plzeň: Aleš Čeněk, 2006. ISBN 978-80-738-0004-8.

Cabada, Ladislav. *Evropa regionů [Europe of Regions]*. Aleš Čeněk, s. r. o., 2009. ISBN 978-80-7380-163-2.

Calvet, Marc S. *Quebec, Scotland and Catalonia: How Secessionist Political Parties Legitimize Political Independence*. Available online: http://paperroom.ipsa.org/papers/paper_13615.pdf

Camp, Edwige. The Scottish National Party (SNP): A Party of Government in the Early 21st Century. *Revue LISA/LISA e-Journal* [En ligne], 2014, 12(8), mis en ligne le 20 décembre 2014, consulté le 26 octobre 2019. DOI: 10.4000/lisa.7008. Available online: http://journals.openedition.org/lisa/7008

Cappon, David. Oil Campaign. *New Scientist*, 8th November 1973, 60(871). ISSN 0262-4079.

Cartera, Evan C., Mccullougha, Michael E., Kim-Spoon, Jungmeen, Carolina, Corralesa, Adam, Blakea. Religious People Discount the Future Less. *Evolution and Human Behavior*, 2012, 33(3), pp. 224–231. http://dx.doi.org/10.1016/j.evolhumbehav.2011.09.006

'Centro de Investigaciones Sociológicas. *Religion in Spain.* Centro de Investigaciones Sociológicas. Barómetro de enero, 2015.

CEO. *Barómetre d'Opinió Política*. Generalitat de Catalunya, 2018.

Charles, Victoria, Carl, Klaus. *The Viennese Secession.* Parkstone International, 2014. ISBN 978-17-8310-394-2.

Clark, Barry, et al. *The Annotated Secessionist Papers*. 2nd edition. The Calhoun Institute, 2018. ISBN 978-19-8325-504-5.

Clayes, Peter, Martire, Federico. If You Want Me to Stay, Pay: A Model of Asymmetric Federalism in Centralised Countries. *Environment and Planning C: Government and Policy*, 2015, 33(2), pp. 305–320.

Coakley, John. *The Territorial Management of Ethnic Conflict*. Psychology Press, 2003. ISBN 978-07-14649887.

Coca. *Corpus of Contemporary American English*. Available online: https://corpus.byu.edu/coca/

Coffé, Hilde, Bolzendahl, Catherine. Same Game, Different Rules? Gender Differences in Political Participation. *Sex Roles*, 2010, 62(5–6), pp. 318–333. DOI: 10.1007/s11199-009-9729-y

Collier, Paul, Elliott, V. Lani, Hegre, Håvard, Hoeffler, Anke, Reynal-Querol, Marta, Sambanis, Nicholas. Breaking the conflict trap: *Civil War and Development Policy* [online]. Washington, DC: World Bank a Oxford University Press, 2003.

Collier, Paul, Hoeffler, Anke. *The Political Economy of Secession*. World Bank, Development Research Gropu, 2002.

Collier, Paul, Hoeffler, Anke. Greed and Grievance in Civil War. *Oxford Economic Papers*, 2004, 56(4), pp. 563–595. https://doi.org/10.1093/oep/gpf064

Connolly, Christopher, K. Independence in Europe: Secession, Sovereignty, and the European Union. *Duke Journal of Comparative & International Law*, 2013, 24(51), pp. 51–105.

Constitution of the Principality of Lichtenstein. *Issued by Legal Service of the Government of the Principality of Lichtenstein*, 2003. Available online: http://hrlibrary.umn.edu/research/liechtenstein-constitution.pdf

Coughlan, Sean. Basque Reinvent Themselves as Education Power. *BBC News*, 15th June 2016. Available online: www.bbc.com/news/business-36517928

Cox, Robert H., Frankland, Erich G. The Federal State and the Breakup of Czechoslovakia: An Institutional Analysis. *Publius*, 1995, 25(1), pp. 71–88.

Coyle, Diane. *GDP: A Brief But Affectionate History*. Princeton, NJ: Princeton University Press, 2014.

Cramér, Harald. *Mathematical Methods of Statistic*. Princeton, NJ: Princeton University Press, 1946. ISBN 0-691-08004-6.

Crepaz, Katharina. *The Impact of Europeanization on Minority Communities*. Springer, 2016. ISBN 978-36-5812-116-7.

'Deacon, Bernard. *The Cornish Paradox: Ethnoregionalism in a Hybrid Territory*. Working paper, University of Exeter, 2003.

Delledonne, Giacomo, Martinico, Giuseppe. *The Canadian Contribution to a Comparative Law of Secession: Legacies of the Quebec Secession Reference*. Springer, 2018. ISBN 978-30-3003-469-6.

Deng, Xiaohao, Hartog, Joop, Sun, Yuze. *Can We Measure Individual Risk Attitudes in a Survey?* Tinbergen Institute Discussion Papers, Tinbergen Institute, 2010, No 10-027/3.

Deprez, Kas, Vos, Louis. *Nationalism in Belgium: Shifting Identities, 1780–1995*. Springer, 2016. ISBN 978-13-4926-868-9.

Detrez, Raymond. *Historical Dictionary of Bulgaria*. Rowman & Littlefield, 2014. ISBN 978-14-4224-180-0.

De Wilde, Dirk. Belgians' Pride in EU Role Quells Euroscepticism. *EU Observer*, 6th May 2014. Available online: https://euobserver.com/eu-elections/123886

Dolan, Paddy, Connolly, John. *Sport and National Identities: Globalization and Conflict*. Abingdon, UK: Routledge, 2017. ISBN: 978-13-1551-911-1.

Dowling, Andrew. The Catholic Church in *Catalonia*: From Cataclysm in the Civil War to the 'Euphoria' of the 1950s. *CatalanReview*, 2006, 10, pp. 83–100.

Doyle, Don Harrison. *Secession as an International Phenomenon: From America's Civil War to Contemporary Separatist Movements*. Athens: University of Georgia Press, c2010. ISBN 978-08-2033-712-8.

Drazen, Alan. *Political Economy in Macroeconomics*. Princeton, NJ: Princeton University Press, 2000. ISBN 978-0-691-09257-7.

Dudáková, Barbora. Volby do parlamentu Alandských ostrovů 2007. *European Electoral Studies*, 2008, 3(2), pp. 140–153.

Dugard, John. *The Secession of States and Their Recognition in the Wake of Kosovo*. The Hague: Hague Academy of International Law, 2013. ISBN 978-90-04-25748-1.

Dvořáková, Kateřina, Ferrarová, Miroslava. Separatistické tendence v současné Evropě: Katalánsko, Skotsko a Vlámsko na cestě k nezávislosti? [Separatist Tendencies in Contemporary Europe: Catalonia, Scotland and Flanders on Their Way to Independence?]. *Politologická revue [Czech Political Science Revue]*, 2014, 20(2), pp. 31–62. ISSN 1211-0353.

EC. *Eurydice: Population: Demographic Situation, Languages and Religion*, 2019. Available online: https://eacea.ec.europa.eu/national-policies/eurydice/national-description_en

*The Economist*. Fiscal Devolution in Scotland: A Taste for More, 9th April 2016.

EFA. *What's EFA and History*, 2018. Available online: www.e-f-a.org/about-us/whats-efa-and-history/

EIA. *Crude Oil Prices: Brent: Europe*. Available online: www.eia.gov/

Eurobarometer 83.4. *GESIS*. Available online: https://dbk.gesis.org/dbksearch/sdesc2.asp?no=6595&db=e&doi=10.4232/1.12442

Eurobarometer 386. March 2012.

European Comission, 2016. Available online: http://ec.europa.eu/regional_policy/cs/policy/evaluations/data-for-research/

Europe Review, 2003/04. *The Economic and Business Report.*Kogan Page Publishers, 2003, ISBN 9780749440671.

Eurostat.*Flash Eurobarometer 427*, 2015. Available online: https://data.europa.eu/euodp/cs/data/dataset/S2102_427_ENG

Eurostat. *Regional Statistics by NUTS Classification*, 2016. Available online: www.ec.europa.eu/Eurostat/data/database

Eurostat. *Euro/ECU Exchange Rates: Monthly Data*, 2019. Available online: http://appsso.eurostat.ec.europa.eu/nui/submitViewTableAction.do (accessed on 5th February 2019).

Eurostat.*Flash Eurobarometer 472*, 2019. Available online: http://data.europa.eu/euodp/en/data/dataset/S2219_472_ENG

EVS. *European Values Study 2008: Integrated Dataset (EVS 2008)*, 2016. GESIS Data Archive, Cologne. ZA4800 Data file Version 4.0.0. DOI: 10.4232/1.12458
Fabbrini, Federico. *Economic Governance in Europe: Comparative Paradoxes and Constitutional Challenges*. Oxford: Oxford University Press, 2016.
Felak, James Ramon. *At the Price of the Republic: Hlinka's Slovak People's Party, 1929–1938*. University of Pittsburgh Press, 1995. ISBN 978-08-2297-694-3.
Field, Andy. *Discovering Statistics Using IBM SPSS Statistics*. 5th edition. Thousand Oaks, CA: Sage Publications, 2013. ISBN 9781526419514.
Finlan, Alastair. *The Collapse of Yugoslavia 1991–1999*. Bloomsbury Publishing, 2004. ISBN 978-14-7281-027-4.
Fiordelisi, Franco, Philip, Molyneux. *Shareholder Value in Banking*. England: Palgrave Macmillan, c2006. ISBN 978-14-0399-666-4.
Flynn, Eileen Patricia. *How Just Is the War on Terror: A Question of Morality*. Paulist Press, 2007. ISBN 978-08-0914-509-6.
Fogelquist, Alan. *Politics and Economic Policy in Yugoslavia, 1918–1929*. Lulu.com, 2011. ISBN 978-12-5794-299-2.
Future of Åland. *A Brief Summary of Ålands Framtid*, 2016. Available online: www.alandsframtid.ax/index.php?option=com_content&view=article&id=315&Itemid=125
Gammelgaard, Karen, Holmøyvik, Eirik. *Writing Democracy: The Norwegian Constitution 1814–2014*. Berghahn Books, 2014. ISBN 978-17-8238-505-9.
GESIS. *European Values Study 2017: Variable Report: Integrated Dataset*. Köln, 2018. ISSN 2190-6742. DOI: 10.4232/1.13090
GESIS. *Trust in National and International Institutions*. Available online: www.gesis.org/eurobarometer-data-service/search-data-access/eb-trends-trend-files/list-of-trends/trust-in-institutions/
Gideon, Michael, Hsu, Joanne, Helppie-McFall, Brooke. Heaping at Round Numbers on Financial Questions: The Role of Satisficing. *Survey Research Methods*, 2017, 11(2), pp. 189–214. http://dx.doi.org/10.18148/srm/2017.v11i2.6782
Gillespie, Richard, Gray, Caroline. *Contesting Spain? The Dynamics of Nationalist Movements in Catalonia and the Basque Country*. Abingdon, UK: Routledge, 2015. ISBN 978-13-1740-948-9.
Giuriato, Luisa, Gastaldi, Francesca. *The Domestic Stability Pact in Italy: Rule for Discipline*?, 2009, MPRA Paper No. 15183.
Google. *Google Correlate*, 2019. Available online: www.google.com/trends/correlate/
Gordon, David. *Secession, State and Liberty*. Transaction Publishers, 2002. ISBN 978-14-1283-383-7.
Grable, John E., Lytton, Ruth, H. The Development of a Risk Assessment Instrument: A Follow-Up Study. *Financial Sendees Review*, 2003, 12, pp. 257–274.
Gradstein, Mark. Political Bargaining in a Federation: Buchanan Meets Coase. *European Economic Review*, 2004, 48(5), pp. 983–999.
Graziosi, Gripgoire, R. Secession and the Limits of Taxation: Toward a Theory of Internal Exit: Comment. *American Economic Review*, 1997, 97(1), pp. 534–538.
Green, David, Petrick, Karl. *Banking and Financial Stability in Central Europe: Integrating Transition Economies into the European Union*. Edward Elgar Publishing, 2002. ISBN 978-17-8195-029-6.
Griera, Mar. The Governance of Religious Diversity in Stateless Nations: The Case of Catalonia. *Religion, State & Society*, 2016, 44(1), pp. 13–31. DOI: 10.1080/09637494.2016.1171576
Griffiths, Ryan D. *Age of Secession: The International and Domestic Determinants of State Birth*. Cambridge: Cambridge University Press, 2016.

Grossman, Herschel I., Kim, Minseong. Swords or Plowshares? A Theory of the Security of Claims to Property. *Journal of Political Economy*, 1995, 103(6), pp. 1275–1288.

*The Guardian*. The South Tyrol Identity Crisis: To Live in Italy, But Feel Austrian, 2014. Available online: www.theguardian.com/education/2014/may/30/south-tyrol-live-in-italy-feel-austrian

Guibernau, Montserrat. *Nationalism and Intellectuals in Nations without States: The Catalan Case*. Barcelona: Institut de Ciencies Polítiques i Socials, WP núm. 222, 2003.

Guillemette, Michael A., Yao, Rui, James, Ruseel N. An Analysis of Risk Assessment Questions Based on Loss-Averse Preferences. *Journal of Financial Counseling and Planning*, 2015, 26(1), pp. 17–29.

Guinot, Dolores Luna. *From Al-Andalus to Monte Sacro*. Trafford Publishing, 2014.

Hair, Joseph F., Jr., Black, William C., Babin, Barry J., Anderson, Rolph, E. *Multivariate Data Analysis: Pearson New International Edition*. Pearson Education Limited, 2013. ISBN 978-1-292-02190-4.

Harriman. The Ambassador in the Soviet Union (Harriman) to the Secretary of State, 860F.014/6–2945: Telegram (Moscow, June 29, 1945). In *Foreign Relations of the United States: Diplomatic Papers, 1945, Europe*, Vol. 4, ed. Slany, William, Reid, John, Sappington, G., Houston, N.O. and Douglas, W. Washington, DC: United States Government Printing Office, 1968.

Hartog, Joop, Ferrer-I-Carbonell, Ada, Jonker, Nicole. Linking Measured Risk Aversion to Individual Characteristics. *Kyklos*, 2002, 55, pp. 3–26.

Hauk, Esther, Ortega, Javier. *Schooling, Nation Building and Industrialization: A Gellnerian Approach*. CEP Discussion Paper No 1328, 2015.

Hechter, Michael. *Internal Colonialism: The Celtic Fringe in British National Development: With a New Introduction and a New Appendix by the Author*. London and New York: Routledge, 2017. ISBN 978-0-7658-0475-4.

Heij, Christiaan, Boer, de Paul, Franses, Philip Hans, Kloek, Teun, Dijk, van Herman K. *Econometric Methods with Applications in Business and Economics*. New York: Oxford University Press, 2004. ISBN 0-19-926801-0.

Herger, Nils. *Understanding Central Banks*. Springer, 2019. ISBN 978-30-3005-162-4.

Heywood, Andrew. *Politics*. 4th revised edition. Macmillan International Higher Education, 2013. ISBN 978-11-3727-244-7.

Hierro, María José. Crafting Identities in a Multinational Context: Evidence from Catalonia. *Nations and Nationalism*, 2015, 21(3), pp. 461–482.

Hirschman, Albert O. The Paternity of an Index. *The American Economic Review*, 1964, 54(5), p. 761.

Hobolt, Sara. How Parties Affect Vote Choice in European Integration Referendums. *Party Politics*, 2006, 12(5), pp. 623–647.

Holland, Robert. Cyprus and Malta: Two Colonial Experiences. *Journal of Mediterranean Studies*, 2014, 23(1), pp. 9–20.

Holt, Charles A., Laury, Susan K. Risk Aversion and Incentive Effects. *American Economic Review*, 2002, 92(5), pp. 1644–1655. DOI: 10.1257/000282802762024700

Hörner, Wolfgang, Döbert, Hans, Kopp, von Botho, Mitter, Wolfgang. *The Education Systems of Europe*. Springer Science & Business Media, 2007. ISBN 978-1-4020-4874-6.

Hroch, Miroslav. *V národním zájmu [In the Mational Interest]*, Prague: NLN, 1996, pp. 14–16.

Huntington, Samuel P. *Clash of Civilisations*. Simon & Schuster, 1997. ISBN 978-0-684-84441-1.

Hupchick, Dennis P. The Rise of Romantic Nationalism. In *The Balkans*. New York: Palgrave Macmillan, 2002. ISBN 978-1-4039-6417-5.

Huszka, Beata. *Secessionist Movements and Ethnic Conflict: Debate-Framing and Rhetoric in Independence Campaigns*. Abingdon, UK: Routledge, 2013. ISBN 978-1-1346-8784-8.

Huysseune, Michel. Imagined Geographies: Political and Scientific Discourses on Italy's North-South Divide. In *Secession, History and Social Sciences*, ed. Coppieters, B. VUB Brussels University Press, 2002, pp. 207–226. ISBN 90-5487-312-4.

IBZ. *Service public fédéral Intérieu. Direction des Elections*, 2019. Available online: https://elections.fgov.be/

ICM. *What Scotland Thinks*, 2013. Available online: http://whatscotlandthinks.org/questions/would-you-support-or-oppose-scotland-becoming-independent-if-you-were-convinced

Ihalainen, Pasi. *The Springs of Democracy: National and Transnational Debates on Constitutional Reform in the British, German, Swedish and Finnish Parliaments, 1917–1919*. Books on Demand, 2017. ISBN 978-95-2222-918-2.

ILO. *Structure of the International Standard Classification of Occupations (ISCO-08)*, 2008. Available online: www.ilo.org/public/english/bureau/stat/isco/isco08/index.htm

Jelavich, Charles, Jelavich, Barbara. *The Establishment of the Balkan National States, 1804–1920*. University of Washington Press, 2012. ISBN 978-02-9580-360-9.

John, Marl. Spain Says Won't Recognise Kosovo Independence. *Reuters*, 18th February 2008.

Jowett, Benjamin. Introduction to Plato's Laws. *Project Gutenberg*, 2008. Available online: www.gutenberg.org/files/1750/1750-h/1750-h.htm

Jussila, Osmo, Hentilä, Seppo, Nevakivi, Jukka. *From Grand Duchy to a Modern State: A Political History of Finland Since 1809*. C. Hurst & Co. Publishers, 1999. ISBN 978-18-5065-528-2.

Kahneman, Daniel, Tversky, Amos. 1979. Prospect Theory: An Analysis of Decision under Risk. *Econometrica*, 1979, 47(2), p. 263. DOI: 10.2307/1914185

Kassimeris, Christos. Fascism, Separatism and the Ultrás: Discrimination in Italian Football. *Soccer and Society*, 2011, 12(5), pp. 677–688.

Keating, Michael. Plurinational Democracy in a Post-Sovereign Order. *Queen's Papers on Europeanisation*, 2002, (1).

Keating, Michael. European Integration and the Nationalities Question. *Politics & Society*, 2004, 32(3), pp. 367–388.

Kemayou, Yanick. *More Class in Management Research: The Relationship between Socioeconomic Background and Managerial Attitudes*. Springer, 2016. ISBN 978-36-5812-063-4.

Kemezis, Paul. The People of Flanders Achieve Status in Language: The Dutch They Speak. *The New York Times*, 3rd February 1974. Available online: www.nytimes.com/1974/02/03/archives/the-people-of-flanders-achieve-status-in-languagethe-dutch-they.html

Keynes, John M. *The Economic Consequence of the Peace*. New York: Harcourt, Brace and Howe, 1920.

Keynes, John M. *How to Pay for the War: A Radical Plan for the Chancellor of the Exchequer*. London: Macmillan and Co. Limited, 1940.

Khan, Mehreen. The Economics of Catalan Secession. *Financial Times*, 6th October 2017. Available online: www.ft.com/content/2c4aa308-aa63-11e7-ab55-27219df83c97

Knight, David B. Identity and Territory: Geographical Perspectives on Nationalism and Regionalism. *Annals, Association of American Geographers*, 1982, 72(4), pp. 514–531.

Knight, David B. Territory and People or People and Territory? Thoughts on Postcolonial Self-Determination. *International Political Science Review*, 1985, 6(2), pp. 248–272.

Koffka, Kurt. *Principles of Gestalt Psychology*. New York: Harcourt, Brace and Company, 1935. ISBN 978-07-1003-121-1.

Kokaisl, Petr, Hamouzová, Kateřina, Hromádková, Michaela, Jarolímková, Tereza. 'Německá' kultura ve Francii – Alsasko a Alsasané. *Kulturní studia*, 2013, pp. 20–44.

Kotler, Philip, Keller, Kevin, Lane. *Marketing Management*. Prague: Grada, 2007. ISBN 978-80-2471-359-5.

Krajewska, Barbara. Napoleon and the Corsican Dilemma. *Revue du Souvenir Napoléonien*, 2005, 457, pp. 12–18.

Kuzminski, Adrian. Money and Liberty. In *Most Likely to Secede: What the Vermont Independence Movement Can Teach Us about Reclaiming Community and Creating a Human-Scale Vision for the 21st Century*, ed. Miller, Ron and Williams, Rob. Chelsea Green Publishing, 2013. ISBN 978-16-0358-502-6.

Kuzniak, Stephen, Rabbani, Abed, Heo, Wookjae, Ruiz-Menjivar, Jorge, Grable, John E. The Grable and Lytton Risk-Tolerance Scale: A 15-Year Retrospective. *Financial Services Review*, 2015, 24(2), pp. 177–192.

Leblanc, David C. *Statistics: Concepts and Applications for Science*. Subsequent edition. Jones & Bartlett Publishers, 2004. ISBN 978-0763717292.

'Leeson, David M. Post-War Conflict (Great Britain and Ireland). In *1914–1918-Online International Encyclopedia of the First World War*, ed. Daniel, Ute, Gatrell, Peter, Janz, Oliver, Jones, Heather, Keene, Jennifer, Kramer, Alan, and Nasson, Bill. Berlin: Freie Universität Berlin, 2016. DOI: 10.15463/ie1418.10816

Leeson, Peter T., Smith, Daniel J., Snow, Nicholas A. Hooligans. *Review d'Économie Politique*, 2012, 122(2).

Lefevre, Marie-Anne. Corsica: A National Gamble. *The Brooking Institution*, 2003. Available online: https://www.brookings.edu/wp-content/uploads/2016/06/lefevre.pdf

Levy, Roger. 1990. *Scottish Nationalism at the Crossroads*. Scottish Academy Press, 154 p. ISBN 978-0-70730-595-0.

Lichfield, John. *Corsica: Installation of Nationalist Government Sparks Concern in Paris Amid Renewed Calls for Independence*, 2015. Available online: www.independent.co.uk/news/world/europe/corsica-islands-new-nationalist-government-sparks-concern-in-paris-amid-renewed-calls-for-a6787016.html (accessed on 4th April 2016).

Lincoln, Abraham. *First Inaugural Address*, 4th March 1861. Available online: http://avalon.law.yale.edu/19th_century/lincoln1.asp

Lipovská, Hana. Territorial Claims and Right to Secede. In *New Approaches to the National Security*, ed. Náplavová, Magdalena and Pochobradská, Kateřina. Brno: University of Defence in Brno, 2017, pp. 267–273. ISBN 978-80-7231-402-7.

The Local. *Goodbye Denmark? Faroese Weigh Pulling Free of Danish Grip*, 19th June 2018. Available online: www.thelocal.dk/20180619/goodbye-denmark-faroese-weigh-pulling-free-of-danish-grip

Maddens, Bart. *Secessionist Strategies: The Case of Flanders*. Collección Mongrafiás. Barcelona: CIDOB, 2017, pp. 55–62. ISBN: 978-84-92511-53-2.

Malley-Morrison, Kathleen, McCarthy, Sherri, Hines, Denise. *International Handbook of War, Torture and Terrorism*. Springer Science & Business Media, 2012. ISBN 978-14-6141-638-8.

Manski, Charles F., Francesca, Molinari. Rounding Probabilistic Expectations in Surveys. *Journal of Business & Economic Statistics*, 2010, 28(2), pp. 219–231.

Mas-Collel, Andreu, Whinston, Michael D., Green, Jerry R. *Microeconomic Theory*. Oxford: Oxford University Press, 1995. ISBN 978-01-9507-340-9.

Massetti, Emanuele, Schakel, Arjan H. Between Autonomy and Secession: Decentralization and Regionalist Party Ideological Radicalism. *Party Politics*, 2013, published online first, 16 December 2013, 22(1), pp. 59–79.

Mates, Neven. Currency Splits: When a Monetary Union Falls Apart: The Experience of Former Yugoslavia in 1990–92. *CERGE-EI Insight*, 2011, 1.

Mchenry, Dean E. Is Economic Inequality a Foundation of Separatist Identity? An Examination of Successful and Unsuccessful Movements in India. *Working Papers, presented at Annual Meeting of Asian Studies on the Pacific Coast (ASPAC) held on June 15–17*, 2007, Honolulu.

Melander, Erik, Petterson, Therése, Themnér, Lotta. Organized Violence, 1989–2015. *Journal of Peace Research*, 2016, 53(5), pp. 727–742.

Millard, Gregory. *Secession and Self: Quebec in Canadian Thought*. McGill-Queen's Press, 2008. ISBN 978-07-7357-486-1.

Miller, Vaughne, Lunn, Jon, Lang, Arabella, Walekr, Nigel, Robinson, Tim, McGrath, Francesca. *Independence and Constitutional Referendums around the World*. London: House of Commons Library, 2013.

Minahan, James B. *Encyclopedia of Stateless Nations: Ethnic and National Groups around the World*. 2nd edition. ABC-CLIO, 2016. ISBN 978-16-1069-954-9.

Ministerio Del Interior. *26J Elecciones Generales Cognreso. Resumen de circunscripciones*, 2017. Available online: http://resultados2016.infoelecciones.es/99CO/DCO99000CI.htm?lang=es

Mises, Ludwig von. Liberal Foreign Policy. In *The Political Economy of Secession: A* Source *Book*, ed. Backhaus, Jürgen G., Doering, Detmar. Neue Zürcher Zeitung Publishing, 2004. ISBN 3-03823-102-9.

Mohebbi, Matt, Vanderkam, Dan, Kodysh, Julia, Schonberger, Rob, Choi, Hyunyoung, Kumar, Sanjiv. *Google Correlate Whitepaper*, 2011. Available online: www.google.com/trends/correlate/whitepaper.pdf

Montesquieu, Charles de Secondat. *The Spirit of Laws*. Kitchener: Batoche Books, 2001 [1748], translated by Thomas Nugent [1752].

Montserrat Guibernau. *Catalan Nationalism: Francoism, Transition and Democracy Routledge*. ISBN 9781134353255, 2004.

Mrak, Mojmir, Arhar, France. Succession Issues in Allocating the External Debt of SFR Yugoslavia and Achieving Slovenia's Financial Independence. In *Slovenia: From Yugoslavia to the European Union*, ed. Mrak, V.M., Rojec, M., and Silva-Jauregui, C. Washington: The World Bank, 2004.

Mudde, Cas. Can Soccer Unite the Belgians? *The Washington Post*, 2014. Available online: www.washingtonpost.com/news/monkey-cage/wp/2014/06/16/can-the-red-devils-unite-the-belgians/?utm_term=.2e70947ade8a

Munoz, Jordi, Tormos, Raül. Economic Expectations and Support for Secession in Catalonia between Causality and Rationalization. *European Political Science Review*, 2015, 7(2), pp. 315–341.

Mustafa, Erdogdu. *Comparative Political and Economic Perspectives on the MENA Region*. IGI Global, 2015. ISBN 978-14-6669-602-0.

Narita, Futoshi, Yin, Rujun. *In Search of Information: Use of Google Trend's Data to Narrow Information Gaps for Low-Income Developing Countries*. International Monetary Fund, 2018.

Natsios, Andrew S., Abramowitz, Michael. Sudan's Secession Crisis: Can the South Part From the North without War? *Foreign Affairs*, 2011, January/February Issue.

New Flemish Alliance. *The N-VA's Ideology and Purpose*, 2016. Available online: https://english.n-va.be/frequently-asked-questions#ideology

Norman, Wayne. The Ethics of Secession as the Regulation of Secessionist Politics. In *National Self-Determination and Secession*, ed. Moore, M. Oxford: Oxford University Press, 1998, pp. 34–61.

Norwegian Centre for Research Data. *European Election Database*, 2016. Available online: www.nsd.uib.no/european_election_database

Oates, Wallace. *Fiscal Federalism*. New York: Harcourt Brace Jovanovich, 1972.

OECD. *Development Centre Seminars Different Paths to a Market Economy: China and European Economies in Transition*. OECD Publishing, 1998. ISBN 978-92-6416-301-0.

OECD. *OECD Data on Skills: Employment by Industry and Occupation*. Economic Analysis and Statistics Division. STI Working Papers, 1998/4.

OECD. *Purchasing Power Parities (PPP) (Indicator)*, 2019. DOI: 10.1787/1290ee5a-en (accessed on 2nd February 2019).

O'Leary, Brendan. *Analysing Partition: Definition, Classification and Explanation*. Institute for British-Irish Studies. MFFP Working Paper No 27, 2006. ISSN 1649-0304.

OPEC. *OPEC Basket Price Monthly*, 2019.

OUP. *Oxford English Dictionary*. Available online: https://public.oed.com

Panizza, Ugo. Decentralisation as a Mechanism to Prevent Secession. *Economic Notes*, 1998, 27, pp. 263–279.

Parlament de Catalunya. *Declaration of the Legitimate Representatives of Catalonia*, 2017.

Party of Sardinians. *Manifesto*, 2016. Available online: www.ilpartitodeisardi.eu/chi-siamo/manifesto/

Pastiurko, Natalka, Campbell, John L., Hall, John A. Measuring Cultural Diversity: Ethnic, Linguistic and Religious Fractionalization in the OECD. *Ethnic and Racial Studies*, 2011, 35(2), pp. 195–217.

Patočka, Jan. Filosofie českých dějin [Philosophy of the Czech History]. *Sociologický časopisy [Czech Sociological Review]*, 1969, 5(5), pp. 457–463.

Pavkovic, Aleksandar, Radan, Peter. *Creating New States: Theory and Practice of Secession*. Ashgate Publishing Ltd., 2013. ISBN 978-14-0949-841-4.

Pearson, Raymond. *The Longman Companion to European Nationalism 1789–1920*. Abingdon, UK: Routledge, 2014. ISBN 978-13-1789-777-4.

Pendakur, Krishna, Pendakur, Ravi. Speak and Ye Shall Receive: Language Knowledge as Human Capital. In *New Canadian Perspectives*. Ottawa: Canadian Heritage, 1998.

Perman, Dagmar. *The Shaping of the Czechoslovak State, Diplomatic: History of the Boundaries of Czechoslovakia, 1914–1920*. Leiden: Brill Archive, 1962.

Petty, William. Treaties of Taxe, [1662]. In *The Economic Writings of Sir William Petty, together with The Observation Upon Bills of Mortality, More Probably by Captain John Granut*, ed. Hull, Charles Henry. Cambridge: Cambridge University Press, 1899.

Pfőstl, Eva. Tolerance Established by Law: The Autonomy of South Tyrol in Italy. *Mahanirban Calcutta Research Group*. Available online: www.mcrg.ac.in/EURAC_RP2.pdf

Pigou, Arthur C. *The Political Economy of War*. London: Macmillan Press, 1921.

Pipes, Richard. *Vlastnictví a svoboda [Property and Freedom]*. Argo, 2008.

Pittock, Murray G.H. *Scottish Nationality*. Palgrave Macmillian, 2001. ISBN: 978-0-23062-906-6.

Plaid Cymru. *Wales' Voice in Europe*, 2016. Available online: www.partyof.wales/europe-1/

Plato. *Laws*. Plato with an English Translation IX by R.G. Bury. Cambridge, MA: Harvard University Press, London: William Heinemann Ltd., 1961.

Pogge, Thomas W. Cosmopolitanism and Sovereignty. *Ethics*, 1992, 103(1), pp. 48–75.

Pouw, Brandon. *The Recognition of Kosovo: A Political Affair*. Leiden University, Political Science Department-International Organisation, 2016, s1754076.

Putnam, Ruth. *Luxemburg and Her Neighbours: A Record of the Political Fortunes of the Present Grand Duchy from the Eve of the French Revolution to the Great War, with a Preliminary Sketch of Events from 963 to 1780*. G. P. Putnam's Sons, 1919.

Rae, Douglas W. *The Political Consequences of Electoral Laws, 1945–85*. New Haven: Yale University Press, 1967.
RAND. *The Nobel Prize and RAND*, 2018. Available online: www.rand.org/about/history/nobel.html
Rejzek, Jiří. *Český etymologický slovník*. Praha: LEDA, 2015.
Renan, Ernest. *What Is a Nation?* 1882. Conference at the Sorbonne (*Qu'est-ce qu'une nation?*), translated by Ethan Rundell. Press-Pocket, 1992, Paris.
Requejo Coll, Ferran, Caminal I Badia, Miquel. *Political Liberalism and Plurinational Democracies*. New York: Routledge, 2011. ISBN 978-0-4155-6450-2.
Requejo Coll, Ferran, Nagel, Klaus-Jürgen. *Politics of Religion and Nationalism: Federalism, Consociationalism and Secession*. Abingdon, UK: Routledge, 2014. ISBN 978-1-3175-6606-9.
Rettman, Andrew. Spain Tells EU to Cut Kosovo from Enlargement Plan. *EU Observer*, 30th January 2018. Available online: https://euobserver.com/enlargement/140771
Řezanková, Hana. Cluster Alanysis of Economic Data. *Statistika*, 2014, 94(1), pp. 73–86.
Ricks, David, Beaton, Roderick. *The Making of Modern Greece: Nationalism, Romanticism, and the Use of the Past (1797–1896)*. Ashgate Publishing Ltd., 2013. ISBN 978-14-0948-027-3.
Rodríguez-Pose, Andreas, Gill, Nicholas. On the 'Economic Dividend' of Devolution. *Regional Studies*, 2005, 39(4), pp. 405–420.
Rodríguez-Pose, Andrés, Stermšek, Marko. *The Economics of Secession: Analysing the Economic Impact of the Collapse of the Former Yugoslavia*. GEN Working Paper, 2014.
Roeder, Phillip G. *National Secession: Persuasion and Violence in Independence Campaigns*. Ithaca, NY: Cornell University Press, 2018. ISBN 978-15-0172-599-9.
Rosůlek, Přemysl. *Politický secesionismus & Etické teorie: Allen Buchanan a jeho kritici*. Brno: Barrister & Principal, 2014. ISBN 978-80-7485-037-0.
Roszkowski, Michael J., Grable, John E. Estimating Risk Tolerance: The Degree of Accuracy and the Paramorphic Representations of the Estimate. *Financial Counseling and Planning*, 2005, 16(2), pp. 29–47.
The Royal Swedish Academy of Sciences. *Press Release*, 10th October 2005. Available online: www.nobelprize.org/prizes/economics/2005/press-release/
Ruano, Jose, Profiroiu, Marius (Eds.). *The Palgrave Handbook of Decentralisation in Europe*. Palgrave Macmillan. 2016.
Saideman, Stephen M. *The Ties That Divide: Ethnic Politics, Foreign Policy, and International Conflict*. Columbia University Press. 2001. ISBN 978-02-3150-627-4.
San Martín, Inés. *Catalonia Referendum Divides the Churche as It Does the People*. Crux, 2017. Available online: https://cruxnow.com/global-church/2017/09/30/catalonia-referendum-divides-church-people/
Schrijver, Frans. *Regionalism after Regionalisation: Spain, France and the United Kingdom*. Amsterdam University Press, 2006: ISBN 978-90-5629-428-1.
Scottish Government. *Government Expenditure & Revenue: Scotland 2012–2013*. APS Group Scotland, 2014. ISBN: 978-1-78412-338-3.
Scottish Government. *Oil and Gas Production Statistics 2017–18*, 2018. Available online: https://www2.gov.scot/Topics/Statistics/Browse/Economy/oilgas1718
Scottish National Party. 2016. *What Is the SNP's Position on the EU?* Available online: www.snp.org/pb_what_is_the_snp_s_position_on_the_eu
Sebastian, Ashwini. *Is Divorce a Credible Threat? Unilateral Separation Laws, Household Bargaining and Women's Labor in Egypt*. University of Maryland. Preliminary Working Paper, 2011.

Sinn, Hans-Werner. The ECB's Fiscal Policy. *International Tax and Public Finance*, 2018, 25(2), pp. 1–30. https://doi.org/10.1007/s10797-018-9501-8
Sklenářová, Sylva. *Spojené království nizozemské (1815–1830)*. Oftis. ISBN 978-80-7405-150-0.
Šleivyte, Janina. *Russia's European Agenda and the Baltic States*. Abingdon, UK: Routledge, 2009: ISBN 978-11-3518-111-6.
Smout, T. Chrisophet. *Scotland and the Sea*. Rowman & Littlefield, 1992. 232 p. ISBN 978-0-85976-338-7.
Sobel, Lester A. *Energy Crisis: 1974–75*. Facts on File, 1975. 213 p. ISBN 978-0-87196-278-2.
Sorens, Jason P. *Secessionism: Identity, Interest, and Strategy*. McGill-Queen's Press-MQUP, 2012. ISBN 978-07-7358-751-9.
Sorens, Jason P. Secession Risk and Fiscal Federalism. *Publius: The Journal of Federalism*, 2016, 46(1), pp. 25–50.
Soubeyran, Antoine, Tomini, Agnes. Water Shortage and Conflict. *Revue d'Économie Politique*, 2012, 122(2).
Soytas, Mehmet A., Kose, Tekin. *Does Heterogeneity in Individual Discount Rates Explain the Gender Gap in Self-Assessed Health Status?* Working Paper, 2014.
Speir, John P. Reviewed Work: *The Economics of Secession* by Milica Zarkovic Bookman. *Southern Economic Journal*, 1994, 60(3), pp. 794–795.
Staal, Klaas. Incentives for Separation and Incentives for Public Good Provision. *Public Choice*, 2010, 145(3–4), pp. 531–546.
Stalin, Joseph V. The Independence of Finland: Speech Delivered in the All-Russian Central Executive Committee, December 22, 1917 (Newspaper Report). In *J. V. Stalin Works Volume 4, November 1917–1920*. Moscow: Foreign Language Publishing House, 1953.
Stegarescu, Dan. The Effects of Economic and Political Integration of Fiscal Decentralization: Evidence from OECD Countries. *The Canadian Journal of Economics*, 2009, 42(2), pp. 694–718.
Südtiroler Volkspartei. *Das Wahlprogramm*, 2016. Available online: www.svp.eu/de/themen/
Suksi, Markku. *Sub-State Governance through Territorial Autonomy: A Comparative Study in Constitutional Law of Powers, Procedures and Institutions*. Springer Science & Business Media, 2011.
Szayna, Thomas S. *Identifying Potential Ethnic Conflict: Application of a Process Model*. RAND Corporation, 2000. ISBN 0-8330-2842-1.
Talmon, Stefan. *Acceptance of Recognition of Kosovo's Independence: Does It Make a Difference?* German Practice in International Law, 2018. Available online: https://gpil.jura.uni-bonn.de/2018/04/acceptance-recognition-kosovos-independence-make-difference/
Tavares, Rodrigo. *Paradiplomacy: Cities and States as Global Players*. Oxford: Oxford University Press, 2016. ISBN 978-019-0462-14-7.
Thompson, Wayne. *Western Europe 2015–2016*. Rowman & Littlefield, 2015. ISBN 978-14-7581-885-7.
Tibco Software Inc. Statistica (Data Analysis Software System), Version 13. *Statistica Electronic Manual*, 2017.
Tiebout, Charles M. A Pure Theory of Local Expenditures. *The Journal of Political Economy*, 1956, 64(5), pp. 416–424.
Tomz, Michael R. *The Morality of Secession*. Oxford, 1994. Available online: https://web.stanford.edu/~tomz/working/secede.pdf
UEFA. *Member Associations*, 2019. Available online: www.uefa.com/insideuefa/member-associations/

UNCTADstat. Data Center. *Merchandise: Product Concentration and Diversification Indices on Exports and Imports, Annual, 1995–2016*. Available online: http://unctadstat.unctad.org/wds/TableViewer/tableView.aspx

United Nations General Assembly Resolution 1514: *Declaration on the Granting of Independence to Colonial Countries and Peoples,* 1960. Available online: https://www.sfu.ca/~palys/UN-Resolution%201514.pdf

Vaďura, Vladimír. Politická ekonomie konfliktu – nový směr výzkumu vnitrostátních konfliktů? [The Political Economy of Conflict: A New Direction of Research on Internal Conflicts?] *Vojenské rozhledy (Czech Military Review)*, 2010, 19(51), pp. 138–154.

Varian, Hal R. *Variants in Economic Theory: Selected Works of Hal R. Varian*. Edward Elgar Publishing, 2000. ISBN 978-17-8254-362-6.

Vaubel, Roland. Secession in the European Union. *Economic Affairs*, 2013, 33(3), pp. 288–302.

Vlaams Belang. *The Flemish Republic*, 2016. Available online: www.flemishrepublic.org

Vokáč, Petr. *Země v srdci Evropy: české země do roku 1526 v kontaktu s ostatní Evropou*. Praha: Baronet Publishers, 2006. 108 s. ISBN 978-80-7214-887-5.

Vos, Louis. Reconstruction of the Past in Belgium and Flanders. In *History and Social Sciencese*, ed. Coppieters, B. VUB Brussels University Press, 2002, pp. 179–206.

Walker, Neil. *Beyond Secession? Law in the Framing of the National Policy*. Europa Working Paper No 2014/11, 2014. Edinburgh School of Law Research Paper Series.

Walter, Christian, von Ungern-Sternberg, Antje, Abushov, Kavus. *Self-Determination and Secession in International Law*. Oxford: Oxford University Press, 2014. ISBN 9780191006913.

Watts, Duncan. *European Union*. Edinburgh University Press, 2008. ISBN 978-074-8632-25-1.

Weber, Max. *From Max Weber: Essays in Sociology*. New York: Oxford University Press, 1946.

Weiss, Moritz. The 'Political Economy of Conflicts': A Window of Opportunity for CFSP? *Journal of Contemporary European Research*, 2008, 4(1), pp. 1–17.

Wellman, Christopher H. The Morality of Secession. In *Secession as an International Phenomenon: From America's Civil War to Contemporary Separatist Movements*. University of Georgia Press, 2010. ISBN 978-80-2033-737-1.

Wood, John R. Secession: A Comparative Analytical Framework. *Canadian Journal of Political Science*, 1981, 14(1), pp. 107–134.

World Atlas. *What Languages Are Spoken in Croatia?* Available online: www.worldatlas.com/articles/what-languages-are-spoken-in-croatia.html

World Bank. *Breaking the Conflict Trap: Civil War and Development Policy*. World Bank Publications, 2003. 240 p. ISBN 978-0-82138-641-5.

World Bank. *World Development Report 2011: Conflict, Security and Development*. Washington, DC: The International Bank for Reconstruction and Development/The World Bank.

Woodrow Wilson, [1918] 2017. The Fourteen Points Speech. Squid Ink Classics. ISBN 9781548159412.

The World Factbook. CIA. *Independence*, 2018. Available online: www.cia.gov/library/publications/the-world-factbook/fields/2088.html

Young, Robert A. How Do Peaceful Secessions Happen? *Canadian Journal of Political Science*, 1994a, 27(4), pp. 773–792.

Young, Robert A. *The Breakup of Czechoslovakia*. Institute of Intergovernmental Relations, Research Paper No. 32, 1994b.

Young, Robert A. *The Secession of Quebec and the Future of Canada*. McGill-Queen's Press, 1998. ISBN 978-07-7351-530-7.

Young, Robert A. *Struggle for Quebec*. McGill-Queen's Press, 1999. ISBN 978-07-7351-851-3.

Young, Robert A. Secession as Revolution. *Homo Economicus*, 2004, 21(2), pp. 373–395.

Young, Robert A. The Road to Secession: Estimating the Costs of Independence in Advanced Industrial States. *LSE*, 2013. Available online: http://blogs.lse.ac.uk/europpblog/2013/12/05/the-road-to-secession-estimating-the-costs-of-independence-in-advanced-industrial-states/

Žáček, Rudolf. *Dějiny Slezska v datech*. Praha: Libri, 2004. 546 s. ISBN 978-80-7277-172-1

Žídek, Libor. *Dějiny světového hospodářství, 2. vydání*. Aleš Čeněk s.r.o., 2009. ISBN 978-80-7380-184-7.

Zipfel, Frank, Vetter, Stefan. Better on Their Own? *Deutsche Bank Research: EU Monitor, European Integration*, 2015, pp. 1–20. ISSN 1612-0272.

Zwet, Arno van der. Operationalising National Identity: The Cases of the Scottish National Party and Frisian National Party. *Nations and Nationalism*, 2015, 21(1), pp. 62–82. ISSN 1354-5078. http://dx.doi.org/10.1111/nana.12091

# Index

Note: Page numbers in *italics* indicate figures and page numbers in **bold** indicate tables on the corresponding page. A page number with an "n" indicates a note. age, secessionist attitudes and 83–149

For Product Safety Concerns and Information please contact our EU representative GPSR@taylorandfrancis.com
Taylor & Francis Verlag GmbH, Kaufingerstraße 24, 80331 München, Germany

www.ingramcontent.com/pod-product-compliance
Ingram Content Group UK Ltd.
Pitfield, Milton Keynes, MK11 3LW, UK
UKHW020201200926
475702UK00004B/559

* 9 7 8 0 3 6 7 8 9 6 4 7 8 *